# Study Guide

to accompany

# The Micro Economy Today

# Study Guide

to accompany

# The Micro Economy Today

## Eighth Edition

Bradley R. Schiller
*The American University*

Prepared by
Linda Willson
*University of Texas-Arlington*

Tom Anderson
*Montgomery College*

Boston   Burr Ridge, IL   Dubuque, IA   Madison, WI   New York   San Francisco   St. Louis
Bangkok   Bogotá   Caracas   Lisbon   London   Madrid
Mexico City   Milan   New Delhi   Seoul   Singapore   Sydney   Taipei   Toronto

**McGraw-Hill Higher Education** 🐾

*A Division of The McGraw-Hill Companies*

Study Guide to accompany
THE MICRO ECONOMY TODAY

2 3 4 5 6 7 8 9 0 QPD/QPD 9 0 0 8 7 6 5 4 3 2 1

ISBN 0-07-242956-9

http://www.mhhe.com

# STUDY GUIDE
# Table of Contents

# STUDY GUIDE

# Preface

This study guide is written to accompany *The Micro Economy Today*, 8th edition, by Bradley R. Schiller. The overall focus of the Study Guide is to reinforce the economic principles and concepts presented in the textbook. Each section of each chapter has a particular objective.

The *Quick Review* and *Learning Objectives* sections provide brief summaries of the basic contents of the corresponding text chapters.

The *Using Key Terms* section allows students to practice using the words defined in each chapter in a crossword puzzle format.

The *True or False* and *Multiple Choice* sections help students apply economic principles in a familiar problem-solving setting. This will help greatly in the preparation for exams.

The *Problems and Applications* section lets students discover economic principles for themselves. Students not only learn the techniques that economists use, but they also discover the basis for the economic concepts they have learned.

Semester after semester, students have difficulty with the same concepts and make the same mistakes. The section called *Common Errors* addresses some of these problems, and provides an explanation using appropriate economic principles.

# Acknowledgments

We thank the McGraw-Hill staff for their support, especially Paul Shensa and Miller Murray. We also thank Thomas Jarrett for providing graphic design, layout modifications, and technical support for this edition.

Linda L. Wilson
The University of Texas at Arlington

Thomas Anderson
Montgomery College, Maryland

# CHAPTER 1

# Economics: The Core Issues

## Quick Review

Throughout history, people have strived to increase the level of output given the available resources and technology. As we move into the 21st century, the quest for more output continues. But what approach should be used to manage society's scarce resources? This question has generated much debate. Adam Smith believed we should allow the market mechanism to allocate resources and rely on a minimum of government intervention. Karl Marx said the government should decide the allocation of all resources and should even own the resources or factors of production. John Maynard Keynes called on government to play an active role in maintaining balance in the economy to prevent the excesses which result from a "hands off" approach.

The debate over how resources should be allocated is not unique to the United States, and is heard increasingly in other parts of the world as countries try to adjust to the collapse of the communist systems in Eastern Europe and elsewhere. The emerging consensus indicates that the market mechanism relied on in the United States (and elsewhere) is vastly superior to the central-planning mechanism which characterized the communist world. This result leads us to focus on two central questions:

- What forces determine economic outcomes?
- What can we do to improve economic outcomes?

To begin the study of economics, we note that the U.S. economy produces an output of over $7 trillion per year. In the process it must allocate its land, labor, capital, and entrepreneurship to competing uses. Resources are considered scarce, even when they seem abundant, because there are not enough of them to satisfy all of society's wants. Thus, every society confronts the problem of scarcity and must somehow answer these basic questions:

- WHAT is to be produced?
- HOW should it be produced?
- FOR WHOM should the output be produced?

Because of the imbalance between society's wants and resources, choosing to produce one thing means choosing not to produce something else. Economists illustrate these choices by drawing a production-possibilities curve. This curve shows the combinations of goods and services a society could produce if it were operating efficiently and all of its resources were fully employed. The production-possibilities curve appears bowed out from the origin because of the law of increasing opportunity costs. To an economist, cost is measured by the best alternative opportunity forgone when choosing a course of action.

In the United States, our choices are largely accomplished through the market mechanism. The "invisible hand" of the market mechanism coordinates the production and consumption decisions of millions of individuals and directly affects the allocation of the economy's resources. Changes in relative prices (called price signals) are what make the system go.

The individual decisions of households and firms are supplemented with generous doses of public-sector activity. When the market mechanism fails to provide goods and services efficiently and equitably – a situation called "market failure" – the public sector must provide assistance. For example, market systems do not automatically generate pollution-control mechanisms which assure us of clean air and water. Such market imperfections must be overcome by government activity. In some economies the market mechanism has not been allowed to work. Planned (or command) economies, like that of the old Soviet Union, are good examples of this. But even in mixed economies "government failure" can make things worse.

In the study of the economy, it is useful to break economics into two categories: microeconomics and macroeconomics. Microeconomics focuses on a specific individual, firm, industry, or government agency; macroeconomics focuses on the entire economy. It should be noted that economics is not a settled body of doctrine. There is much controversy over how the economy works. That is what makes it so interesting.

## Learning Objectives

After reading Chapter 1 and doing the following exercises, you should:

1.  Understand the debate concerning market allocation vs. government allocation of resources.
2.  Understand that economics is the study of how to allocate society's scarce resources – land, labor, capital, and entrepreneurship.
3.  Know that scarcity results because resources are not sufficient to satisfy all of society's wants.
4.  Be able to define and illustrate opportunity costs using a production-possibilities curve.
5.  Understand the law of increasing opportunity costs.
6.  Be able to demonstrate efficiency, growth, unemployment, and underemployment using a production-possibilities curve.
7.  Know why every economy must answer the same basic questions – WHAT, HOW, FOR WHOM.
8.  Be able to distinguish macroeconomic issues from microeconomic issues.
9.  Be able to describe how the market mechanism seeks to allocate society's resources to their most valued use.
10. Be aware that there is serious debate and controversy over how the economy works.
11. Be able to discuss the tradeoffs inherent in the "peace dividend."
12. Be able to describe the mixed economy and distinguish market failure from government failure.

## Using Key Terms
Fill in the puzzle on the opposite page with the appropriate term from the list of Key Terms at the end of the chapter in the text.

### *Across*
1.  The reason there is no such thing as a "free lunch".
3.  Occurs when government intervention fails to improve economic outcomes.
6.  Represented by land, labor, capital, and entrepreneurship.
7.  Economic study concerned with the behavior of individuals, firms, and government agencies.
11. The study of how best to allocate society's scarce resources.
14. Referred to as the "invisible hand" by Adam Smith.
16. Latin term meaning "other things remaining equal."
17. Economic policy supported by Adam Smith.

### *Down*
2.  The curve represented in Figure 1.1 in the text.
4.  The assembling of resources to produce new or better products.

5.     The study of the economy as a whole.
8.     The use of both market signals and government directives to select the mix of output.
9.     Illustrated in Figure 1.4 in the text by the outward shift of the production-possibilities curve.
10.    Occurs when the market mechanism results in the wrong mix of output.
12.    Final goods used to produce other goods.
13.    The idea that there are not enough resources available to satisfy all desires.
15.    According to the *World View* article on page 5 in the text, the Chinese government has been experimenting with a market-driven economy to increase output and _____.

## Puzzle 1.1

# True or False: *Circle your choice and explain why any false statements are incorrect.*

T  F  1.  Scarcity is only a problem in the very poor countries of the world.

T  F  2.  Students do not pay tuition in elementary school, so from society's point of view, there is no opportunity cost involved in their education.

T  F  3.  A production-possibilities curve can be drawn only if a scarce resource prevents unlimited production of a product.

T  F  4.  One reason that the production-possibilities curve is bowed outward is that more production means the economy is less efficient in producing output.

T  F  5.  If the economy is fully and efficiently employing its resources, then the only way to acquire more of one good, *ceteris paribus*, is to accept less of something else.

T  F  6.  The opportunity cost of a good increases as more of the good is produced because resources are not equally well suited to the production of all goods.

T  F  7.  The economy achieves the greatest efficiency when it is inside the production-possibilities curve.

T  F  8.  An economy will never be able to produce a combination of goods and services outside of its existing production-possibilities curve.

T  F  9.  A market driven economy is not capable of solving the problems created by pollution without intervention by government.

T  F  10.  Price signals direct the answers to the WHAT, HOW, and FOR WHOM decisions in a laissez-faire economy.

# Multiple Choice: *Select the correct answer.*

_____ 1.  Which of the following is the best description of the origin of the economic problem of scarcity?
  (a)  Humans have limited wants for goods and services and resources are also limited.
  (b)  Humans have limited wants for goods and services and resources are unlimited.
  (c)  Humans have unlimited wants for goods and services but resources are limited.
  (d)  Humans have unlimited wants for goods and services and resources are also unlimited.

_____ 2.  Which of the following best describes the term "resource allocation"?
  (a)  Which goods and services society will produce with available factors of production.
  (b)  How society spends the income of individuals based on resource availability.
  (c)  How society purchases resources, given its macroeconomic goals.
  (d)  How individual market participants decide what to produce given fixed resource constraints.

_____ 3.  A consequence of the economic problem of scarcity is that:
  (a)  Choices have to be made about how resources are used.
  (b)  There is never too much of any good or service produced.
  (c)  The production of goods and services has to be controlled by the government.
  (d)  The production possibilities curve is bowed outward.

_____ 4. Which of the following is *not* a factor of production?
- (a) A teacher.
- (b) A ball-point pen.
- (c) The $100,000 used to start a new business.
- (d) Ten acres of forest.

_____ 5. Centrally planned economies are most likely to underestimate the value of:
- (a) Land.
- (b) Labor.
- (c) Capital.
- (d) Entrepreneurship.

_____ 6. Which of the following describes how resources are typically allocated in the U.S. economy?
- (a) By tradition.
- (b) By democratic vote.
- (c) By markets.
- (d) By government.

_____ 7. I plan on going to a $5 movie this evening instead of studying for an exam. The total opportunity cost of the movie:
- (a) Depends on how I score on the exam.
- (b) Is $5.
- (c) Is what I could have purchased with the $5 plus the study time I forgo.
- (d) Is the forgone studying I could have done in the same time.

_____ 8. The opportunity cost of installing a traffic light at a dangerous intersection is:
- (a) Negative, since it will reduce accidents.
- (b) The best possible alternative bundle of other goods or services that must be forgone in order to build and install the traffic light.
- (c) The time lost by drivers who approach the intersection when the light is red.
- (d) The cost of the stoplight plus the cost savings from a reduction in the number of accidents.

_____ 9. Which of the following events would cause the production-possibilities curve to shift inward?
- (a) The labor supply grows.
- (b) An unexpected freeze destroys many U.S. crops.
- (c) A technological breakthrough occurs.
- (d) New factories are built.

_____ 10. Which of the following events would cause the production-possibilities curve to shift outward?
- (a) The economy's capital stock increases.
- (b) A new, strong plastic is developed for use in building houses.
- (c) More women enter the labor force.
- (d) All of the above.

_____ 11. The slope of the production-possibilities curve provides information about:
- (a) The growth of the economy.
- (b) Technological change in the economy.
- (c) Opportunity costs in the economy.
- (d) All of the above.

_____ 12. The law of increasing opportunity cost explains:
- (a) How everything becomes more expensive as the economy grows.
- (b) The shape of the production-possibilities curve.
- (c) Inflation.
- (d) All of the above.

13. When an economy is producing efficiently it is:
    (a) Producing a combination of goods and services outside the production-possiblities curve.
    (b) Getting the most goods and services from the available resources.
    (c) Experiencing decreasing opportunity costs.
    (d) All of the above are correct.

14. In a market economy, the answer to the WHAT to produce question is determined by:
    (a) Direct negotiations between consumers and producers.
    (b) Producer profits and sales.
    (c) Government directives.
    (d) A democratic vote of all producers.

15. In a market economy, the answer to the HOW to produce question is determined by:
    (a) Government planners.
    (b) The production possibilities curve.
    (c) The least-cost method of production.
    (d) The method of production which uses the least amount of labor.

16. The trend toward greater reliance on the market mechanism by former communist societies is evidence of:
    (a) Government failure.
    (b) Market failure.
    (c) The failure of a mixed economy.
    (d) *Ceteris paribus*.

17. Which of the following are major macroeconomic goals of the economy?
    (a) Full employment.
    (b) Control of inflation.
    (c) Economic growth.
    (d) All of the above.

18. Microeconomics focuses on the performance of:
    (a) Individual consumers, firms and government agencies.
    (b) Firms only.
    (c) Government agencies only.
    (d) The economy as a whole.

19. Reread the *World View* article "Free Enterprise Blooms in Wenzhou, China, Out of the Party's Sight." The article best illustrates:
    (a) The success of Karl Marx's view of market-based economies.
    (b) Market failure.
    (c) The concepts described in *The Wealth of Nations*.
    (d) The scarcity of resources.

20. Reread the *World View* article "North Korea Says It Is Running out of Food." Implicitly, the article is suggesting that the maintenance of an army results in:
    (a) An opportunity cost in terms of consumer goods.
    (b) An opportunity cost in terms of investment goods only.
    (c) No opportunity cost because the army keeps the country safe.
    (d) No opportunity cost because the soldiers are being paid.

_____ 21. The slope of a curve at any point is given by the formula:
    (a) The change in $y$ coordinates between two points divided by the change in their $x$ coordinates.
    (b) The change in $x$ coordinates between two points divided by the change in their $y$ coordinates.
    (c) The percentage change in $y$ coordinates between two points divided by the percentage change in their $x$ coordinates.
    (d) The percentage change in $x$ coordinates between two points divided by the percentage change in their $y$ coordinates.

_____ 22. When the relationship between two variables changes:
    (a) There is movement from one point on a linear curve to another point on the same curve.
    (b) The entire curve shifts.
    (c) The labels on the axes must be changed.
    (d) The curve becomes linear.

_____ 23. A linear curve can be distinguished by:
    (a) The continuous change in its slope.
    (b) The same slope throughout the curve.
    (c) The changing relationship between the two variables.
    (d) A shift in the curve.

# Problems and Applications

## Exercise 1

Suppose you have only 20 hours per week to allocate to study or leisure. The following table indicates the tradeoff between leisure time (not studying) and the grade-point average achieved as a result of studying.

### Table 1.1

|                              | (a) | (b) | (c)  | (d) | (e) |
|------------------------------|-----|-----|------|-----|-----|
| Leisure time (hours / week)  | 20  | 18  | 14.5 | 10  | 0   |
| Grade-point average          | 0   | 1.0 | 2.0  | 3.0 | 4.0 |

1. In Figure 1.1, draw the production-possibilities curve that represents the possible combinations from Table 1.1.

**Figure 1.1**

2. Using the information above, what is the opportunity cost of raising your grade-point average from 2.0 to 3.0? _____

3. What is the opportunity cost of raising your grade-point average from 3.0 to 4.0?

   _____

4. Why does the opportunity cost of improving your grade-point average increase?

   _____

## Exercise 2

This exercise is similar to the problem at the end of Chapter 1 in the text. It provides practice in drawing and interpreting a production-possibilities curve and demonstrating shifts of such a curve.

1. A production-possibilities schedule showing the production alternatives between corn and lumber is presented in Table 1.2. Plot combination *A* in Figure 1.2 and label it. Do the same for combination *B*. In going from combination *A* to combination *B*, the economy has sacrificed _____ billion board feet of lumber production per year and has transferred the land to production of _____ billion bushels of corn per year. The opportunity cost of corn in terms of lumber is _____ board feet per bushel.

**Table 1.2**

| Combination | Quantity of corn (billions of bushels per year) | Quantity of lumber (billions of board feet per year) |
|---|---|---|
| A | 0 | 50 |
| B | 1 | 48 |
| C | 2 | 44 |
| D | 3 | 38 |
| E | 4 | 30 |
| F | 5 | 20 |
| G | 6 | 0 |

2.  In answering Question 1 you determined the opportunity cost of corn when the economy is initially producing only lumber (combination *A*). Using the information in Table 1.2, plot the rest of the production-possibilities combinations in Figure 1.2 and label each of the points with the appropriate letter.

**Figure 1.2**

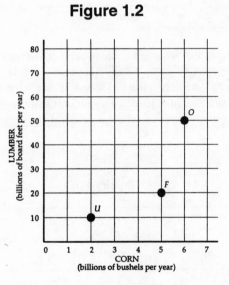

3.  When Table 1.3 is completed, it should show the opportunity cost of corn at each possible combination of lumber and corn production in the economy. Opposite "1st billion bushels" insert the number of board feet per year of lumber sacrificed when the economy shifts from combination *A* to combination *B*. Complete the table for each of the remaining combinations.

**Table 1.3**

| Corn production (billions of bushels per year) | Opportunity cost of corn in terms of lumber (billions of board feet per year) |
|---|---|
| 1st billion bushels | _____ |
| 2nd billion bushels | _____ |
| 3rd billion bushels | _____ |
| 4th billion bushels | _____ |
| 5th billion bushels | _____ |
| 6th billion bushels | _____ |

4.  In Table 1.3, as more corn is produced (as the economy moves from combination *A* toward combination *G*), the opportunity cost of corn (falls, rises, remains the same), which illustrates the law of _____.

5.  Suppose that lumber companies begin to clear-cut forest areas instead of cutting them selectively. Clear-cutting improves the economy's ability to produce lumber but not corn. Table 1.4 describes such a situation. Using the information in Table 1.4, sketch the new production-possibilities curve in Figure 1.2 as you did the initial production-possibilities curve based on Table 1.3. For which combination does clear-cutting fail to change the amount of corn and lumber produced?
    _____

**Table 1.4**

| Combination | Corn (billions of bushels per year) | Lumber (billions of board feet per year) |
|---|---|---|
| A' | 0 | 75 |
| B' | 1 | 72 |
| C' | 2 | 66 |
| D' | 3 | 57 |
| E' | 4 | 45 |
| F' | 5 | 30 |
| G' | 6 | 0 |

6.  After the introduction of clear-cutting most of the new production-possibilities curve is (outside, inside, the same as) the earlier curve. The opportunity cost of corn has (increased, decreased) as a result of clear-cutting.

7.  Study your original production-possibilities curve in Figure 1.2 and decide which of the combinations shown (*U, F, O*) demonstrates each of the following. (*Hint:* Check the answers at the end of the chapter to make sure you have diagrammed the production-possibilities curve in Figure 1.2 correctly.)
    (a) Society is producing at its maximum potential. Combination_____.
    (b) Society has some unemployed or underemployed resources. Combination _____.
    (c) Society cannot produce this combination. Combination _____.
    (d) Society might be able to produce this combination if technology improved but cannot produce it with current technology. Combination _____.
    (e) If society produces this combination, some of society's wants will go unsatisfied unnecessarily. Combination _____.

## Exercise 3

This exercise requires the understanding of scarcity, opportunity cost and production possibilities. Answer the following questions based on the information on pages 4 through 9 in the text.

_____  1.  The term "peace dividend," refers to the:
            (a) Difference between a market economy and a mixed economy.
            (b) Availability of scare resources for the production of civilian goods.
            (c) Tradeoff between consumption and investment.
            (d) Tradeoff between food and civilian goods.

_____  2.  For the U.S., the share of total output devoted to military goods:
            (a) Has remained fairly constant since 1940.
            (b) Is currently about 25 percent.
            (c) Has decreased since the end of the Cold War.
            (d) Is fairly low and results in no opportunity cost.

_____  3.  According to Figure 1.1 in the text, as the mix of output moves from point *B* to point *C*:
            (a) There is an increase in the production of televisions.
            (b) There is no opportunity cost because point *C* represents the optimal mix of output.
            (c) More factors of production are available for both shoes and televisions.
            (d) All of the above are true.

_____  4.  According to the text, the North Korean army:
            (a) Is the largest in the world in terms of number of personnel.
            (b) Absorbs approximately 25 percent of the country's resources.
            (c) Absorbs a large share of output because North Korea is such a large country.
            (d) All of the above are true.

_____  5.  Which of the following is the opportunity cost of maintaining an army in North Korea?
            (a) There is no opportunity cost because North Korea needs a large army to protect its citizens.
            (b) There is no opportunity cost because North Korea is producing the optimal mix of output.
            (c) Only the money spent on military equipment and salaries.
            (d) The food and other consumer goods that must be given up.

# Exercise 4

This exercise provides practice in the use of graphs.

Use Figure 1.3 below to answer the following questions.

## Figure 1.3

The slope of a line is the rate of change between two points or the vertical change divided by the horizontal change.

1.  The vertical distance between the two points equals _____ .

2.  The horizontal distance between the two points equals _____ .

3.  The slope of the line equals _____ .

4.  The slope of the line is (positive, negative) because as one variable increases the other variable (increases, decreases).

5.  The line has the same slope at every point implying a (constant, changing) relationship between the two variables.

6.  When the slope of a line is the same at every point, the curve is (linear, nonlinear).

# Common Errors

The first statement in each "common error" below is incorrect. Each incorrect statement is followed by a corrected version and an explanation.

1. Words mean the same thing in economics that they do in our everyday conversation. WRONG!

   Words used in everyday conversation *very often* have different meanings when they are used in economics. RIGHT!

   You'll have to be very careful here. Words are used with precision in economics. You'll have difficulty if you confuse their everyday meanings with their economic meanings. For example, the term "capital" in economics means simply "man-made instruments of production." In everyday usage it may mean money, machines, a loan, or even the British response to the question "How are you feeling?"

2. Economic models are abstractions from the real world and are therefore useless in predicting and explaining economic behavior. WRONG!

   Economic models are abstractions from the real world and *as a result* are useful in predicting and explaining economic behavior. RIGHT!

   You have to be willing to deal with abstractions if you want to get anything accomplished in economics. By using economic models based on specific assumptions, we can make reasonable judgments about what's going on around us. We try not to disregard any useful information. However, to try to include everything (such as what cereal we like for breakfast) would be fruitless. For example, the production-possibilities frontier is an abstraction. No economist would argue that it is an economy! But it certainly is useful in focusing on public-policy choices, such as the choice between guns and butter.

3. Because economics is a "science," all economists should come up with the same answer to any given question. WRONG!

   Economics is a science, but there is often room for disagreement in trying to answer a given question. RIGHT!

   Economics is a social science, and the entire society and economy represent the economist's laboratory. Economists cannot run the kind of experiments that are done by physical scientists. As a result, two economists may attack a given problem or question in different ways using different models. They may come up with different answers, but since there is no answer book, you cannot say which is right. The solution is, then, to do more testing, refine our models, compare results, and so on. By the way, the recent space probes have given physicists cause to reevaluate much of their theory concerning the solar system, and there is much controversy concerning what the new evidence means. But physics is still a science, as is economics!

4. Increasing opportunity cost results from increasing inefficiency. WRONG!

   Increasing opportunity cost occurs even when resources are being used at their peak efficiency. RIGHT!

   Increasing opportunity cost and inefficiency are confused because both result in a lower amount of output per unit of input. However, inefficiency results from poor utilization or underemployment of resources, while increasing opportunity results from the increasing difficulty of adapting resources to production as more of a good is produced. Inefficiency can be represented as a movement inward from the production-possibilities curve, while increasing opportunity cost can be measured in movements along the production-possibilities curve. As the slope becomes steeper because of a movement down the production-possibilities curve, the good on the *x*-axis experiences increasing opportunity cost (a steeper slope). Similarly, a movement up along the production-possibilities curve represents a higher opportunity cost for the good on the *y*-axis – this time in the form of a flatter slope as more of the good on the *y*-axis is produced.

# •ANSWERS•

## Using Key Terms

### *Across*

1. opportunity cost
3. government failure
6. factors of production
7. microeconomics
11. economics
14. market mechanism
16. ceteris paribus
17. laissez faire

## Down

2. production possibilities
4. entrepreneurship
5. macroeconomics
8. mixed economy
9. economic growth
10. market failure
12. capital
13. scarcity
15. efficiency

## True or False

1. F   All societies experience the problem of scarcity because human wants for goods and services will always exceed society's ability to produce goods and services.
2. F   Factors of production are required to produce education. These factors could have been used to produce other goods and services. The opportunity cost of education is the value of the best goods and services given up to get education.
3. T
4. F   Efficiency is maximized along a given production-possibilities curve. The production-possibilities curve bows outward because of the law of increasing opportunity costs, i.e. resources are not perfectly transferable from the production of one good to the production of another. Efficiency means "getting the most from what you have."
5. T
6. T
7. F   The economy achieves the greatest efficiency when it is on the curve.
8. F   An economy could produce a combination of goods and services outside its existing curve in the future if technology improves and/or the quantity of resources increase sufficiently.
9. T
10. T

## Multiple Choice

| | | | | | | | | | |
|---|---|---|---|---|---|---|---|---|---|
| 1. c | 5. d | 9. b | 13. b | 17. d | 21. a |
| 2. a | 6. c | 10. d | 14. b | 18. a | 22. b |
| 3. a | 7. c | 11. c | 15. c | 19. c | 23. b |
| 4. c | 8. b | 12. b | 16. a | 20. a | |

## Problems and Applications

### Exercise 1

1. **Figure 1.1 Answer**

2. 4.5 hours of leisure time.

3. 10 hours of leisure time.

4. Higher grades are harder to get, particularly if the class is graded on a curve, with higher grades being received by a decreasing number of students. The "law" of increasing opportunity cost is evident in the economy and in the classroom.

## Exercise 2

1.  2, 1, 2

2.  **Figure 1.2 Answer**

3.  **Table 1.3 Answer**

| Corn production (billions of bushels per year) | Opportunity cost of corn in terms of lumber (billions of board feet per year) |
|---|---|
| 1st billion bushels | 2 |
| 2nd billion bushels | 4 |
| 3rd billion bushels | 6 |
| 4th billion bushels | 8 |
| 5th billion bushels | 10 |
| 6th billion bushels | 20 |

4.  Rises, increasing opportunity costs
5.  See Figure 1.2 answer; combination *G*.
6.  Outside, increased
7.  a . *F;*  b . *U;*  c . *O;*  d .*O;*  e . *U*

## Exercise 3

1.  b
2.  c
3.  a
4.  b
5.  d

16

# *Exercise 4*

1. 2
2. 4
3. Slope = vertical change/horizontal change = 2/4 = 1/2 or 0.5
4. Positive, increases
5. Constant
6. Linear

# CHAPTER 2

# The U.S. Economy: A Global View

## Quick Review

To understand the American economy, we must look to the answers it generates to the following questions:

- WHAT goods and services does the United States produce?
- HOW is that output distributed?
- FOR WHOM is the output produced?

The WHAT question is answered by a summary measure called gross domestic product (GDP). GDP is the total dollar value of all final goods and services produced *in a country* during a given time period. Although there are several ways to break up the GDP, a frequently used technique is to classify the *output which is produced* by the groups which purchase it: consumer goods by households, investment goods by business, and output taken by government at the federal, state, and local levels. In addition we must account for goods and services produced here and sold abroad (exports) and those which are produced abroad and sold here (imports).

The HOW question is answered by entrepreneurs who make decisions about how the nation's factors of production (which vary in quantity, quality and mobility) will be allocated within the framework provided by government. Government provides the legal rules of the game under which economic activity takes place. Government also intervenes to protect the environment from the negative third-party effects which accompany the pursuit of profits within the market mechanism. Government provides protection to consumers, labor and the environment through laws and regulations.

The economy never stands still, and we have observed in this century both the decline of agriculture and manufacturing and the rise of the service sector in the U.S. economy. The relative importance (both in size and numbers) of various forms of business organization – proprietorships, partnerships and corporations – has undergone substantial revision as well.

The FOR WHOM question is answered by the nation's income distribution, where those at the upper end of the distribution receive incomes which are disproportionate to their numbers.

In the future society will demand different answers to the WHAT, HOW, and FOR WHOM questions as new concerns cause us to revise our priorities. Both market signals and government directives will be assigned significant roles as questions concerning possible income stagnation, environmental destruction, and widening inequality and others are debated.

## Learning Objectives

After reading Chapter 2 and doing the following exercises, you should:

1. Be able explain why GDP and its components are an answer to the WHAT question.
2. Understand that factors of production differ in quantity, quality, and mobility in the United States and elsewhere.
3. Be able to trace the broad changes in industry structure in the United States from 1900 to the present.
4. Understand the role of government intervention as the economy answers the HOW question.
5. Know the basic types and relative importance of business organizations in the United States.
6. Understand that the economy's answer to the FOR WHOM question lies in the income distribution.
7. Expect that new market signals and government directives will change the answers to the WHAT, HOW, and FOR WHOM questions.

## Using Key Terms

Fill in the puzzle on the opposite page with the appropriate term from the of Key Terms at the end of the chapter in the text.

### *Across*

1. Account for nearly half of all federal government spending but are not part of GDP.
6. Used in Table 2.2 in the text to divide the population and then rank by income level.
9. The ability of a country to produce a good at a lower opportunity cost than another country.
10. The high level of _____ in the U.S. is explained to some extent by the level of education according to the article on page 34 in the text.
12. Goods and services bought from other countries.
13. A market situation in which the government intervenes to protect consumers from exploitation.
14. The costs or benefits of a market activity that affect a third party.
15. The resources used to produce goods and services.
16. A high ratio of capital to labor in the production process.

### *Down*

2. Goods and services sold to other countries.
3. The sum of consumption, investment, government expenditure, and net exports.
4. The knowledge and skills possessed by the labor force.
5. An expansion of production possibilities.
7. Used to compare the average living standards in the article on page 28 in the text.
8. The value of exports minus imports.
11. Equals 15 percent of GDP in Figure 2.3 in the text.

# Puzzle 2.1

## True or False: *Circle your choice and explain why any false statements are incorrect.*

T   F   1.   The United States produces about 25 percent of the world's output.

T   F   2.   If the economic growth rate exceeds the population growth rate, per capita GDP will increase.

T   F   3.   Federal government purchases of goods and services make up approximately 20 percent of GDP.

T   F   4.   Food stamps, medicare, and veterans' benefits are counted as government expenditures in the GDP.

T   F   5.   Industrialized countries tend to use the more capital-intensive methods of production than poor countries.

T   F   6.   Output by the U.S. manufacturing sector has declined since World War II.

T   F   7.   If a business installs outdoor lighting which makes it difficult for you to sleep, this is an externality.

T   F   8.   The corporation is the dominant form of business organization in the United States in terms of numbers, assets, and sales.

T   F   9.   In developed countries the richest quintile of the population gets a smaller proportion of total income than that quintile receives in poor, developing nations.

T   F   10.   Income transfers are intended to alter the market's answer to the HOW question.

## Multiple Choice: *Select the correct answer.*

_____ 1.   The economic growth rate of the economy is best measured by:
    (a)   The percentage change in the GDP between two points in time.
    (b)   The percentage change in per capita GDP between two points in time.
    (c)   The sum of the value of the factors of production used to produce output in a country.
    (d)   A measure of output divided by a measure of population.

_____ 2.   The standard of living will decline:
    (a)   Whenever the GDP falls.
    (b)   If the percentage change in per capita GDP rises.
    (c)   If the rate of population growth exceeds the rate of economic growth.
    (d)   If factor growth exceeds economic growth.

_____ 3.   Suppose that during the course of a year, an economy produces $4.8 trillion consumer goods, $1.2 trillion investment goods, $1.4 trillion government services, $0.6 trillion exports, and $0.8 trillion imports. For that economy, GDP would be:
    (a)   $8,000 trillion.
    (b)   $7,000 trillion.
    (c)   $8,800 trillion.
    (d)   $7,200 trillion.

_____ 4.   Which of the following countries (or regions) annually produces the most output?
    (a)   Japan.
    (b)   United States.
    (c)   China.
    (d)   The combined European Union.

_____ 5. Since 1900 the change in the relative importance of different sectors in the U.S. economy is best characterized as:
(a) Relative growth in farm output share.
(b) Relative growth in manufacturing output share.
(c) Relative growth in service output share.
(d) Relative decrease in service output share.

_____ 6. As the United States economy relies more and more heavily on the production of services rather than goods:
(a) GDP will decrease since there will be less "real" production.
(b) International trade will become more difficult.
(c) Mass unemployment will result.
(d) None of the above are likely to occur.

_____ 7. Which of the following has contributed to the increase in international trade in the United States since the 1920s?
(a) Reduced trade barriers.
(b) Improved communication systems.
(c) The growing share of services in U.S. production.
(d) All of the above.

_____ 8. Most of the United States GDP is used by:
(a) Consumers.
(b) Federal, state and local governments.
(c) Businesses.
(d) Foreign individuals and businesses.

_____ 9. Investment goods:
(a) Both maintain and expand production possibilities.
(b) Maintain production possibilities but do not expand them.
(c) Expand production possibilities but do not maintain them.
(d) Include consumption goods.

_____ 10. Which of the following are included in the GDP?
(a) Social security benefits.
(b) Net exports.
(c) Imports.
(d) Welfare checks.

_____ 11. Which of the following explains the low productivity of workers in poor, developing countries?
(a) Labor intensity of their production processes.
(b) The low factor mobility.
(c) The low quality of labor as a result of poor education.
(d) All of the above.

_____ 12. An increase in the level of human capital in an economy, *ceteris paribus*, will have the following effect on the economy's production possibilities curve.
(a) Shift the curve inward.
(b) Result in a movement from inside the curve to a point on the curve.
(c) Shift the curve outward.
(d) Result in a movement along the curve.

_____ 13. The primary way to distinguish among corporations, partnerships, and proprietorships is through:
   (a)   Their ownership characteristics.
   (b)   The size of firms.
   (c)   The market share of leading firms.
   (d)   The number of firms in each classification.

_____ 14. Which of the following would *not* be a common government activity in the U.S. economy?
   (a)   The distribution of goods and services.
   (b)   The regulation of water pollution.
   (c)   Enforcing child labor laws.
   (d)   Requiring producers to label the contents of baby food.

_____ 15. When the production of a good creates external costs:
   (a)   Profits for the producer of the good will be lower.
   (b)   Production of the good will be lower.
   (c)   Society's collective well being will be lower.
   (d)   The level of environment pollution will be lower.

_____ 16. When monopolies exist:
   (a)   Prices tend to be higher.
   (b)   Production tends to be lower.
   (c)   Quality tends to be lower.
   (d)   All of the above can occur.

_____ 17. The result of government intervention in the market in the case of market failure is that:
   (a)   Society is always better off.
   (b)   The production possibilities curve will always shift outward.
   (c)   Society may be worse off.
   (d)   Society will always be worse off.

_____ 18. Which of the following statements about the way markets allocate resources is most accurate from society's perspective?
   (a)   The market always allocates resources in the best way.
   (b)   The market may allocate resources in a way that is not in society's best interest.
   (c)   Resource allocation by markets may not be perfect but it is always better than when the government allocates resources.
   (d)   Markets often fail to allocate resources properly so we must rely on governments to determine the proper use of our resources.

_____ 19. Inequalities in income caused by market forces:
   (a)   Are always undesirable.
   (b)   Can provide incentives and rewards for achievements.
   (c)   Cannot be addressed by government action.
   (d)   Inequalities in income caused by market forces do not exist.

_____ 20. Market signals:
   (a)   Are sent by consumer purchases.
   (b)   Provide incentives for improving efficiency.
   (c)   Are answered by resource reallocations.
   (d)   All of the above.

# Problems and Applications

## Exercise 1

Each January the president has the Council of Economic Advisers prepare an economic report on the state of the U.S. economy called *The Economic Report of the President*. It summarizes the essential features of the economy's performance and describes the policy initiatives that are likely to be undertaken. This exercise uses the kind of information that is developed in this publication.

1. Table 2.1 shows the real GDP and the nominal GDP for the years 1990-97.

### Table 2.1
### Real GDP and nominal GDP, 1990-97

| Year | Real GDP (in billions of dollars per year) | Nominal GDP (in billions of dollars per year) | Percentage growth in real GDP | Percentage growth in nominal GDP | U.S. population (in millions) | Real GDP per capita |
|------|------|------|------|------|------|------|
| 1990 | 6,136.3 | 5,743.8 | ------------ | ----------- | 249.9 | _____ |
| 1991 | 6,079.4 | 5,916.7 | _____ | _____ | 252.6 | _____ |
| 1992 | 6,244.4 | 6,244.4 | _____ | _____ | 255.4 | _____ |
| 1993 | 6,389.6 | 6,558.1 | _____ | _____ | 258.1 | _____ |
| 1994 | 6,610.7 | 6,947.0 | _____ | _____ | 260.6 | _____ |
| 1995 | 6,742.1 | 7,265.4 | _____ | _____ | 263.0 | _____ |
| 1996 | 6,928.4 | 7,636.0 | _____ | _____ | 265.5 | _____ |
| 1997 | 7,191.4 | 8,083.4 | _____ | _____ | 267.9 | _____ |

2. From the information in Table 2.1, calculate the percentage growth in nominal and real GDP for each of the years 1991-97 and insert your answers in the appropriate columns.
   Use the following formula:

$$\text{Percentage growth in real GDP} = \frac{\text{real GDP}_t - \text{real GDP}_{t-1}}{\text{real GDP}_{t-1}} \times 100\%$$

where $t$ = current year

$t - 1$ = previous year

For example, for 1991 real GDP grew by the following percentage:

$$\frac{\text{real GDP}_t - \text{real GDP}_{t-1}}{\text{real GDP}_{t-1}} = \frac{\$6,079.4 - \$6,136.3}{\$6,136.3} \times 100\% = -0.9\%$$

3. T    F    When nominal GDP grows, real GDP must grow.
4. By what nominal-dollar amount did nominal GDP grow from 1990 to 1997? $_____
5. By what constant-dollar amount did real GDP grow from 1990 to 1997? $_____
6. The U.S. population for the years 1990–97 is presented in column 6 of Table 2.1. Calculate the real GDP per capita in column 7.
7. T    F    When real GDP rises, real GDP per capita must also rise.

# Exercise 2

This problem is designed to help you understand the mix of output in the United States.

1. Calculate the percentage of total output accounted for by each of the expenditure categories in Table 2.2. Then compare your answers to Figure 2.3 in the text. Figures will not be exact due to rounding.

**Table 2.2. U.S. national-income aggregates, 1997 (billions of dollars per year)**

| Expenditure categories | | Percentage of total output |
|---|---|---|
| Consumption goods and services | $5,489 | _____ |
| Investment goods | 1,238 | _____ |
| Exports | 959 | _____ |
| Imports | 1,056 | _____ |
| Federal government purchases | 525 | _____ |
| State and local government purchases | 929 | _____ |

2. Are net exports positive or negative in Table 2.2? _____

3. T  F    When net exports are negative, an economy uses more goods and services than it produces.

# Exercise 3

This exercise focuses on the growth rates for GDP, population, and per capita GDP.

Refer to Table 2.1 in the text to answer questions 1-5.

1. Which country had the lowest growth rate of per capita GDP during this time period? _____

2. Which country had the highest growth rate of per capita GDP during this time period? _____

3. In Kenya, the growth rate of GDP during this time period was _____ percent and the growth rate of population was _____ percent. When the population growth rate is greater than the GDP growth rate, then per capita GDP must (increase, decrease).

4. In general, the population of high-income countries grew more (rapidly, slowly) which made it easier to raise living standards.

5. T  F    Since the GDP growth rate for Nigeria was greater than the GDP growth rate for Zimbabwe, during this time period, then Nigeria experienced a greater increase in per capita GDP than did Zimbabwe.

# Common Errors

The first statement in each "common error" below is incorrect. Each incorrect statement is followed by a corrected version and an explanation.

1.  A higher GDP means an increase in the standard of living. WRONG!

    A high per capita GDP is an imperfect measure of the standard of living. RIGHT!

    Many developing countries experience a rise in GDP, but their population grows faster. This means that there is actually less income per person and the standard of living falls! The growth in population must be taken into account in measuring the standard of living, which is the reason that the per capita GDP, not just the GDP, is used. However, even the per capita GDP measure fails to take into account the distribution of income.

2.  Investors make an economic investment when they invest in the stock market. WRONG!

    Economic investment occurs only with the *tangible* creation or maintenance of capital goods. RIGHT!

    A distinction must be made between financial investment and economic investment. Common usage usually refers to financial investment in which individuals purchase a financial security backed by a financial institution. Such an activity is called saving, which is the alternative to immediate consumption. Such saving may eventually be used by financial corporations to make loans that will eventually lead to economic investment. But economists have found that there are a lot of things that can happen to saving before it turns into tangible production of capital goods. Therefore economists analyze saving and investment separately.

3.  As the United States imports more, consumption rises and therefore so does the GDP. WRONG!

    Imports replace consumption of goods produced in the United States and lower the GDP. RIGHT!

    The GDP is the sum of consumption, investment, government purchases and *net exports*. Net exports are computed by *subtracting* imports from exports. So, let's look at the GDP as an equation:
    GDP = consumption + investment + government purchases + exports - imports

    Greater imports mean a lower GDP, *ceteris paribus*! Consumption of foreign goods is not the concept of U.S. consumption used by economists. Economists focus on the output that is actually produced *in the United States* to satisfy U.S. consumers, not all of the expenditures that consumers make.

4.  Export goods are not included in the GDP because they are not consumed by Americans. WRONG!

    Export goods are produced in the United States and therefore are included in the GDP. RIGHT!

    The GDP is the sum of consumption, investment, government purchases and *net exports*. Once again the equation appears as follows:
    GDP = consumption + investment + government purchases + exports - imports

    Larger exports mean a higher GDP! The GDP focuses on the output of the economy and our use of resources to produce that output, regardless of who consumes it.

# •ANSWERS•

## Using Key Terms

### Across

1. income transfers
6. income quintile
9. comparative advantage
10. productivity
12. imports
13. monopoly
14. externalities
15. factors of production
16. capital intensive

### Down

2. exports
3. gross domestic product
4. human capital
5. economic growth
7. per capita GDP
8. net exports
11. investment

## True or False

1. T
2. T
3. F   Federal government purchases of goods and services only make up approximately 8 percent of GDP.
4. F   These are income transfers and are not included in GDP. No good or service is directly provided in exchange for these payments.
5. T
6. F   Manufacturing output has increased by approximately 4 times since just 1950. However, since GDP has increased by more than 4 times since 1950, manufacturing's share of total GDP has decreased.
7. T
8. F   The corporation is dominant in sales and assets, but the single proprietorship is the most common form of business structure in the U.S.
9. T
10. F   Income transfers alter the market's answer to the FOR WHOM question.

## Multiple Choice

| | | | | |
|---|---|---|---|---|
| 1. a | 5. c | 9. a | 13. a | 17. c |
| 2. c | 6. d | 10. b | 14. a | 18. b |
| 3. d | 7. d | 11. d | 15. c | 19. b |
| 4. b | 8. a | 12. c | 16. d | 20. d |

# Problems and Applications

## *Exercise 1*

1. **Table 2.1 Answer**

| Year | Real GDP (in billions of dollars per year) | Nominal GDP (in billions of dollars per year) | Percentage growth in real GDP | Percentage growth in nominal GDP | U.S. population (in millions) | Real GDP per capita |
|------|------|------|------|------|------|------|
| 1990 | 6,136.3 | 5,743.8 | ---- | ---- | 249.9 | 24,555 |
| 1991 | 6,079.4 | 5,916.7 | -0.9 | 3.0 | 252.6 | 24,067 |
| 1992 | 6,244.4 | 6,244.4 | 2.7 | 5.5 | 255.4 | 24,449 |
| 1993 | 6,389.6 | 6,558.1 | 2.3 | 5.0 | 258.1 | 24,756 |
| 1994 | 6,610.7 | 6,947.0 | 3.5 | 5.9 | 260.6 | 25,367 |
| 1995 | 6,742.1 | 7,265.4 | 2.0 | 4.6 | 263.0 | 25,635 |
| 1996 | 6,928.4 | 7,636.0 | 2.8 | 5.1 | 265.5 | 26,096 |
| 1997 | 7,191.4 | 8,083.4 | 3.8 | 5.9 | 267.9 | 26,844 |

2. See Table 2.1 answer, columns 4, 5
3. F
4. $2,339.6 billion

5. $1,055.1 billion
6. See Table 2.1 answer, column 7
7. F

## *Exercise 2*

1. **Table 2.2 Answer**

| Expenditure categories | | Percentage of total output |
|------|------|------|
| Consumption goods and services | $5,489 | 67.9 |
| Investment goods | 1,238 | 15.3 |
| Exports | 959 | 11.9 |
| Imports | 1,056 | 13.1 |
| Federal government purchases | 525 | 6.5 |
| State and local government purchases | 929 | 11.5 |

2. Negative
3. T

## *Exercise 3*

1. Haiti
2. China
3. 2.0, 2.6, decrease
4. slowly
5. F

# CHAPTER 3
# Supply and Demand

## Quick Review

Nations around the world have abandoned central planning as a means of answering the WHAT, HOW, and FOR WHOM questions and are hastily turning to free markets for solutions instead. To understand how a market economy solves these same questions requires an understanding of the essential features of market-directed activity—demand and supply. To focus our discussion, we examine the following questions:

- What determines the price of a good or service?
- How does the price of a product affect its production or consumption?
- Why do prices and production levels often change?

All market participants have a common characteristic. They try to maximize some goal subject to one or more constraints. They do so by participating in markets.

Let's look at some market participants and see how they interact. Households and firms exchange factors of production in factor markets and goods and services in product markets. The quantity supplied of factors or products in a market is the quantity that sellers are willing and able to sell at a particular price. Market prices are likely to affect the quantity supplied. Economists represent the relationship between price and the quantity supplied in a supply schedule or supply curve. Supply represents the ability and willingness to sell specific quantities of a good at alternative prices in a given time period, *ceteris paribus*.

The quantity demanded of factors or products in a market is the quantity that buyers are willing and able to buy at a particular price. When prices fall, people tend to buy more. Economists represent the relationship between price and the quantity purchased in the form of a demand schedule or demand curve. Demand is the ability and willingness to buy specific quantities of a good at alternative prices in a given time period, *ceteris paribus*. Demand and supply do not determine what is actually exchanged, nor do they tell why an exchange occurs.

Market supply and market demand curves can be used to find the equilibrium price and rate of production in a market. A market supply curve is the sum of the supply curves of the sellers in the market. Similarly, a market demand curve is the sum of the individual demand curves of buyers in the market. When the market demand curve intersects the market supply curve, the market is in equilibrium. The market mechanism moves price toward the equilibrium price level as follows:

1. If the market price is above the equilibrium price, surpluses appear. To get rid of the surplus, sellers lower prices and production rates. Buyers purchase more at lower prices.
2. If the market price is below equilibrium price, shortages occur. Buyers bid up the price of the commodity and sellers raise production rates in response to the increased price.

In both cases, price and production rates change until the market reaches the equilibrium price and equilibrium quantity production rate - the price and quantity that clears the market. The market mechanism is not perfect and may fail if there are externalities. It may not allocate income in a desirable way, but it does answer the questions WHAT to produce, HOW to produce, and FOR WHOM to produce.

Market demand and market supply curves shift for a variety of reasons. Changes in the price or availability of other goods, tastes, income, expectations, and the number of buyers can alter market demand. Changes in resource prices, in technology, in expectations, in taxes, and in the number of sellers can alter market supply. With each shift the market finds its way, through trial and error, back to equilibrium. Governments sometimes feel compelled to interfere with the market mechanism by establishing maximum prices (price ceilings) for certain things. No matter how laudable the goals of the program for which they are instituted, price ceilings result in shortages. In some cases the results have been so perverse that public-sector intervention moves society away from, rather than toward, preferred economic outcomes. Participants in the market for rent-controlled apartments in New York and Moscow can attest to this.

## Learning Objectives

After reading Chapter 3 and doing the following exercises, you should:

1. Know the basic questions in economics and how the U.S. economy answers the questions.
2. Be able to describe the different types of markets and the motivations of participants in those markets.
3. Understand how a demand schedule represents demand and how a supply schedule represents supply.
4. Be able to define and graph supply and demand curves.
5. Know why supply and demand curves shift.
6. Know what causes movements along demand and supply curves.
7. Know the difference between individual demand and supply vs. market demand and market supply.
8. Be able to explain shortages and surpluses and the effects of price ceilings and price floors.
9. Be able to describe how and why markets move toward equilibrium.

## Using Key Terms

Fill in the puzzle on the opposite page with the appropriate term from the list of Key Terms at the end of the chapter in the text.

### *Across*

3.  The result of rent controls discussed on page 62-63 in the text.
6.  Changes from $2.00 to $3.00 in Figure 3.7 in the text.
7.  The willingness and ability to sell various quantities of a good at alternative prices.
10. The willingness and ability to buy a particular good at some price.
12. The assumption by economists that nothing else changes.
15. Where businesses purchase the factors of production.
16. The use of market price and sales to signal desired output.
17. Refers to the inverse relationship between price and quantity.

### *Down*

1.  The result of an income change in Figure 3.3 in the text.
2.  According to the cyber note on page 50 in the text, consumers reveal their _____ to Priceline.
3.  The sum of all producers' sales intentions.
4.  The name of the table from which Figure 3.2 in the text is drawn.
5.  Where goods and services are exchanged.
8.  According to Figure 3.6 in the text, at a price of $2.50 per page, a _____ of 32 pages per semester exists.
9.  The response of some local governments, including New York City, to high rent prices according to the text.
11. Explains why the curve in Figure 3.5 in the text is upward sloping.

13. The value of the most desirable forgone alternative.
14. The name for the final curve on the right in Figure 3.4 in the text.

# Puzzle 3.1

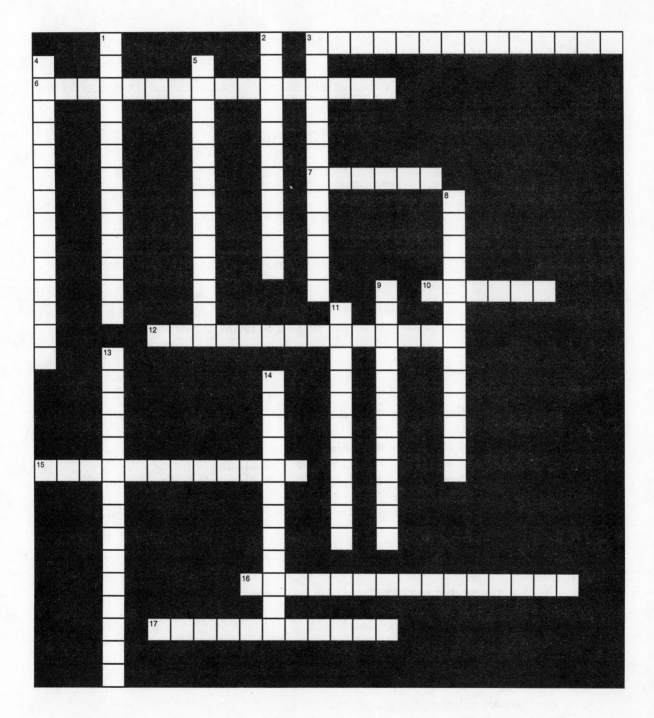

## True or False: *Circle your choice and explain why any false statements are incorrect.*

T   F   1.   The demand curve shows how much of a good a buyer will actually buy at a given price.

T   F   2.   A change in one of the determinants of demand causes a movement along the demand curve for the good.

T   F   3.   An increase in the price of one good can cause the demand for another good to increase if the goods are substitutes.

T   F   4.   Supply curves reflect the potential behavior of the sellers or producers of a good or service, not of the buyers.

T   F   5.   The "law of supply" has nothing to do with opportunity costs.

T   F   6.   When the number of suppliers in a market changes, the market supply curve also changes, even if the individual supply curves of original suppliers do not shift.

T   F   7.   The equilibrium price can be determined through the process of trial and error by both the buyers and the sellers in a market.

T   F   8.   There are never shortages or surpluses when the price in a market is equal to the equilibrium price for the market.

T   F   9.   When economists say that the market mechanism provides an "optimal" allocation of resources they mean that all consumer desires are satisfied and business profits are maximized.

T   F   10.  In a market economy, producers earn profits by producing the goods and services that consumers want the most.

## Multiple Choice: *Select the correct answer.*

_____  1.   The goals of the principal actors in the economy are:
   (a)   Income for consumers, profits for businesses, and taxes for government.
   (b)   Goods and services for consumers, scarce resources for businesses, and resources not used by businesses for government.
   (c)   Satisfaction from purchases for consumers, profits for businesses, and general welfare for government.
   (d)   Available goods and services for consumers, scarce resources for businesses, and general welfare for government.

_____  2.   The incentives for economic interaction among market participants include:
   (a)   Limited ability to produce what we need.
   (b)   Constraints on time, energy, and resources.
   (c)   The gains possible from specialization.
   (d)   All of the above.

_____  3.   Consumers:
   (a)   Provide dollars to the product market.
   (b)   Receive dollars from the product market.
   (c)   Provide dollars to the factor market.
   (d)   Receive goods and services from the factor market.

34

4. The law of demand states that:
   (a) As price falls, quantity demanded falls, *ceteris paribus.*
   (b) As price falls, quantity demanded increases, *ceteris paribus.*
   (c) As price falls, demand falls, *ceteris paribus.*
   (d) As price falls, demand increases, *ceteris paribus.*

5. Which of the following must be held constant according to the *ceteris paribus* assumption in defining a demand schedule?
   (a) The price of the good itself.
   (b) Expectations of sellers.
   (c) Income.
   (d) Technology.

6. The quantity of a good that a consumer is willing to buy depends on:
   (a) The price of the good.
   (b) The consumer's income.
   (c) The opportunity cost of purchasing that good.
   d) All of the above.

7. Jon's demand schedule for donuts indicates:
   (a) How much he likes donuts.
   (b) His opportunity cost of buying donuts.
   (c) Why he likes donuts.
   (d) How many donuts he will actually buy.

8. According to the law of supply, a supply curve:
   (a) Has a negative slope.
   (b) Has a positive slope.
   (c) Is a horizontal, or flat, line.
   (d) Will always be less than the demand curve.

9. When a seller sells a good, *ceteris paribus*:
   (a) There is no change in supply or the quantity supplied.
   (b) The supply curve shifts to the left, but quantity supplied remains the same.
   (c) The quantity supplied of the good falls, but supply remains unchanged.
   (d) The supply curve shifts to the left, and the quantity supplied falls.

10. If corn and wheat are alternative pursuits for a farmer, a change in the supply of corn will take place:
    (a) When the price of corn changes.
    (b) When the price of wheat changes.
    (c) When the demand for corn changes.
    (d) When consumers want to buy more corn at the same price.

11. Suppose that this spring the MC birdhouse Co. announced that they need higher prices than last year to sell the same quantity of birdhouses. We can conclude that:
    (a) There has been an increase in demand.
    (b) There has been a decrease in demand.
    (c) There has been a decrease in the company's supply.
    (d) There has been an increase in the company's supply.

12. To calculate market supply we:
    (a) Add the quantities supplied for each individual supply schedule horizontally.
    (b) Add the quantities supplied for each individual supply schedule vertically.
    (c) Find the average quantity supplied at each price.
    (d) Find the difference between the quantity supplied and the quantity demanded at each price.

_____ 13. Market supply and market demand are similar in that both:
  (a)  Involve the willingness and ability of a supplier to sell a product or service.
  (b)  Can be derived by adding horizontally all the respective supply and demand curves of the individuals in the market.
  (c)  Are affected by income.
  (d)  Have price on the x-axis and production rate(quantity) on the y-axis.

_____ 14. In a market, the equilibrium price is determined by:
  (a)  What buyers are willing and able to purchase.
  (b)  What sellers are willing and able to offer for sale.
  (c)  Both demand and supply.
  (d)  The government.

_____ 15. A leftward shift in a demand curve and a leftward shift in a supply curve both result in a:
  (a)  Lower equilibrium quantity.
  (b)  Higher equilibrium quantity.
  (c)  Lower equilibrium price.
  (d)  Higher equilibrium price.

_____ 16. Supply and demand do not necessarily tell us:
  (a)  The actual quantities produced and bought in a market.
  (b)  The reasons that a particular quantity is demanded or supplied.
  (c)  Who actually produces or receives the quantity supplied or demand.
  (d)  All of the above.

_____ 17. In a market economy, the people who receive the goods and services produced are the people who:
  (a)  Need the goods and services.
  (b)  Want the goods and services the most.
  (c)  Have the most political power.
  (d)  Are willing and able to pay the market price.

_____ 18. When economists talk about "optimal outcomes" in the marketplace, they mean that:
  (a)  The allocation of resources by the market is perfect.
  (b)  All consumer desires are satisfied and business profits are maximized.
  (c)  The allocation of resources by the market is likely to be the best possible given scare resources and income constraints.
  (d)  Everyone that wants a good or service can get it.

_____ 19. When effective price ceilings are set for a market:
  (a)  Quantity supplied will be less than the equilibrium quantity, and price will be less than the equilibrium price.
  (b)  Quantity supplied will be less than the equilibrium quantity, and price will be greater than the equilibrium price.
  (c)  Quantity supplied will be greater than the equilibrium quantity, and price will be less than the equilibrium price.
  (d)  Quantity supplied will be greater than the equilibrium quantity, and price will be greater than the equilibrium price.

_____ 20. One *World View* article described the difficulty faced by consumers of electricity who were already "severely pinched by . . . the new, real-world prices for food, rents, and other services." The determinant that is shifting the market demand for electricity on the basis of this quotation is:
  (a)   The price of electricity.
  (b)   The price of other goods.
  (c)   Seller expectations.
  (d)   Income.

## Problems and Applications

## *Exercise 1*

This exercise provides practice in graphing demand and supply curves for individual buyers and sellers as well as graphing market demand and market supply curves.

1.  Suppose you are willing and able to buy 20 gallons of gasoline per week if the price is $1 per gallon, but if the price is $3 per gallon you are willing and able to buy only the bare minimum of 10 gallons. Complete the demand schedule in Table 3.1.

### Table 3.1
### Your demand schedule for gasoline

| Price (dollars per gallon) | Quantity (gallons per week) |
| --- | --- |
| $1 | _____ |
| 3 | _____ |

2.  Use the demand schedule in Table 3.1 to draw the demand curve in Figure 3.1. Assume the demand curve is a straight line.

### Figure 3.1
### Your demand curve for gasoline.

If you have drawn your demand curve correctly, it should go through point *A*.

3. Suppose that 999 other people in your town have demand curves for gasoline that are just like yours in Figure 3.1. Fill out the town's market-demand schedule in Table 3.2 at each price. (Remember to include your own quantity demanded along with everyone else's at each price.)

### Table 3.2
### Market-demand schedule for gasoline in your town

| Price (dollars per gallon) | Quantity (gallons per week) |
|:---:|:---:|
| $1 | _____ |
| 3 | _____ |

4. Using the market-demand schedule in Table 3.2, draw the market-demand curve for gasoline for your town in Figure 3.2. Assume that the curve is a straight line, and label it *D*.

### Figure 3.2
### Market supply and demand curves for gasoline in your town

If you have drawn the demand curve correctly, it should pass through point *A*.

5. Suppose the friendly neighborhood gas station is willing to sell 250 gallons of gasoline per week at $1 per gallon and 1,250 gallons per week at $3 per gallon. Fill in the supply schedule for this gas station in Table 3.3.

### Table 3.3
### Supply schedule for neighborhood gas station

| Price (dollars per gallon) | Quantity (gallons per week) |
|:---:|:---:|
| $1 | _____ |
| 3 | _____ |

6.  Graph the supply curve for the gas station in Figure 3.3 using the information in Table 3.3. Assume that the supply curve is a straight line.

## Figure 3.3
## Supply curve for neighborhood gas station

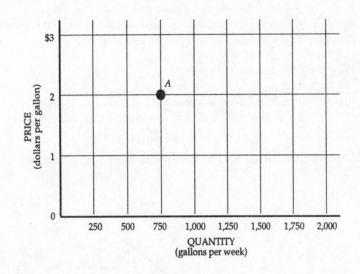

If you have drawn the supply curve correctly, it should pass through point *A*.

7.  Suppose that nineteen other gas stations in your town have the same supply schedule as your neighborhood gas station (Table 3.3). Fill out the market-supply schedule for gasoline of the 20 gas stations in your town in Table 3.4.

## Table 3.4
## Market supply schedule for gasoline in your town

| Price (dollars per gallon) | Quantity (gallons per week) |
|---|---|
| $1 | _____ |
| 3 | _____ |

8.  Using the market supply schedule in Table 3.4, draw the market supply curve for gasoline for your town in Figure 3.2. Assume that the market supply curve is a straight line. If you have drawn the curve correctly, it should pass through point *A*. Label the supply curve *S*.

9.  The equilibrium price for gasoline for your town's 20 gas stations and 1,000 buyers of gasoline (see Figure 3.2) is:
    (a)    Above $2.
    (b)    Exactly $2.
    (c)    Below $2.

10. At the equilibrium price:
   (a)  There is a shortage.
   (b)  There is a surplus.
   (c)  There is an excess of inventory.
   (d)  The quantity demanded equals the quantity supplied.

## Exercise 2

This exercise shows the market mechanics at work in shifting market-demand curves.

1. In Figure 3.4, the supply ($S_1$) and demand ($D_1$) curves for gasoline as they might appear in your town are presented. The equilibrium price and quantity are:
   (a)  $3 per gallon and 20,000 gallons.
   (b)  $2 per gallon and 20,000 gallons.
   (c)  $2 per gallon and 15,000 gallons.
   (d)  $1 per gallon and 15,000 gallons.

### Figure 3.4
### Market demand and supply curves for gasoline in your town

2. Assume that one-half of the people in your town move away. Because of this, suppose that the remaining buyers are willing and able to buy only half as much gasoline at each price as was bought before. Draw the new demand curve in Figure 3.4 and label it $D_2$.

3. When the number of buyers in a market changes, the market demand curve for goods and services shifts and there is a change in (demand, quantity demanded).

4. When half of the buyers move from your town and the demand curve shifts, the new equilibrium price:
   (a)  Is above the old equilibrium price.
   (b)  Remains the same as the old equilibrium price.
   (c)  Is below the old equilibrium price.
   (*Hint:* See the second demand curve, $D_2$, in Figure 3.4.)

40

5. Given the new demand curve, if the market price remains at the old equilibrium price of $2 then:
   (a) A surplus of gasoline will occur.
   (b) A shortage of gasoline will occur.
   (c) The quantity demanded will equal the quantity supplied.

6. When there is a surplus in a market:
   (a) Buyers do not wish to buy as much as sellers want to sell.
   (b) Sellers are likely to offer discounts to eliminate expensive excess inventories.
   (c) Buyers who cannot buy commodities at the current market price are likely to make offers to buy at lower prices that sellers will now accept.
   (d) All the above.

7. When there is a leftward shift of the market-demand curve, market forces should push:
   (a) Market prices upward and market quantity downward.
   (b) Market prices upward and market quantity upward.
   (c) Market prices downward and market quantity upward.
   (d) Market prices downward and market quantity downward.

8. Whenever there is a rightward shift of the market demand curve, market forces should push:
   (a) Market prices upward and market quantity downward.
   (b) Market prices upward and market quantity upward.
   (c) Market prices downward and market quantity upward.
   (d) Market prices downward and market quantity downward.

# Exercise 3

This exercise gives practice in computing market demand and market supply curves using the demand and supply curves of individuals in a market. It is similar to a problem for chapter 3 in the text.

1. Table 3.5 shows the weekly demand and supply schedules for various individuals. Fill in the total market quantity that these individuals demand and supply.

## Table 3.5
## Individual demand and supply schedules

| Price | $4 | $3 | $2 | $1 |
|---|---|---|---|---|
| **Buyers** | | | | |
| Al's quantity demanded | 2 | 3 | 5 | 6 |
| Betsy's quantity demanded | 2 | 2 | 2 | 3 |
| Casey's quantity demanded | 1 | 2.5 | 3 | 3.5 |
|   Total market quantity demanded | ____ | ____ | ____ | ____ |
| | | | | |
| **Sellers** | | | | |
| Alice's quantity supplied | 4 | 3 | 2 | 1 |
| Butch's quantity supplied | 6 | 5 | 4 | 2 |
| Connie's quantity supplied | 5 | 4 | 3 | 2 |
| Ellen's quantity supplied | 5 | 3 | 1 | 0 |
|   Total market quantity supplied | ____ | ____ | ____ | ____ |

Use the data in Table 3.5 to answer questions 2-4.

2. Construct and label market-supply and market-demand curves in Figure 3.5.

3. Identify the equilibrium point and label it *EQ* in Figure 3.5.

4. What is the situation in terms of quantity demanded versus quantity supplied at a price of $1 in Figure 3.5?

## Figure 3.5
## Market-supply and market-demand curves for buyers and sellers

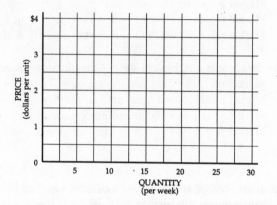

# Exercise 4

This exercise provides examples of events that would shift demand or supply curves. It is similar to a problem at the end of the chapter in the text.

## Figure 3.6
## Shifts of curves

Choose the letter of the appropriate diagram in Figure 3.6 that best describes the shift that would occur in each of the following situations. The shifts are occurring in the market for U.S. defense goods. (*Hint:* Ask yourself if the change first affects buyers or the sellers. Refer to the nonprice determinants for demand and supply listed in the text if necessary).

42

_____ 1.  Because of increased protectionism for steel, steel producers are able to raise the price of specialty steel, which is a key resource in the production of defense goods.

_____ 2.  A new superior engineering design is developed that reduces the amount of materials needed to produce nuclear submarines.

_____ 3.  New buyers enter the market to purchase defense goods.

_____ 4.  A large firm in the defense industry closes down when it loses a defense contract.

_____ 5.  A country that previously bought U.S. defense goods enters into a peace agreement.

## Exercise 5

The media often provide information about supply and demand shifts. This exercise uses one of the articles in the text to show the kind of information to look for.

Reread the *In the News* article entitled "Orange Prices Start to Rise After California Freeze." Then answer the following questions:

1.  Which of the four diagrams in Figure 3.6 in the previous exercise best represents the shift in the orange market caused by the freeze?   a   b   c   d     (circle one)

2.  The change in the orange market is referred to as a:
    (a) Change in demand.
    (b) Change in quantity demanded.
    (c) Change in supply.
    (d) Change in quantity supplied.

3.  What is the expected change in price and quantity in the orange market?
    _____

## Common Errors

The first statement in each "common error" below is incorrect. Each incorrect statement is followed by a corrected version and an explanation.

1.  If a large number of people petition the government in order to get something, then there is a large demand for that item. WRONG!

    If a large number of people desire a commodity *and have the ability to pay for it,* then there is a large demand for that item. RIGHT!

    People want something, but there is no "demand" for it unless they are able to pay for it. Economists use the word "demand" in a way that is quite different from normal usage. People who want (desire; have preferences, a taste, or liking for) a commodity are seen as going to a market to purchase the commodity with money. "Demand" does not mean claiming the right to something when a person hasn't the ability to buy it.

43

2. Market price is the same thing as equilibrium price. WRONG!

The market price moves by trial and error (via the market mechanism) toward the equilibrium price. RIGHT!

When demand and supply curves shift, the market is temporarily out of equilibrium. The price may move along a demand or supply curve toward the new equilibrium.

3. Since the quantity bought must equal the quantity sold, every market is always in equilibrium by definition. WRONG!

Although quantity bought equals quantity sold, there may be shortages or surpluses. RIGHT!

Although the quantity actually bought does equal the quantity actually sold, there may still be buyers who are willing and able to buy more of the good at the market price (market shortages exist) or sellers who are willing and able to sell more of the good at the market price (market surpluses exist). If the market price is above the equilibrium price, there will be queues of goods (inventories). Prices will be lowered by sellers toward the equilibrium price. If the market price is below the equilibrium price, there will be queues of buyers (shortages). Prices will be bid up by buyers toward the equilibrium price.

4. The intersection of supply and demand curves determines how much of a good or service will actually be exchanged and the actual price of the exchange. WRONG!

The intersection of supply and demand curves shows only where buyers and sellers intend and have the ability to exchange the same amount of a commodity. RIGHT!

Many institutional interferences may prevent the market from ever reaching the equilibrium point, where supply and demand curves intersect. All that can be said is that, given a free market, prices and production will tend to move toward equilibrium levels.

5. A change in price changes the demand for goods by consumers. WRONG!

A change in price changes the quantity demanded by consumers in a given time period. RIGHT!

Economists differentiate the terms "quantity demanded" and "demand." A change in the quantity demanded usually refers to a movement along the demand curve as a result of a change in price. A change in demand refers to a shift of the demand curve as a result of a change in incomes, tastes, prices or availability of other goods, or expectations.

6. A change in price changes the supply of goods produced by a firm. WRONG!

A change in price changes the quantity supplied of a good by a firm in a given time period. RIGHT!

Economists differentiate the terms "quantity supplied" and "supply." A change in the quantity supplied usually refers to a movement along a supply curve as a result of a change in price or production rate. A change in supply refers to a shift of the supply curve as a result of a change in technology, prices of resources, number of sellers, other goods, expectations, or taxes.

# •ANSWERS•

## Using Key Terms

### Across

3.   market shortage
6.   equilibrium price
7.   supply
10.  demand
12.  ceteris paribus
15.  factor market
16.  market mechanism
17.  law of demand

### Down

1.   shift in demand
2.   demand curve
3.   market supply
4.   demand schedule
5.   product market
8.   market surplus
9.   price ceiling
11.  law of supply
13.  opportunity cost
14.  market demand

## True or False

1.   F   The demand curve indicates how much a buyer would like to buy and is able to pay for. How much is actually bought also depends on supply.
2.   F   A change in one of the determinants of demand results in a shift in the demand curve.
3.   T
4.   T
5.   F   The quantity of a good that a producer is willing and able to produce and offer for sale at any price depends on the value of the alternative goods that could have been produced with those same resources, i.e. the opportunity costs.
6.   T
7.   T
8.   T
9.   F   An optimal outcome does not mean that all consumer desires are satisfied and business profits are maximized. It simply means that the market outcome is likely to be the best possible given scarce resources and income constraints.
10.  F   In a market economy, producers earn profits by producing the goods and services that consumers demand, i.e. are willing and able to pay for.

## Multiple Choice

| | | | | | |
|---|---|---|---|---|---|
| 1. c | 5. c | 9. a | 13. b | 17. d |
| 2. d | 6. d | 10. b | 14. c | 18. c |
| 3. a | 7. b | 11. c | 15. a | 19. a |
| 4. b | 8. b | 12. a | 16. d | 20. b |

# Problems and Applications

## *Exercise 1*

1.  **Table 3.1 Answer**

| p | q |
|---|---|
| $1 | 20 |
| 3 | 10 |

2.  **Figure 3.1 Answer**

3.  **Table 3.2 Answer**

| p | q |
|---|---|
| $1 | 20,000 |
| 3 | 10,000 |

46

4.  See Figure 3.2 Answer, curve D.

## Figure 3.2 Answer

5.  ## Table 3.3 Answer

| p | q |
|---|---|
| $1 | 250 |
| 3 | 1,250 |

6.  ## Figure 3.3 Answer

7.  ## Table 3.4 Answer

| p | q |
|---|---|
| $1 | 5,000 |
| 3 | 25,000 |

8.  See Figure 3.2 Answer, curve S.

47

9.   b
10.   d

## Exercise 2

1.   c

2.   Figure 3.4 Answer

3.   demand
4.   c
5.   a
6.   d
7.   d
8.   b

## Exercise 3

1.   **Table 3.5 Answer**

| Price | $4 | $3 | $2 | $1 |
|---|---|---|---|---|
| *Buyers*<br>Total market quantity demanded | 5 | 7.5 | 10 | 12.5 |
| *Sellers*<br>Total market quantity supplied | 20 | 15 | 10 | 5 |

2.    **Figure 3.5 Answer.**

3.    See point *EQ* in Figure 3.5.
4.    The quantity demanded is greater than the quantity supplied or there is a shortage of 7.5 units (12.5 minus 5).

## Exercise 4

1.  a
2.  b
3.  d
4.  a
5.  c

## Exercise 5

1.  a
2.  c
3.  an increase in price and a decrease in quantity

49

# CHAPTER 4
# The Public Sector

## Quick Review

The combined levels of government—federal, state, and local—have a tremendous impact on the answers to the questions WHAT, HOW, and FOR WHOM in the U.S. economy. In this chapter we focus initially on the following questions:

- Do we need a public sector?
- What goods and services are best produced by the government?
- How large a public sector is desirable?

There are several ways to justify the existence of the public sector. One justification is market failure, the failure of the market mechanism when left on its own to produce an "optimal mix" of output. This first justification for government intervention resides in the concept of "public goods." These goods and services are consumed jointly, both by those who pay and by those who don't. Those who don't pay are termed "free riders." National defense is a good example, because the consumption of national defense is communal. Consumption by one person does not preclude consumption by another. Public goods are different from private goods, because consumption of a private good by one person generally does preclude consumption by another.

The existence of externalities—costs or benefits of a market activity that are borne by a third party—is often cited as justification of public-sector activity, too. Externalities can be negative (such as the pollution from a steel mill) or positive (such as the enrichment of the surrounding community when education is produced and consumed). Because the market has no way of accounting for all the costs and benefits of some forms of economic activity, it tends to underproduce those that generate external benefits and overproduce those that generate external costs.

The existence of market power—the ability of a single firm to alter the market price of a specific product—also justifies public-sector intervention. Market power—whether bestowed by a legal sanction (copyrights, patents, and the like), efficiencies of large-scale production, or some other factor—can be used to restrict output and raise prices. The public sector counters market power by antitrust activity and/or regulation (as with cable TV).

Finally, lack of equity in the answer to the FOR WHOM question is the basis for a large measure of public-sector activity. The market mechanism, left on its own, would provide too little for some (the aged, the infirm, some of the very young) than is thought fair. Since the public at large is thought to benefit from expenditures made to address this problem, income redistribution—for example, through transfer payments—is considered a public good.

The examples above focus on micro failures (i.e., where *we are on* the production-possibilities curve). Macro failures can also occur, such as when *we fail to reach* our production-possibilities curve or experience inflation. Thus, government is expected to intervene at the macro level to alleviate the problem of unemployment and stabilize the price level.

The role of government has grown dramatically in recent decades. The budget of the federal government is $1.8 trillion per year, but it still takes a slightly smaller share (of the now much larger economy) than it did in 1950. State and local government activity exceeds that of the federal government and has grown much more rapidly in recent decades. Transfer payments have increased much faster than purchases of goods and services, and they account for the largest part of the observed increase in the size of the entire public sector.

Federal expenditures on goods and services, transfer payments, interest on the public debt, and general aid to state and local governments are supported by the federal personal income tax, social security taxes, corporate income taxes, excise taxes, and other taxes. State and local governments rely most heavily on sales taxes and on property taxes, respectively. Their expenditures go primarily to education, streets and highways, and other services we find close to home.

Whether government is "too big" depends on one's perception of the private-sector activity forgone when government absorbs resources and changes the mix of the economy's output. Cost-benefit analysis and mechanisms that allow taxpayers to vote on projects are ways of trying to ensure that we get the amount and kind of government we want.

Critics of public-sector activity emphasize the role of public officials' self-interest in the decision-making process. In fact, public-choice theory essentially extends the analysis of market behavior to political behavior. Public officials are viewed as utility maximizers pursuing their own individual goals rather than public goals.

## Learning Objectives

After reading Chapter 4 and doing the following exercises, you should:

1. Be able to explain the different types of micro failure that justify public-sector intervention.
2. Understand how macro failure justifies public-sector activity.
3. Recognize the opportunity costs of public-sector activity.
4. Know how the mechanism of public decision making differs from the market mechanism.
5. Be able to compute and use cost-benefit ratios.
6. Know the effects of externalities and how they should be handled in the economy.
7. Know the different tax structures and the level of government for which they are particularly important.
8. Be able to determine whether a given tax is progressive or regressive.
9. Know some of the important policy issues connected with taxation, expenditure and borrowing.
10. Understand the essentials of public choice.

## Using Key Terms

Fill in the puzzle on the opposite page with the appropriate term from the list of Key Terms at the end of the chapter in the text.

### Across

1. The most desired goods and services that are given up in order to obtain something else.
5. An increase in the average level of prices.
8. Referred to as the "invisible hand."
10. The likely outcome of government intervention according to the survey titled "Rising Doubts about Government Waste" in the text.
14. An industry in which a single firm achieves economies of scale over the entire range of output.
16. State lotteries are categorized in this way according to the article titled "Some Taxing Facts about Lotteries" in the text.
18. A form of government intervention to address the FOR WHOM question.
19. Theory which emphasizes the role of self-interest in public decision making.
20. The ability to alter the market price of a good or service.
21. The fee paid for the use of a public-sector good or service.

### Down

2. Labeled as point X in Figure 4.1 in the text.
3. Occurs when people are willing to work but are unable to find jobs.

4. The market failure discussed in the article "The Human Cost of Secondhand Smoke" in the text.
6. A tax system in which tax rates rise as incomes rise.
7. For a _____, consumption by one person excludes consumption by others.
9. Federal grants to state and local governments for specific purposes.
11. Represented by point M in Figure 4.1 in the text.
12. Can be consumed jointly.
13. Only one producer in an industry.
15. One who does not pay but still enjoys the benefits.
17. The legislation used to prevent or break up concentrations of market power such as Microsoft.

## Puzzle 4.1

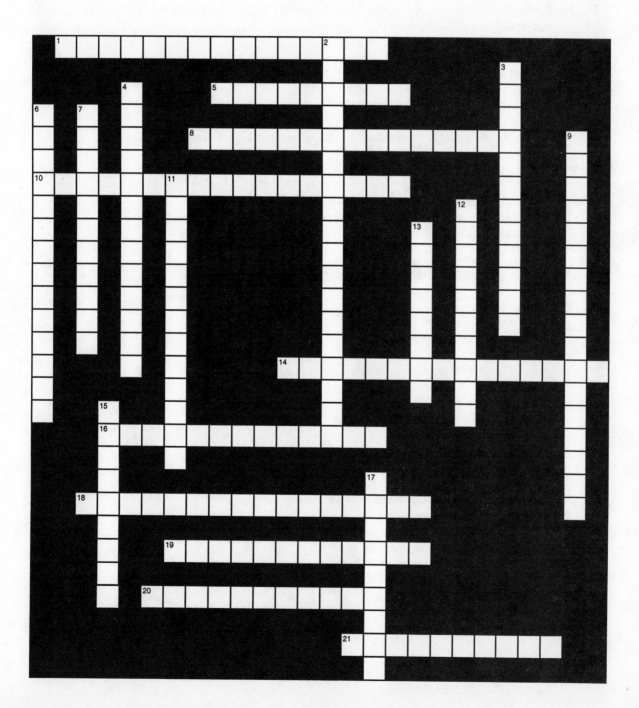

53

## True or False: *Circle your choice and explain why any false statements are incorrect.*

T  F  1.  Market failure implies that the forces of supply and demand have not led to the best point on the production-possibilities curve.

T  F  2.  Government intervention is not necessary even when the market mix of output equals the optimal mix of output.

T  F  3.  The existence of public goods and externalities causes resource misallocations.

T  F  4.  Police protection is an example of a service that involves the free-rider problem.

T  F  5.  If you burn garbage in your backyard and the smoke damages a neighbor's house, the damage is considered an externality.

T  F  6.  Markets will overproduce goods that yield external benefits and underproduce goods that yield external costs.

T  F  7.  Market power creates a flawed response to an accurate price signal.

T  F  8.  Monopolies will tend to overproduce goods and charge a higher than competitive price.

T  F  9.  The federal government in the U.S. economy has grown in both relative and absolute terms since the 1950s.

T  F  10.  When the government intervenes in the economy, the market mix of goods and services is always improved.

## Multiple Choice: *Select the correct answer.*

_____  1.  In a market economy, producers will produce the goods and services:
(a)  That consumers desire the most.
(b)  That consumers need the most.
(c)  That consumers demand.
(d)  That optimize consumer utility.

_____  2.  Market failure includes:
(a)  Externalities.
(b)  Market power.
(c)  Inequity in the distribution of goods and services.
(d)  All of the above.

_____  3.  Market failure suggests that the market mechanism, left alone, will:
(a)  Produce too many public goods and too few private goods.
(b)  Produce too many private goods and too few public goods.
(c)  Produce the optimal mix of output.
(d)  Result in too few resources being allocated to private goods.

4. The market will sometimes fail to produce society's optimum output because:
   (a) Producers do not always measure the same benefits and costs as society.
   (b) Producers will not produce certain types of important goods and services that cannot be kept from consumers who do not pay.
   (c) When producers have market power, they will tend to underproduce goods and services.
   (d) All of the above are correct.

5. When the market fails, which of the following is true?
   (a) The mix of goods and services is inside the production-possibilities curve.
   (b) Government intervention will improve the mix of goods and services.
   (c) The mix of goods and services is at the wrong point on the production-possibilities curve.
   (d) All of the above could be true.

6. Which of the following is most likely a private good?
   (a) Computers.
   (b) National defense.
   (c) Roads.
   (d) Flood control dams.

7. When public goods are marketed like private goods:
   (a) Public goods are underproduced.
   (b) Many consumers want to buy the goods.
   (c) Public goods are overproduced.
   (d) Government failure results.

8. For which of the following goods and services is the government likely to encourage production because of the existence of external benefits?
   (a) Education.
   (b) Health services for the poor.
   (c) A neighborhood renovation project.
   (d) All of the above.

9. The federal government's role in antitrust enforcement is justified by considerations of:
   (a) Equity in the distribution of goods and services.
   (b) Public goods and externalities.
   (c) Underproduction by firms with market power.
   (d) Macro failure.

10. The development of market power by a firm is considered to be a market failure because firms with market power:
    (a) Produce more and charge a lower price than what is socially optimal.
    (b) Tend to ignore external costs.
    (c) Produce less and charge a higher price than what is socially optimal.
    (d) Do not respond to consumer demand.

11. Transfer payments are an appropriate mechanism for correcting:
    (a) Market power.
    (b) Government failure.
    (c) Inflation.
    (d) Inequity in the distribution of goods and services.

_____ 12. Which of the following are both examples of macro failure?
- (a) Externalities and market power.
- (b) Inflation and unemployment.
- (c) Inflation and regulation.
- (d) Regulation and antitrust.

_____ 13. The primary function of taxes is to:
- (a) Transfer command over resources from the private sector to the public sector.
- (b) Increase the purchasing power of the private sector.
- (c) Increase private saving.
- (d) Make it possible to sell bonds to finance the U.S. budget deficit.

_____ 14. Government intervention in the market:
- (a) Involves an opportunity cost.
- (b) Never involves an opportunity cost because only market activities result in other goods and services being given up.
- (c) Does not involve an opportunity cost if market outcomes are improved.
- (d) Results in the "free-rider dilemma."

_____ 15. The largest single source of revenue for the federal government is:
- (a) Borrowing (selling government bonds).
- (b) Social security taxes.
- (c) The corporate profits tax.
- (d) The personal income tax.

_____ 16. Which of the following can be classified as a regressive tax?
- (a) The federal corporate income tax.
- (b) The federal personal income tax.
- (c) The state sales tax.
- (d) All of the above.

_____ 17. Which of the following is an example of a progressive tax?
- (a) The excise tax on distilled spirits.
- (b) The federal tax on gasoline.
- (c) The federal personal income tax.
- (d) All of the above.

_____ 18. States receive most of their tax revenues from :
- (a) Sales taxes.
- (b) State income taxes.
- (c) Property taxes.
- (d) User charges.

_____ 19. If government production forces the economy inside the production-possibilities curve, the following will occur:
- (a) Government failure.
- (b) Waste.
- (c) Inefficiency.
- (d) All of the above.

56

_____ 20. Which of the following would *not* support the theory of public choice?
  (a) The governor of the state vetoes a highway bill even though the highway would enhance the value of property he owns.
  (b) The local mayor campaigns in favor of a bond issue for the construction of sewer lines that will raise the value of his property.
  (c) The local police chief fails to give the mayor a speeding ticket because the mayor might fire him.
  (d) A college president asks the board of regents to allow her to remain in office so she can bolster her retirement income, even though she has reached the mandatory retirement age.

# Problems and Applications

## *Exercise 1*

Assume point *A* represents the optimal mix of output in Figure 4.1.  Determine which letter best represents the following situations.  Then answer questions 4-7.

### Figure 4.1

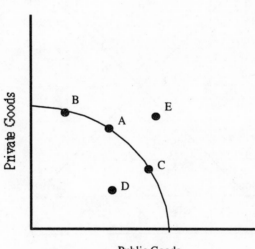

Public Goods

_____ 1. Government failure at the micro level that results in an overproduction of public goods.

_____ 2. The free-rider dilemma.

_____ 3. Macro failure in the marketplace.

4. The market mechanism tends to _____ private goods and _____ public goods.

5. In terms of the production-possibilities curve, _____ failures imply that society is at the wrong point on the curve and _____ failures imply that society is inside the curve.

6. Market failures justify government _____.

7. If government involvement fails to improve market outcomes then there is _____
_____.

## Exercise 2

This exercise examines the difference between internal and external costs and the impact on the demand curve.

Assume that the consumption of the good represented in Figure 4.2 generates external costs of $2 per unit.

1. Draw the social demand curve in Figure 4.2 and label it.

### Figure 4.2

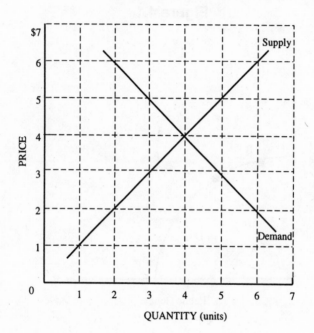

QUANTITY (units)

2. Market equilibrium occurs at a price of _____ and a quantity of _____ in Figure 4.3.

3. The socially optimal level of production occurs at a price of _____ and a quantity of _____.

4. External costs cause the market to produce (more, less) of a good than is optimal.

5. T  F     The market price of $4.00 does not reflect the external costs.

58

# Exercise 3

This exercise focuses on the changes in public-sector spending in the U.S.

Refer to figure 4.4 in the text titled "Government Growth" to answer questions 1-4.

1. The large increase in total government purchases between 1940 and 1945 was the result of an increase in (only federal, both state and local and federal) government spending.

2. Compared to the level of federal spending in 1960, the projected level of federal spending for 2000 is (greater, less, the same).

3. State and local government spending increased from approximately 6 percent of national output in 1950 to approximately _____ percent in 1990.

4. The decrease in total government purchases during the 1990s was primarily due to the decrease in (federal, state and local) purchases.

# Exercise 4

This exercise examines progressive and regressive tax structures.

## Table 4.1.

|  | Income | Tax paid | Percentage of income paid in taxes |
|---|---|---|---|
| Country A | $30,000 | $3,000 | _____ |
|  | $60,000 | $7,200 | _____ |
| Country B | $30,000 | $4,500 | _____ |
|  | $60,000 | $7,800 | _____ |

1. Calculate the percentage of income paid in taxes in Table 4.1.

2. According to Table 4.1, the tax structure in Country A is _____ because the tax rate _____ as income rises.

3. According to Table 4.1, the tax structure in Country B is _____ because the tax rate _____ as income rises.

## Common Errors

The first statement in the "common error" below is incorrect. The incorrect statement is followed by a corrected version and an explanation.

1.  Fire protection, police protection, education, and other services can be produced more efficiently by the private sector than by the public sector. WRONG!

    The public sector can produce many services more efficiently than the private sector. RIGHT!

    You should recognize now that the existence of externalities and the free-rider problem force society to produce some goods and services through public-sector expenditures. Many of the goods and services we take for granted (such as education) would not be produced in sufficient quantities if left to the private sector. And can you imagine trying to provide for your own defense against foreign countries?

## •ANSWERS•

## Using Key Terms
### Across
|    |                  |
|----|------------------|
| 1. | opportunity cost |
| 5. | inflation        |
| 8. | market mechanism |
| 10.| government failure |
| 14.| natural monopoly |
| 16.| regressive tax   |
| 18.| transfer payments |
| 19.| public choice    |
| 20.| market power     |
| 21.| user charge      |

### Down
|     |                      |
|-----|----------------------|
| 2.  | optimal mix of output |
| 3.  | unemployment         |
| 4.  | externalities        |
| 6.  | progressive tax      |
| 7.  | private good         |
| 9.  | categorical grants   |
| 11. | market failure       |
| 12. | public good          |
| 13. | monopoly             |
| 15. | free rider           |
| 17. | antitrust            |

## True or False

1.  T
2.  F   Equity considerations may necessitate government intervention.
3.  T
4.  T
5.  T
6.  F   Markets will underproduce goods that yield external benefits and overproduce goods that yield external costs.

7. T

8. F Monopolies will tend to underproduce goods and are therefore able to charge a higher price.

9. F The federal government has grown in absolute terms since the 1950s but its relative share of production has declined, i.e. it has grown more slowly than the private sector.

10. F Sometimes government intervention worsens the market mix of goods and services. This is an example of "government failure."

## Multiple Choice

| | | | | |
|---|---|---|---|---|
| 1. c | 5. d | 9. c | 13. a | 17. c |
| 2. d | 6. a | 10. c | 14. a | 18. a |
| 3. b | 7. a | 11. d | 15. d | 19. d |
| 4. d | 8. d | 12. b | 16. c | 20. a |

## Problems and Applications

### Exercise 1

1. c
2. b
3. d
4. overproduce, underproduce

5. micro, macro
6. intervention
7. government failure

### Exercise 2

1. See Figure 4.2 answer

**Figure 4.2 Answer**

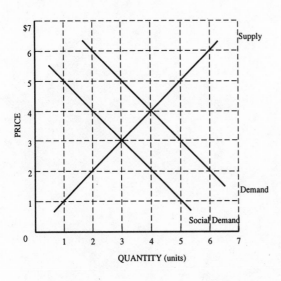

2. $4.00, 4 units
3. $3.00, 3 units
4. more
5. T

61

## Exercise 3

1. only federal
2. less
3. 12 percent
4. federal

## Exercise 4

1. See Table 4.1 Answer

### Table 4.1 Answer

|  | Income | Tax Paid | Percentage of income paid in taxes |
|---|---|---|---|
| Country A | $30,000 | $3,000 | 10% |
|  | $60,000 | $7,200 | 12% |
| Country B | $30,000 | $4,500 | 15% |
|  | $60,000 | $7,800 | 13% |

2. progressive, rises
3. regressive, falls

## CHAPTER 5

# The Demand for Goods

## Quick Review

Demand and supply were introduced in Chapter 3 to demonstrate how markets operate. In this chapter we look at demand in greater depth. Specifically, the chapter looks at the following questions:

- How do we decide how much of any good to buy?
- How does a change in a product's price affect the quantity we purchase or the amount of money we spend on it?
- Why do we buy certain products but not others?

Other concepts are developed too, but these three questions organize our early discussion.

Demand for goods and services is more than just the desire for goods and services and it has nothing to do with the sellers of those goods or services or even with the availability of the goods or services. In fact, demand can exist even if there are no purchases by buyers at all. When people starve as a result of a drought, they have the desire for food but not the ability to pay for it. Demand reflects both the willingness and the ability to buy goods and services. Consumers' tastes, their incomes, the prices (and availability) of other goods, and people's expectations (about tastes, incomes, and prices) determine what individuals are willing and able to buy. If any of these determinants of demand change, then the demand curve shifts. Shifts in the demand curve are likely to cause changes in price and purchases in the marketplace. To understand the market, we must look carefully at tastes, incomes, prices, and expectations.

Utility theory helps clarify much of what we know about consumer tastes and preferences. Consumers buy only those things that give them satisfaction, or utility. Since consumers have a limited income, they must ask what gives them maximum satisfaction for that income. Usually a variety of goods and services is available. Consumers compare the available goods and services—and their relative prices—then choose the amounts that will give them the greatest satisfaction, or utility, for the income available. As a person consumes more and more of any one product, other goods and services become relatively more desirable. This is the law of diminishing marginal utility at work: as we consume more of a product, we receive smaller and smaller *increments* of pleasure from it.

The law of diminishing marginal utility translates readily into the law of demand. The law of demand asserts that we will be willing to buy increasing quantities of a product as its price falls; that is, an inverse relationship exists between quantity demanded and price. This law is graphically illustrated by a downward-sloping demand curve. The demand curve itself relates the quantity of a good demanded to its price, under the assumption that all other things are held constant (*ceteris paribus*). The downward slope of the demand curve indicates that larger quantities of a good will be purchased at lower prices.

The demand curve provides information about the total revenue that a firm could receive. By computing the price elasticity of demand, the firm can even determine how its total revenue changes for a given change in price and how responsive quantity demanded is to a change in price. Income elasticity and cross-price elasticity

63

provide information on how demand curves shift in response to changes in income and the prices of other goods, respectively. The role of advertising can be understood in terms of demand theory—it is to shift the demand curve for a product to the right.

## Learning Objectives

After reading Chapter 5 and doing the following exercises, you should:

1. Be able to distinguish the demand for a good from the desire for it.
2. Be able to show how any change in the price of a good, in the price of a substitute, in the price of a complement, in incomes, in tastes, or in expectations will affect the demand curve.
3. Know how the law of diminishing marginal utility and the law of demand relate to each other.
4. Be able to draw a demand curve from a demand schedule and create a demand schedule by looking at a demand curve.
5. Be able to distinguish between a change in demand (a shift of the curve) and a change in quantity demanded (a movement along the demand curve).
6. Know the determinants of elasticity.
7. Be able to compute the price elasticity of demand between two points on the demand curve.
8. Be able to determine on the basis of the elasticity of demand what will happen to total revenue when price changes.
9. Understand income elasticity, cross-price elasticity and their role in demand theory.
10. Know how a consumer makes the optimal consumption decision.
11. Understand the role of advertising in the theory of demand.

## Using Key Terms

### *Across*

1. Items for which an increase in the price of good X causes a decrease in the demand for good Y.
6. In the cartoon in the text, the fourth hamburger does not provide as much satisfaction as the first hamburger because of the law of _____.
12. Explains why the curve in Figure 5.3 in the text is downward sloping.
13. The satisfaction obtained from the entire consumption of a good.
14. The quantity of a product sold times the price at which it is sold.
15. According to Figure 5.8 in the text, candy and popcorn are _____.
17. Equal to the percentage change in quantity demanded divided by the percentage change in income.
18. Equal to the percentage change in quantity demanded of good X divided by the percentage change in the price of good Y.
19. The best forgone alternative.

### *Down*

2. Influenced by tastes, income, expectations, and other goods.
3. Measures the response of consumers to a change in price.
4. The combination of goods which maximizes the total utility attainable from available income.
5. Positive but diminishing for the first five boxes of popcorn in Figure 5.2 in the text.
7. The result of a successful advertising campaign in Figure 5.9 in the text.
8. An item for which quantity demanded falls when income rises.
9. Affected by advertising in Figure 5.9 in the text.
10. Consumers buy more of such an item when their incomes rise.
11. The assumption that everything else is constant.
16. Satisfaction obtained from goods and services.

# Puzzle 5.1

65

# True or False: *Circle your choice and explain why any false statements are incorrect.*

T  F  1.  Sellers use advertising to change the consumer's utilities, thus causing a shift in the consumer's demand curve.

T  F  2.  The law of demand differs from the law of diminishing marginal utility in that it considers what a person is able to pay for a good or service, not just the person's desire for a good or service.

T  F  3.  When the price of a good is expected to fall next month, then the current demand curve should shift to the right.

T  F  4.  According to the law of diminishing marginal utility, the total utility we obtain from a product declines as we consume more of it.

T  F  5.  If there is no budget constraint, utility maximization is achieved when marginal utility is zero.

T  F  6.  If demand is elastic, a rise in price raises total revenue.

T  F  7.  Elasticity of demand is constant along straight-line demand curves.

T  F  8.  The price elasticity of demand is influenced by all the determinants of demand.

T  F  9.  A demand curve is perfectly elastic if consumers reduce their quantity demanded to zero if price rises by even the slightest amount.

T  F  10.  A negative cross-price elasticity indicates goods are substitutes because a positive percentage increase in one good results in a negative percentage increase in the other.

# Multiple Choice: *Select the correct answer.*

_____  1.  As more of a good is consumed, then total utility typically:
   (a)  Increases at a decreasing rate.
   (b)  Decreases as long as marginal utility is negative.
   (c)  Decreases as long as marginal utility is positive.
   (d)  Is negative as long as marginal utility is decreasing.

_____  2.  Which of the following statements exemplifies the law of diminishing marginal utility?
   (a)  Spinach gives me no satisfaction, so I won't spend my income for any of it.
   (b)  The more soda I drink, the more I want to drink.
   (c)  The more I go to school, the more I want to do something else.
   (d)  Since we need water more than we need diamonds, water is more valuable.

_____  3.  Both the law of demand and the law of diminishing marginal utility:
   (a)  State that quantity and price are inversely related.
   (b)  Reflect declining increments of satisfaction from consuming additional units of product.
   (c)  Reflect both the willingness and the ability of buyers to buy goods and services.
   (d)  Can be illustrated by means of demand curves.

_____ 4. Which of the following is a reason why a demand curve is typically downward sloping?
   (a)   The law of diminishing marginal utility.
   (b)   Consumers are not willing to pay as much for a good with low marginal utility than for a good with a high marginal utility.
   (c)   Consumers have limited budgets.
   (d)   All of the above are reasons.

_____ 5. The price elasticity of demand:
   (a)   Compares the absolute change in quantity demanded with the percentage change in price.
   (b)   Provides information about how responsive consumers are to a change in price.
   (c)   Is the same as the slope of the demand curve.
   (d)   Refers to the response of producers to a change in price.

_____ 6. Which of the following causes demand to be more elastic with respect to price?
   (a)   Shorter periods of time to adjust to a change in price.
   (b)   A steeper demand curve for a given price and quantity.
   (c)   More substitutes.
   (d)   If the good takes up a larger portion of the consumer's budget.

_____ 7. Which of the following is likely to have the most elastic price elasticity of demand?
   (a)   Food.
   (b)   Fruit.
   (c)   Peaches.
   (d)   Farmer Betty's peaches ( which are exactly like all the other farmer's peaches).

_____ 8. Assume that the price elasticity of demand for U.S. Frisbee Co. frisbees is -0.6. If the company increases the price of each frisbee from $6 to $8, the number of frisbees sold will:
   (a)   Decrease by 17.1 percent.
   (b)   Decrease by 47.6 percent.
   (c)   Increase by 28.6 percent.
   (d)   Increase by 17.1 percent.

_____ 9. A demand curve is described as perfectly elastic if:
   (a)   The same quantity is purchased regardless of price.
   (b)   The same price is charged regardless of quantity sold.
   (c)   Only price can change.
   (d)   It is vertical.

_____ 10. Total revenue declines when demand is:
   (a)   Elastic and price rises, causing a demand shift.
   (b)   Elastic and price rises, causing a movement along the demand curve.
   (c)   Inelastic and price rises, causing a demand shift.
   (d)   Inelastic and price rises, causing a movement along the demand curve.

_____ 11. One of the airline industry's arguments against deregulation of air fares was that the resulting fall in prices would lower airline total revenue. Instead, total revenue rose. Assuming the increase in total revenue was due solely to the lower fares, it can be concluded that:
   (a)   Airline representatives thought demand for plane trips was elastic.
   (b)   Quantity demanded of airline service increased by a greater percentage than the percentage fall in price.
   (c)   Demand for airline service increased with the fall in prices.
   (d)   Airlines were more profitable after deregulation.

12. If a state legislature wishes to raise revenue by increasing certain sales taxes, it would increase sales taxes on goods that:
    (a) Are illegal.
    (b) Are bought by those with high incomes.
    (c) Have inelastic demand.
    (d) Have elastic demand.

13. Assume that a good has a downward sloping, linear demand curve. As the price of this good increases, total revenues:
    (a) Increase indefinitely.
    (b) Decrease indefinitely because the quantity sold will decrease.
    (c) Remain constant.
    (d) Increase then decrease.

14. Assume that the price elasticity of demand for Great Fit Shoe Co. shoes is -1.5. If the company decreases the price of each pair of shoes, total revenues will:
    (a) Increase because more shoes will be sold.
    (b) Decrease because the company will be receiving less revenue per pair of shoes.
    (c) Increase because the percentage increase in the number sold is greater than the percentage decrease in the price.
    (d) Impossible to predict because we do not know the percentage change in price.

15. When the price of postage stamps increases, the demand for long-distance telephone service increases, *ceteris paribus*. Postage stamps and long-distance service are therefore:
    (a) Elastic.
    (b) Inelastic.
    (c) Complements.
    (d) Substitutes.

16. Which of the following elasticities would be most useful in determining the impact of a recession on the demand for airline travel?
    (a) The income elasticity of air travel.
    (b) The price elasticity of demand for air travel.
    (c) The cross-price elasticity of demand for air travel with respect to income.
    (d) The cross-price elasticity of income with respect to air travel.

17. Suppose the cross-price elasticity of demand for automobiles with respect to the gasoline price is -0.20. If gasoline prices rise 20 percent, then automobile sales should, *ceteris paribus*:
    (a) Fall 4 percent.
    (b) Fall 100 percent.
    (c) Rise 4 percent.
    (d) Rise 100 percent.

18. Optimal consumption when two or more goods are being consumed is achieved when:
    (a) Opportunity costs relative to utility are zero for all goods.
    (b) Marginal utility equals zero.
    (c) Marginal revenue equals zero.
    (d) The ratio of marginal utility to price is the same for all goods.

_____ 19. To maximize utility when purchasing two or more goods, the consumer should choose that good which:
   (a)   Is priced the lowest.
   (b)   Has the highest price elasticity.
   (c)   Delivers the most marginal utility per dollar.
   (d)   Provides the most satisfaction.

_____ 20. The objective of advertising is to:
   (a)   Increase demand and increase the price elasticity of demand.
   (b)   Increase demand and decrease the price elasticity of demand.
   (c)   Increase demand only.
   (d)   Decrease demand and make the price elasticity of demand unitary.

## [CHAPTER 5 APPENDIX QUESTIONS]

_____ 21. An indifference curve shows:
   (a)   The maximum utility that can be achieved for a given consumer budget.
   (b)   The maximum utility that can be achieved for different amounts of a good.
   (c)   The combinations of goods giving equal utility to a consumer.
   (d)   The optimal consumption combinations between two goods.

_____ 22. A budget line represents:
   (a)   Consumption possibilities.
   (b)   The combinations of goods giving equal utility to a consumer.
   (c)   The combinations of goods a consumer can afford.
   (d)   The amount of income that is required to purchase a given amount of a good.

_____ 23. Where the budget line and an indifference curve are tangent, there is:
   (a)   An optimal consumption point.
   (b)   A point indicating the quantity and price that would appear on a demand curve.
   (c)   A point where the ratio of marginal utility to price is equal for two goods.
   (d)   All of the above.

# Problems and Applications

## Exercise 1

This exercise will help you draw demand curves using demand schedules. It should also give you practice in constructing market demand curves.

   1.   Market demand is:
   (a)   The total quantity of a good or service that people are willing and able to buy at alternative prices in a given period of time, _ceteris paribus_.
   (b)   The sum of individual demands.
   (c)   Represented as the horizontal sum of individual demand curves.
   (d)   All of the above.

2. Table 5.1 presents a hypothetical demand schedule for cars manufactured in the United States.

## Table 5.1 Demand for U.S. cars

| Price | Number of new U.S. cars (millions per year) |
|---|---|
| $10,000 | 9.0 |
| 9,000 | 10.0 |

Graph this demand curve in Figure 5.1.

## Figure 5.1

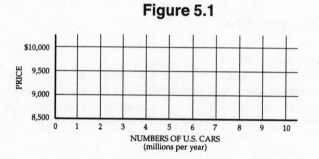

3. Table 5.2 presents a similar demand schedule for imported cars.

## Table 5.2
## Demand for foreign cars

| Price | Number of new foreign cars (millions per year) |
|---|---|
| $10,000 | 1.0 |
| 9,000 | 2.0 |

Graph this demand curve in Figure 5.2.

## Figure 5.2

4. In Table 5.3 calculate the demand schedule for cars (both foreign and domestically produced) at the two prices shown.

## Table 5.3
## Market demand for new cars

| Price | Number of new cars (millions per year) |
|---|---|
| $10,000 | _____ |
| 9,000 | _____ |

5. In Figure 5.3 draw the domestic market demand curve for both foreign and domestic cars.

## Figure 5.3

NUMBERS OF CARS
(millions per year)

## *Exercise 2*

This exercise should give you practice in computing and interpreting the price elasticity of demand. This exercise is similar to a problem in the text.

1. T    F    The midpoint formula for the price elasticity of demand is

$$\frac{(p_2 - p_1)/[1/2(p_1 + p_2)]}{(q_2 - q_1)/[1/2(q_1 + q_2)]}$$

2. If you answered "true" to problem 1, you goofed. The percentage change in quantity, $(q_2 - q_1) \div [1/2(q_1 + q_2)]$, should be on the top, not the bottom. The correct formula is

$$\frac{(q_2 - q_1)/[1/2(q_1 + q_2)]}{(p_2 - p_1)/[1/2(p_1 + p_2)]}$$

Apply this formula to the information in Table 5.4, which represents a hypothetical demand schedule for cars. Remember to use the absolute value of this expression, which makes the coefficient always positive. (When calculating elasticities, answers will vary depending on the number of decimal places used. To achieve the book answer you will need to round each calculation to 2 decimal places.)

71

## Table 5.4
## Market demand schedule for cars

| Price | Number of new U.S. cars (millions per year) | Elasticity of demand |
|---|---|---|
| $10,000 | 10.0 | —— |
| 9,000 | 12.0 | _____ |
| 8,000 | 14.0 | _____ |
| 7,000 | 16.0 | _____ |

3. According to Table 5.4, the price elasticity of demand for U.S. cars is (elastic, inelastic) between $9000 and $8000.

4. According to Table 5.4, what is the total revenue for new U.S. cars at a price of $8000?

5. If the price of new U.S. cars increases from $8000 to $9000, total revenue will (increase, decrease, stay the same).

6. Graph the first two columns of Table 5.4 in Figure 5.4.

## Figure 5.4
## Market demand curve

7. T  F  The curve is a linear demand curve.

8. What is the slope of the demand curve? _____

9. Moving down a linear demand curve results in:
   (a) More inelastic demand and a changing slope.
   (b) More inelastic demand but a constant slope.
   (c) More elastic demand and a changing slope.
   (d) More elastic demand and a constant slope.

10. T  F  While elasticity reflects a ratio of percentage changes in two variables, the slope reflects only changes in the variables, not percentage changes.

# Exercise 3

This exercise focuses on calculating income elasticity and cross-price elasticity. It is similar to a problem in the text.

1. Use Table 5.5 to calculate the income elasticity of demand for peanut butter. Refer to the formula in the text. (Remember to round to 2 decimal places.)

## Table 5.5

|   | Income (per year) | Demand for peanut butter (jars per year) | | Income elasticity of demand |
|---|---|---|---|---|
| a | $10,000 | 12 | | |
| b | $20,000 | 7 | a to b | _____ |
| c | $40,000 | 3 | b to c | _____ |
| d | $80,000 | 1 | c to d | _____ |

2. Based on Table 5.5, peanut butter is a (normal, inferior) good because as income rises, the quantity demanded of peanut butter (rises, falls), and the income elasticity of demand is (negative, positive).

3. Use Table 5.6 to calculate the cross-price elasticity of demand for jelly when the price of peanut butter changes. Refer to the formula in the text. (Remember to round to 2 decimal places.)

## Table 5.6

|   | Price of peanut butter (per jar) | Demand for jelly (jars per year) | | Cross-price elasticity of demand |
|---|---|---|---|---|
| a | $2.00 | 12 | | |
| b | $3.00 | 10 | a to b | _____ |
| c | $4.00 | 7 | b to c | _____ |
| d | $5.00 | 2 | c to d | _____ |

4. Based upon Table 5.6, peanut butter and jelly are (substitute, complementary) goods because as the price of peanut butter rises, the demand for jelly (falls, rises) and the cross-price elasticity of demand is (negative, positive).

# Exercise 4

This exercise shows the relationship between total and marginal utility. It also gives practice in identifying the law of diminishing marginal utility.

Suppose there are two types of entertainment you enjoy - an evening at home with friends and an "event" entertainment, such as a sports event or a rock concert. The number of times that you experience each type of entertainment during a month determines the total utility of each type of entertainment for that month. Suppose Table 5.7 represents the total utility you achieve from consuming various quantities of the two types of entertainment.

# Table 5.7
## Total and marginal utility of two types of entertainment per month

| Days of entertainment per month | Evening at home Total utility | Evening at home Marginal utility | Event Total utility | Event Marginal utility |
|---|---|---|---|---|
| 0 | 0 | _____ | 0 | _____ |
| 1 | 170 | _____ | 600 | _____ |
| 2 | 360 | _____ | 1,250 | _____ |
| 3 | 540 | _____ | 1,680 | _____ |
| 4 | 690 | _____ | 2,040 | _____ |
| 5 | 820 | _____ | 2,350 | _____ |
| 6 | 930 | _____ | 2,550 | _____ |
| 7 | 1,030 | _____ | 2,720 | _____ |
| 8 | 1,110 | _____ | 2,820 | _____ |
| 9 | 1,170 | _____ | 2,820 | _____ |
| 10 | 1,170 | _____ | 2,760 | _____ |
| 11 | 1,120 | _____ | 2,660 | _____ |
| 12 | 1,020 | _____ | 2,460 | _____ |

1. Complete Table 5.7 by computing the marginal utility of each type of entertainment.

2. The law of diminishing marginal utility means:
   (a) The total utility of a good declines as more of it is consumed in a given time period.
   (b) The marginal utility of a good declines as more of it is consumed in a given time period.
   (c) The price of a good declines as more of it is consumed in a given period of time.
   (d) All of the above.

3. The law of diminishing marginal utility is in evidence in Table 5.7:
   (a) For both types of entertainment.
   (b) For home entertainment only.
   (c) For event entertainment only.
   (d) For neither type of entertainment.

   (Hint: You should be able to tell by looking at the marginal utility columns in Table 5.7. Does the marginal utility become smaller as you go down the column?)

4. In Figure 5.5 graph the total utility curve for evenings at home.

## Figure 5.5

5.  In Figure 5.6 graph the marginal utility curve for evenings at home.

## Figure 5.6

6.  On the basis of the two graphs above, marginal utility becomes zero only when:
    (a)   Total utility is zero.
    (b)   Total utility reaches a maximum.
    (c)   Total utility is rising.
    (d)   Total utility is falling.

7.  When total utility is rising, then:
    (a)   Marginal utility is rising.
    (b)   Marginal utility is negative.
    (c)   Marginal utility is positive.
    (d)   Marginal utility is zero.

# Exercise 5

The principle of utility maximization is used to determine optimal consumption. This exercise builds on the previous exercise.

Suppose you hold a part-time job that gives you $120 a month extra spending money. On any day of the month you can spend that money on either of two types of entertainment—an evening at home with friends, for which you usually spend $10 for snacks and drinks, or an "event" entertainment, which costs $30. Table 5.8 shows the hypothetical marginal utility that each type of entertainment provides for you during the month.

## Table 5.8
## Total and marginal utility of two types of entertainment per month

| Days of entertainment per month | Evening at home (price = $10) | | Event entertainment (price = $30) | |
|---|---|---|---|---|
| | Marginal utility | MU / price | Marginal utility | MU / price |
| 0 | 0 | 0 | 0 | — |
| 1 | 180 | 18 | 600 | ____ |
| 2 | 180 | 18 | 600 | ____ |
| 3 | 170 | 17 | 480 | ____ |
| 4 | 140 | 14 | 360 | ____ |
| 5 | 140 | 14 | 360 | ____ |
| 6 | 140 | 14 | 360 | ____ |
| 7 | 100 | 10 | 360 | ____ |
| 8 | 100 | 10 | 0 | ____ |
| 9 | 100 | 10 | 0 | ____ |
| 10 | 0 | 0 | 0 | ____ |

1. Finding the optimal level of consumption with a given income involves choosing successive *increments* of a good (service), *each of which* yields:
   (a) The largest total utility.
   (b) The largest marginal utility per unit of product or activity purchased.
   (c) The largest marginal utility for each dollar spent.
   (d) All of the above.

2. Divide marginal utility by the price of the event entertainment to complete Table 5.8.

Before you spend any money on any activity:

3. Which activity has the highest MU/$p$ ratio? _____

4. Judging by the MU/$p$ ratio, how many days of event entertainment should you buy before spending anything on at-home entertainment? _____

5. If you had $120 to spend on entertainment, how much money would you have left after buying two days of event entertainment? _____

6. Should you spend the entire balance from question 5 on at-home entertainment? _____

7. After you have bought three at-home nights and two events, how much income is left from the original $120? _____

76

8. Based on MU/*p*, which activity should you purchase with the income remaining in question 7?
_____

9. T   F   When your income is $120, optimal consumption occurs with three evenings of each type of entertainment.

## Appendix
## Exercise 6

This exercise provides practice in interpreting an indifference map and total utility.

For questions 1-7 refer to Figure A.2 in the appendix for Chapter 5.

1. At point E, the consumption combination includes _____ cokes and _____ video games.

2. At point D, the consumption combination includes _____ cokes and _____ video games.

3. Based on the indifference map, the consumer receives:
   (a) Greater satisfaction at point E than at point D.
   (b) Greater satisfaction at point D than at point E.
   (c) Equal satisfaction at point D and at point E.
   (d) Satisfaction cannot be determined from an indifference map.

4. At point B, the consumption combination includes _____ cokes and _____ video games.

5. At point C, the consumption combination includes _____ cokes and _____ video games.

6. Compare combinations B and C to point E. In each case, point E provides (greater, lesser) satisfaction than point B or point C.

7. For the given indifference map, the level of total utility is greatest at any point along curve _____.

## Common Errors

The first statement in each "common error" below is incorrect. Each incorrect statement is followed by a corrected version and an explanation.

1. The law of demand and the law of diminishing marginal utility are the same. WRONG!

   The law of demand and the law of diminishing marginal utility are not the same. RIGHT!

   Do not confuse utility and demand. Utility refers only to expected satisfaction. Demand refers to both preferences and ability to pay. This distinction should help you to keep the law of diminishing marginal utility separate from the law of demand.

2. Figures 5.8a and 5.8b represent simple graphs drawn from a demand schedule.

**Figure 5.8a**

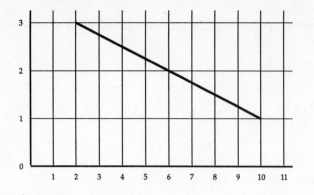

| Price (dollars per unit) | Output quantity per unit of time |
|---|---|
| 10 | 1 |
| 2 | 3 |

WRONG!

**Figure 5.8b**

| Price (dollars per unit) | Output quantity per unit of time |
|---|---|
| 10 | 1 |
| 2 | 3 |

RIGHT!

The first graph has been drawn without any units indicated. It is something of an accidental tradition in economics to show price on the y-axis and quantity on the x-axis. This convention is sometimes confusing to mathematicians, who want to treat quantity as a function of price, according to the definition in the text. In Figure 5.8a the axes have been reversed and incorrect points have been chosen.

*Be careful!* When you are drawing a new graph, make a special effort to understand the units that are placed on the axes. Also, make sure you know the kinds of units in which each axis is measured. If you are drawing a graph from a table (or schedule), you can usually determine what should be on the axes by looking at the heading above the column from which you are reading the numbers.

Make sure price is shown on the y-axis (vertical) and quantity on the x-axis (horizontal). If you mix up the two, you may confuse a graph showing perfectly elastic demand with one showing perfectly inelastic demand.

3.  The formula for the price elasticity of demand is

$$\frac{\text{Change in price}}{\text{Change in quantity}} \qquad \text{WRONG!}$$

The formula for the price elasticity of demand is

$$\frac{\text{Percentage change in quantity}}{\text{Percentage change in price}} \qquad \text{RIGHT!}$$

The concept of elasticity allows us to compare relative changes in quantity and price without having to worry about the units in which they are measured. In order to do this, we compute percentage changes of both price and quantity. A change in price *causes* people to change the quantity they demand in a given time period. By putting the quantity changes in the numerator, we can see that if the quantity response is very large in relation to a price change, the elasticity will also be very large. If the quantity response is small in relation to a price change, then demand is price inelastic (elasticity is small).

*Be careful!* Do not confuse slope and elasticity. The formula for the slope of the demand curve is the *wrong* formula shown above. The formula for the price elasticity of demand is the *right* formula. Remember to take the absolute value of the elasticity too.

4.  A flat demand curve has an elasticity of zero. WRONG!

A flat demand curve has an infinite elasticity. RIGHT!

When price remains constant even when quantity changes, the elasticity formula requires us to divide by a zero price change. In fact, as demand curves approach flatness, the elasticity becomes larger and larger. By agreement we say it is infinite.

5.  The person for whom a good or service has the greatest utility has the greatest desire for more of it. WRONG!

The good that has the greatest *marginal* utility for a person, with respect to price, is the good of which he or she desires more. RIGHT!

Utilities of one good for many people cannot be compared. Utilities of various goods for one person can be compared. Marginal utility with respect to price, not total utility, is the best indicator of how to make a choice.

6.  An expected price change has the same effect as a change in the current price. WRONG!

An unexpected price change shifts the demand curve, whereas a current price change is a movement along the demand curve. RIGHT!

If prices are expected to rise in the near future, people will demand more of the commodity today in order to beat the rise in price. Demand increases and the quantity demanded will rise. However, if the price rises today, by the law of demand people reduce the quantity demanded! Furthermore, demand itself does not change. A current price change and an expected price change have very different effects.

7. When a buyer purchases a good, the demand for the good decreases. WRONG!

When a buyer purchases a good, demand is not affected. RIGHT!

Demand refers only to the *willingness* and *ability* of a buyer to buy. The potential for purchase, not the actual purchase, is the focus of demand. Demand is defined over a given period of time. If a buyer buys a good during that period of time, he or she is still counted as demanding the good—even after it is purchased.

8. Both income and cross-price elasticities must be interpreted using absolute values. WRONG!

The absolute value is used only for the price elasticity of demand. RIGHT!

The law of demand guarantees that the price elasticity of demand would always have a negative sign. However, the income and cross-price elasticities may be either positive or negative, and the sign provides important information about the demand for a good. The sign of the income elasticity indicates if a good is a normal good or an inferior good. The sign on the cross-price elasticity indicates whether a good is a substitute or a complement.

# •ANSWERS•

## Using Key Terms

### Across
1. complementary goods
6. diminishing marginal utility
12. law of demand
13. total utility
14. total revenue
15. substitute goods
17. income elasticity of demand
18. cross-price elasticity
19. opportunity cost

### Down
2. demand
3. price elasticity of demand
4. optimal consumption
5. marginal utility
7. shift in demand
8. inferior good
9. demand curve
10. normal good
11. ceteris paribus
16. utility

# True or False

1. T
2. T
3. F   Consumers will plan to wait until next month's lower prices to purchase this good. The current demand curve will shift to the left.
4. F   The marginal utility will decline. The total utility will increase as long as the marginal utility is positive.
5. T
6. F   A rise in the price will result in lower total revenues. A *decrease* in the price will raise total revenues if demand is elastic.
7. F   Price elasticity of demand will be more elastic (i.e. consumers more responsive) at higher prices. Elasticity cannot be compared to slope.
8. T
9. T
10. F   A *positive* cross-price elasticity indicates substitutes. An *increase* in the price of one good, for example, would result in an *increase* in the demand for the substitute.

# Multiple Choice

| | | | | | |
|---|---|---|---|---|---|
| 1. a | 5. b | 9. b | 13. d | 17. a | 21. c |
| 2. c | 6. c | 10. b | 14. c | 18. d | 22. c |
| 3. b | 7. d | 11. b | 15. d | 19. c | 23. d |
| 4. d | 8. a | 12. c | 16. a | 20. b | |

# Problems and Applications

## Exercise 1

1. d

2. **Figure 5.1 Answer**

3. **Figure 5.2 Answer**

81

4. **Table 5.3 Answer**

| Price | Number of new cars (millions per year) |
|-------|----------------------------------------|
| $10,000 | 10.0 |
| 9,000 | 12.0 |

5. **Figure 5.3 Answer**

# Exercise 2

1. F
2. **Table 5.4 Answer**

| Price | Number of new U.S. cars (millions per year) | Elasticity of demand |
|-------|----------------------------------------------|----------------------|
| $10,000 | 10.0 | --- |
| 9,000 | 12.0 | 1.64 |
| 8,000 | 14.0 | 1.25 |
| 7,000 | 16.0 | 1.00 |

3. elastic
4. $112,000
5. decrease
6. **Figure 5.4 answer**

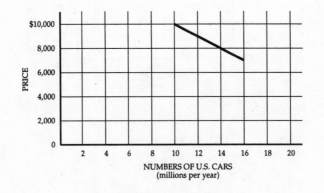

7. T

82

8. The slope can be estimated by using the coordinates of any two points on the demand curve. The slope is computed by dividing the change in the variable on the y-axis by the change in the variable on the x-axis. For example, using the first two points in Table 5.4, we would have

$$\frac{\text{Change in } y\text{-axis}}{\text{Change in } x\text{-axis}} = \frac{p_1 - p_2}{q_1 - q_2} = \frac{10{,}000 - 7{,}000}{10{,}000{,}000 - 16{,}000{,}000} = \frac{3{,}000}{-6{,}000{,}000} = -.0005 \text{ per car}$$

Regardless of what pair of points is chosen, the slope should be the same (except for differences that result from rounding).

9. b    As noted in the previous problem, the slope is the same regardless of which pair of points is tried.

10. T

# Exercise 3

1. **Table 5.5 Answer**

|   | Income (per year) | Demand for peanut butter (jars per year) | | Income elasticity of demand |
|---|---|---|---|---|
| a | $10,000 | 12 | | |
| b | $20,000 | 7 | a to b | -0.79 |
| c | $40,000 | 3 | b to c | -1.19 |
| d | $80,000 | 1 | c to d | -1.49 |

2. inferior, falls, negative.

3. **Table 5.6 Answer**

|   | Price of peanut butter (per jar) | Demand for jelly (jars per year) | | Cross-price elasticity of demand |
|---|---|---|---|---|
| a | $2.00 | 12 | | |
| b | $3.00 | 10 | a to b | -0.45 |
| c | $4.00 | 7 | b to c | -1.21 |
| d | $5.00 | 2 | c to d | -5.05 |

4. complementary, falls, negative.

# Exercise 4

1. **Table 5.7 Answer**

| Days of entertainment per month | Evening at home Marginal utility | Event Marginal utility |
|---|---|---|
| 0 | — | — |
| 1 | 170 | 600 |
| 2 | 190 | 650 |
| 3 | 180 | 430 |
| 4 | 150 | 360 |
| 5 | 130 | 310 |
| 6 | 110 | 200 |
| 7 | 100 | 170 |
| 8 | 80 | 100 |
| 9 | 60 | 0 |
| 10 | 0 | −60 |
| 11 | −50 | −100 |
| 12 | −100 | −200 |

2. b
3. a

4. **Figure 5.5 Answer**

5. **Figure 5.6 Answer**

DAYS OF ENTERTAINMENT AT HOME
(per month)

6. b
7. c

## *Exercise 5*

1. c
2. **Table 5.8 Answer**

|  | Event entertainment (price = $30) | |
| --- | --- | --- |
| Days of entertainment per month | Marginal utility | $\frac{MU}{price}$ |
| 0 | 0 | 0 |
| 1 | 600 | 20 |
| 2 | 600 | 20 |
| 3 | 480 | 16 |
| 4 | 360 | 12 |
| 5 | 360 | 12 |
| 6 | 360 | 12 |
| 7 | 360 | 12 |
| 8 | 0 | 0 |
| 9 | 0 | 0 |
| 10 | 0 | 0 |

3. event entertainment
4. 2
5. $60 [ = $120 - ($30 x 2)]
6. no
7. $30 [ = $120 - $60 - (3 x $10)]
8. event entertainment
9. T

# Exercise 6

1. 3 cokes, 5 video games
2. 2 cokes, 8 video games
3. C
4. 2 cokes, 5 video games
5. 3 cokes, 4 video games
6. greater
7. $I_2$

# CHAPTER 6
# The Costs of Production

## Quick Review

In this chapter we attempt to identify the costs of producing goods and services. We begin by looking at some basic questions:

- How much output can a firm produce?
- How do the costs of production vary with the rate of output?
- Do larger firms have a cost advantage over smaller firms?

Managers of firms must know how costs change when output is changed. Without such knowledge they cannot determine what they should be willing and able to supply in the marketplace. Costs can be computed at different levels of production if management keeps track of all factors that are used in producing output. The production function establishes the maximum quantity that can be produced from a given combination of factors. The production function is therefore the cornerstone for computing a firm's costs at various output levels.

If we know the production function, it is possible to determine factor productivity, efficiency, and various categories of costs. Productivity is simply the amount of output per unit of input that can be produced by a firm. Efficiency is attained if the firm is able to achieve the maximum output from a given set of resources. The law of diminishing returns says that the marginal product of any factor decreases as more of it is employed in the production process when all other factors are held constant. These concepts have important implications for the behavior of cost.

In the short run (when firms are unable to vary some factors of production), the law of diminishing returns causes the marginal costs and average variable costs of production to rise with increased output. In effect, the variable factors of production are limited by the fixed factors, which, by definition, cannot be expanded. Even though average fixed costs fall as output increases, these limitations eventually cause average total costs to rise.

In the long run (when there are no fixed factors), changes in average total cost may occur when the rate of output is increased. If an increase in plant size (scale) causes average total cost to rise, there are diseconomies of scale. If average total cost falls with increased plant size, there are economies of scale. However, it is quite possible that average costs will not change over a wide range of output, in which case there are constant returns to scale.

The short-run cost curves are related to the long-run cost curves. The long-run average total cost curve runs along the lowest points of all possible short-run average total cost curves at each level of output.

Certain rules relate the different cost curves, in both the long-run and the short-run. Whenever the marginal curve is below the average curve, the average curve will fall as output increases. However, if the marginal curve is above the average curve, the average curve will be rising. The marginal cost curve always intersects the average variable cost and average total cost curve at their lowest points.

Global competitiveness of American firms has been called into question. Cheap foreign labor is frequently used as an excuse for the recent trade deficits of the United States. But labor is only one factor in the production process, and low wages generally mean low productivity. Thus, unit labor costs, the wage rate divided by marginal physical product, are the key to measuring labor efficiency. Looked at this way, American labor is highly competitive relative to "cheap" foreign labor.

## Learning Objectives

After reading Chapter 6 and doing the following exercises, you should:

1. Know the relationship between the production function and the firm's ability to produce goods and services.
2. Understand the nature and determinants of marginal productivity.
3. Be able to draw a graph relating the marginal physical product and total product curves.
4. Be able to define and explain the law of diminishing returns.
5. Understand the relationship between the production function and the short-run cost curves.
6. Understand the difference between variable costs and fixed costs.
7. Know how to define and calculate the total, average, and marginal costs of production and be able to show their relationship to marginal productivity.
8. Understand the relationship between average and marginal cost curves.
9. Understand the distinction between economic costs and accounting costs.
10. Know the distinction between long-run costs and short-run costs.
11. Be able to explain economies of scale, diseconomies of scale, and constant returns to scale.
12. Understand the impact of technological improvements on the production function.

## Using Key Terms

Fill in the puzzle on the opposite page with the appropriate term from the list of Key Terms at the end of the chapter in the text.

### *Across*

1. The resources used to produce a good or service.
5. The horizontal curve at $120 in Figure 6.4 in the text.
7. Equals $245 when producing 15 pairs of jeans per day according to Table 6.2 in the text.
9. Equal to the wage rate divided by marginal physical product.
10. The marginal physical product of a variable input declines as more of it is employed with a given quantity of other (fixed) inputs.
12. Maximum output of a good attainable from the resources used.
13. Average total costs minus average fixed costs.
15. Includes both explicit and implicit costs.
16. Equal to 15 for the first worker hired in Figure 6.1 in the text.
19. Used in Table 6.1 in the text to tell how the output of jeans would change if some sewing machines were leased.
20. Output per unit of input.
21. A period in which some inputs are fixed.

### *Down*

2. Drawn with a U-shape in Figure 6.5 in the text.
3. The most desired forgone alternative.
4. Helps to explain why one large firm dominates the funeral business according to the article in the text titled "Funeral Giant Moves In on Small Rivals."
6. A situation in which an increase in plant size does not reduce minimum average costs.
8. Equal to $6 per pair of jeans at an output rate of 20 pairs per day in Figure 6.5 in the text.

11. Determine how fast total costs rise.
14. This curve is typically rising because of the law of diminishing returns.
17. The difference between total revenue and total costs.
18. A period in which all inputs are variable.

## Puzzle 6.1

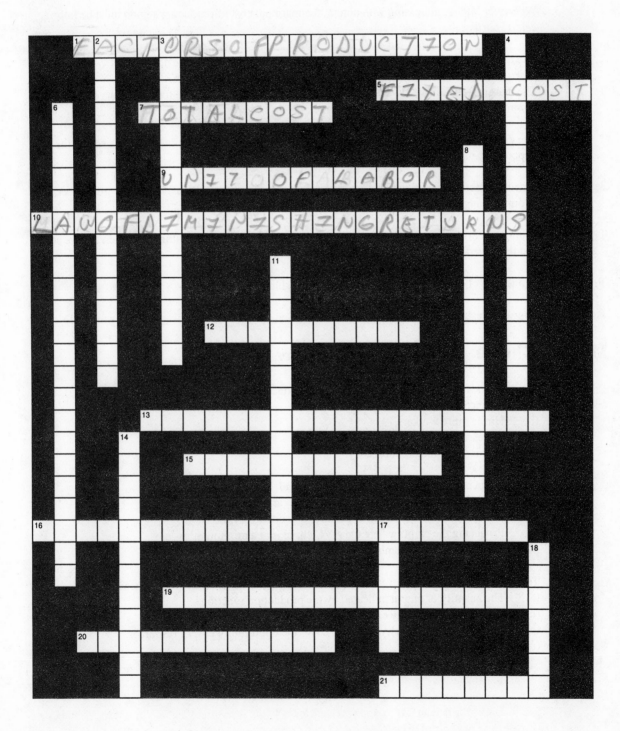

# True or False: *Circle your choice and explain why any false statements are incorrect.*

T   F   1.   The production function can be increased by working the labor input harder.

T   F   2.   The productivity of labor is affected by changes in the mix of other factors being used in the production process.

T   F   3.   Whenever MPP is increasing with output, the marginal cost of producing a good must be falling, *ceteris paribus*.

T   F   4.   The total cost at a zero level of output is always the amount of variable costs.

T   F   5.   The marginal cost curve always intersects the minimum of the average total cost curve and the minimum of the average variable cost curve.

T   F   6.   The difference between the accountant's and the economist's measurement of costs equals the opportunity costs of resources that do not have a value.

T   F   7.   As output increases, marginal costs eventually increase and the MPP eventually decreases because of diminishing returns.

T   F   8.   With greater output, falling average fixed costs eventually outweigh falling average variable costs, and then average total cost starts to rise.

T   F   9.   Economies of scale result from the law of diminishing returns.

T   F   10.  Improved technology shifts the production function upward and the cost curves downward.

# Multiple Choice: *Select the correct answer.*

_____   1.   Which of the following would cause a firm's production function to shift upward?
(a)   An increase in production by the firm.
(b)   Hiring more workers.
(c)   Increased training for the firm's workers.
(d)   An increase in factor costs.

_____   2.   When a firm produces at the least-cost output level, it is:
(a)   Producing the output at the minimum MC curve.
(b)   Using the fewest resources to produce a good or service.
(c)   Producing the output where the AVC curve is at a minimum.
(d)   Producing the best combination of goods and services.

_____   3.   Technical efficiency is achieved for a given set of resources when a firm produces:
(a)   The quantity of output indicated by the production function.
(b)   Below the opportunity cost for the resources.
(c)   The minimum necessary output to cover the opportunity cost of resources.
(d)   All of the above.

_____ 4.  The law of diminishing returns indicates that the greater use of a variable input, holding other factors fixed, results in:
  (a)  A declining rate of increase in total output for each additional unit of input.
  (b)  A rising MC curve.
  (c)  A declining MPP curve.
  (d)  All of the above.

_____ 5.  Rising marginal costs are the result of:
  (a)  The *law of diminishing returns.*
  (b)  Decreasing MPP.
  (c)  Adding more variable factors of production to a fixed quantity of other factors of production.
  (d)  All of the above are correct.

_____ 6.  Given the cost of the variable input, marginal cost will increase with greater output if:
  (a)  Marginal physical product is declining.
  (b)  Marginal physical product is increasing.
  (c)  Total variable cost is decreasing.
  (d)  Total fixed cost is increasing.

_____ 7.  For which of the following costs would the cost curve appear as a flat line and the associated average cost curve decline continuously?
  (a)  Total costs.
  (b)  Variable costs.
  (c)  Fixed costs.
  (d)  Marginal costs.

_____ 8.  If an additional unit of labor costs $10, and has an MPP of 20 units of output, the marginal cost is:
  (a)  $0.20.
  (b)  $0.50.
  (c)  $10.00.
  (d)  $200.00.

_____ 9.  Which of the following can you compute if you know only the total cost at an output level of zero?
  (a)  Fixed cost.
  (b)  Variable cost.
  (c)  Marginal cost.
  (d)  Average total cost.

_____ 10.  When output increases and the marginal cost curve is:
  (a)  Below the ATC, the ATC is downward sloping.
  (b)  Equal to the ATC, the ATC is at its lowest point.
  (c)  Above the ATC, the ATC is upward sloping.
  (d)  All of the above.

_____ 11.  Changes in short-run total costs result from changes in only:
  (a)  Variable costs.
  (b)  Fixed costs.
  (c)  Profit.
  (d)  The price elasticity of demand.

_____ 12.  Which of the following is equivalent to ATC?
  (a)  FC + VC.
  (b)  AFC + AVC.
  (c)  Change in output divided by change in total cost.
  (d)  Total cost times the quantity produced.

_____ 13. The ATC at a given output level multiplied by the number of units produced at that output level equals:
(a) Marginal cost.
(b) Total fixed cost.
(c) Total variable cost.
(d) Total cost.

_____ 14. Which one of the following curves is falling when marginal cost is below it?
(a) Average variable cost curve.
(b) Average total cost curve.
(c) Average fixed cost curve.
(d) All of the above.

_____ 15. Which of the following costs will always increase as output increases?
(a) Total costs.
(b) Average total costs.
(c) Marginal costs.
(d) Fixed costs.

_____ 16. Economies of scale are reductions in:
(a) Average total cost that result from declining average fixed costs.
(b) Average fixed cost that result from reducing the firm's scale of operations.
(c) Average total cost that result from increasing the firm's scale of operations.
(d) Average fixed cost resulting from improved technology and production efficiency.

_____ 17. Which of the following contributes to the typical U shape of the ATC curve?
(a) The initial dominance of diminishing returns.
(b) The eventual dominance of the rising AVC curve.
(c) The steady impact of a rising AFC curve.
(d) All of the above.

_____ 18. The length of the long run in economics is:
(a) A variable time depending on the nature of the business.
(b) Six to nine months.
(c) One year.
(d) More than two years.

_____ 19. In defining economic costs, economists recognize:
(a) Only explicit costs while accountants recognize only implicit costs.
(b) Only explicit costs while accountants recognize explicit and implicit costs.
(c) Explicit and implicit costs while accountants recognize only implicit costs.
(d) Explicit and implicit costs while accountants recognize only explicit costs.

_____ 20. The long-run average cost curve is constructed from:
(a) The minimum points of the short-run marginal cost curves.
(b) The minimum points of the short-run average cost curves.
(c) The lowest average cost for producing each level of output.
(d) The minimum points of the long-run marginal cost curves.

# Problems and Applications

## *Exercise 1*

This exercise shows how to compute and graph the marginal physical product of a factor of production. It also demonstrates the law of diminishing returns.

In Table 6.1 of the text, an example of jeans production was used to show how many sewing machines and workers were needed per day to produce various quantities of jeans per day. This table is very similar.

### Table 6.1
### The production of jeans
### (pairs per day)

| Capital input (sewing machines per day) | Labor input (workers per day) | | | | | | | |
|---|---|---|---|---|---|---|---|---|
| | 0 | 1 | 2 | 3 | 4 | 5 | 6 | 7 |
| 0 | 0 | 0 | 0 | 0 | 0 | 0 | 0 | 0 |
| 1 | 0 | 15 | 34 | 44 | 48 | 50 | 51 | 46 |
| 2 | 0 | 20 | 46 | 64 | 72 | 78 | 81 | 80 |
| 3 | 0 | 21 | 50 | 73 | 82 | 92 | 99 | 102 |

1. Suppose a firm had only two sewing machines and could vary only the amount of labor input. On the basis of Table 6.1, fill in the column 2 of Table 6.2 to show how much can be produced at different levels of labor input when there are only two sewing machines.

### Table 6.2
### The production of jeans with two sewing machines

| (1) Labor input (workers per day) | (2) Production of jeans (pairs per day) | (3) Marginal physical product (pairs per worker) |
|---|---|---|
| 0 | _____ | — |
| 1 | _____ | _____ |
| 2 | _____ | _____ |
| 3 | _____ | _____ |
| 4 | _____ | _____ |
| 5 | _____ | _____ |
| 6 | _____ | _____ |
| 7 | _____ | _____ |

2. Graph the total output curve in Figure 6.1.

**Figure 6.1**

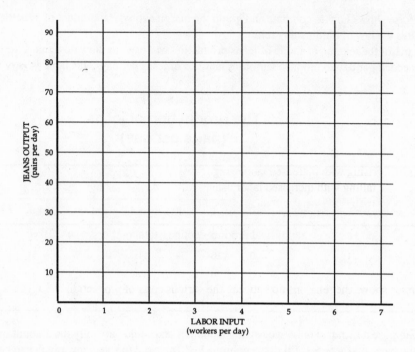

3. Compute the marginal physical product of each extra worker per day. (*Hint:* See Figure 6.2 in the text.) Place the answers in column 3 of Table 6.2.

4. Graph the marginal physical product curve in Figure 6.2.

**Figure 6.2**

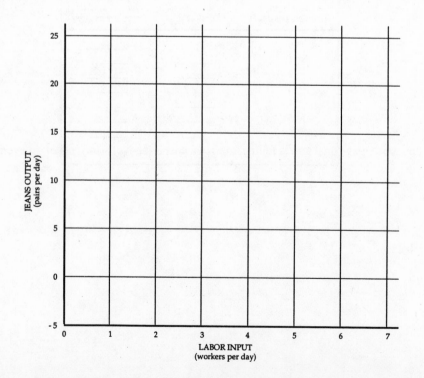

5. The law of diminishing returns states that the marginal physical product of a factor:
   (a) Will become negative as output increases.
   (b) Will decline as output increases.
   (c) Will increase and then decline as output increases.
   (d) Will decline as the amount of a factor used increases.

6. At what amount of labor input does the law of diminishing returns first become apparent in Figure 6.2?
   (a) 0-1.
   (b) 1-2.
   (c) 2-3.
   (d) 3-4.

7. In Figure 6.1 at 3 units of labor, total output:
   (a) Is rising with increased labor usage.
   (b) Is falling with increased labor usage.
   (c) Remains constant with increased labor.

8. T   F   When marginal physical product declines, total output declines.

# Exercise 2

This exercise shows the relationship between the various costs of production.

1. Complete Table 6.3 using the information given about output and the costs of production. (Hint: refer to Figure 6.5 in the text if you need help getting started.)

## Table 6.3  Costs of Production

| Rate of Output | Fixed Cost | Variable Cost | Total Cost | Average Total Cost | Marginal Cost |
|---|---|---|---|---|---|
| 0 | $ _____ | $ _____ | $ 10 | -------- | ------- |
| 1 | _____ | 6 | _____ | $ _____ | $ _____ |
| 2 | _____ | 10 | _____ | _____ | _____ |
| 3 | _____ | 16 | _____ | _____ | _____ |
| 4 | _____ | _____ | 36 | _____ | _____ |
| 5 | _____ | 40 | _____ | _____ | _____ |
| 6 | _____ | _____ | 68 | _____ | _____ |

2. When the average total cost is rising, marginal cost is (above, below, equal to) average total cost.

3. When the average total cost is falling, marginal cost is (above, below, equal to) average total cost.

# Exercise 3

This exercise shows the relationship between fixed costs, variable costs, accounting cost, and economic cost.

1. Fixed costs are defined as:
   (a) Costs that do not change with inflation.
   (b) Costs that are set firmly (without escalator clauses) in a contract.
   (c) Costs of production that do not change when the rate of production is altered.
   (d) Average costs that do not change when the rate of production is altered.

2. Variable costs include:
   (a) Costs of production that change when the rate of production is altered.
   (b) All costs in the long run.
   (c) The difference between total and fixed costs.
   (d) All of the above.

## Table 6.4  Expense statements for parachute business (dollars per week)

| | Parachutes produced per week | | |
|---|---|---|---|
| Weekly expense | 0 | 100 | 200 |
| Lease on building | $1,200 | $1,200 | $1,200 |
| Sewing machines | 500 | 500 | 500 |
| Nylon | 0 | 300 | 700 |
| Utilities (electricity, etc.) | 0 | 150 | 200 |
| Labor | 0 | 650 | 650 |
| Testing and certification | 800 | 800 | 800 |

Use the information in Table 6.4 to answer the following questions.

3. Which items are considered to be fixed costs? _____

4. Calculate variable costs at an output level of 100 parachutes per week. _____

5. Calculate total costs at an output level of 100 parachutes per week. _____

6. Now assume the owner of the parachute business buys the building he is currently leasing so he no longer has a lease expenditure. Calculate the accounting cost at an output level of 200 parachutes per week. _____

7. Assume the owner still owns the building. Calculate the economic cost at an output level of 200 parachutes per week. Explain why there is a difference in the accounting cost at an output level of 200 parachutes and the economic cost. _____

# Exercise 4

This exercise focuses on average total costs. It will help you solve the problems at the end of Chapter 6 in the text.

Table 6.5 represents the cost data for producing cement in three different plants, where Plant 1 is the smallest and Plant 3 is the largest.

## Table 6.5
## Costs associated with three plants

| Output (tons per day) | 1 | 2 | 3 | 4 | 5 | 6 | 7 | 8 | 9 | 10 |
|---|---|---|---|---|---|---|---|---|---|---|
| Average total cost: | | | | | | | | | | |
| Plant 1 | $10 | 9 | 8 | 7 | 8 | 9 | 10 | 11 | 12 | 13 |
| Plant 2 | 12 | 10 | 8 | 6 | 5 | 4 | 5 | 6 | 8 | 10 |
| Plant 3 | 13 | 12 | 11 | 9 | 7 | 5 | 3 | 2 | 3 | 4 |

1. Given the three plant sizes in Table 6.5, the cement industry experiences (economies of scale, diseconomies of scale, constant returns to scale) because as plant size increases the minimum average total cost (increases, decreases, stays the same).

2. Which plant should be used to produce 2 tons of cement per day? _____

3. Which plant should be used to produce 8 tons of cement per day? _____

4. For which levels of output is Plant 2 the best choice? _____

## Exercise 5

Suppose the marginal physical product of worker A is 10 units per hour and her wage is $15 per hour. Suppose the marginal physical product of worker B is 5 units per hour and her wage is $10 per hour. Given this information, answer questions 1-4.

1. Calculate the unit labor cost for worker A. _____

2. Calculate the unit labor cost for worker B. _____

3. T    F    Worker B is less costly per unit because her wage rate is lower.

4. T    F    Unit labor costs can be used to measure productivity.

## Exercise 6

The news media often provide information on events that affect productivity and costs. This exercise will use one of the articles in the text to show the kind of information to look for.

Reread the article in the text titled "Funeral Giant Moves In on Small Rivals," and then answer the following questions.

1. What is the strategy employed by SCI to achieve economies of scale? _____
   _____

2. What phrase(s) indicates how SCI grew to more than 230,000 units? _____
   _____

3. What phrase indicates one way that SCI achieves lower costs than its rivals? _____
   _____

4. What phrase demonstrates that economies of scale have allowed SCI to reap greater profits than its smaller rivals? _____

## Common Errors

The first statement in each "common error" below is incorrect. Each incorrect statement is followed by a corrected version and an explanation.

1. A rising marginal cost means average cost is rising. WRONG!

   A rising average cost curve means the marginal cost curve is above the average cost curve. RIGHT!

It is important to remember the basic relationships between the average cost curves and the marginal cost curve:

(a) When the average cost curve rises, the marginal cost curve is above the average cost curve.

(b) When the average cost curve falls, the marginal cost curve is below the average cost curve.

(c) When the average cost curve is flat, the marginal cost curve equals the average cost curve.

2. Total output starts falling when diminishing returns occur. WRONG!

Diminishing returns set in when marginal physical product begins to decline. RIGHT!

The law of diminishing returns describes what happens to *marginal physical product,* not total output. Marginal physical product will typically begin to decline long before total output begins to decline. For total output to decline, the marginal physical product must be negative.

3. A firm's productivity increases when labor is willing to accept lower wages. WRONG!

A firm's productivity increases when more output can be produced per unit of labor used. RIGHT!

Productivity is not defined on the basis of the prices of factors of production. Productivity depends simply on the amount of output that is produced by the factors of production.

4. The term "economies of scale" refers to the shape of the short-run average cost curve. WRONG!

The term "economies of scale" refers to the shape of the long-run average cost curve. RIGHT!

The short-run average cost curve and the long-run average cost curve may have similar shapes. But the shape of the short-run curve results from the law of diminishing returns. In the long run, all factors, and therefore all costs, are variable. Thus the shape of the long-run average cost curve is the result of other forces, such as the specialization and division of labor, the use of different sources of power, and so on. Remember, even though the long-run average cost curve is a summary of many short-run average cost curves, and even though the shapes of the two curves may be similar, the reasons for the shapes of the curves are quite different. The term "economies of scale" applies only to the long-run average cost curve.

5. The marginal cost curve rises because factor prices rise when more of a good is produced. WRONG!

The marginal cost curve rises because the marginal productivity of the variable factor declines. RIGHT!

The marginal cost curve moves in the direction opposite to that of marginal product curve. Changes in factor prices would shift the whole marginal cost curve but would not explain its shape and would not affect the marginal product curve.

6. Marginal physical product begins to decline because inferior factors must be hired to increase output. WRONG!

Declining marginal physical product occurs even if all of the factors are of equal quality. RIGHT!

Many people incorrectly attribute diminishing returns to the use of inferior factors of production. Diminishing returns result from an increasing ratio of the variable input to the fixed input. There is always a point where the variable input begins to have too little of the fixed input to work with. Result? Diminishing marginal product! The quality of the factors has nothing to do with it. Generally, factors of production are considered homogeneous in economics.

7.  Diminishing returns means there are diseconomies of scale. WRONG!

    Diminishing returns refers to the short run shape of a marginal physical product curve and diseconomies of scale refers to the shape of the long run average cost curve. RIGHT!

    As suggested in the previous Common Error, diminishing returns is a short run phenomenon; at least one input in the production process is fixed. Diminishing returns is reflected in diminishing marginal productivity and a rising short run marginal cost curve. However, when all factors are variable—as they are in the long run—then it is possible to talk about economies or diseconomies of scale. Diseconomies of scale results in a rising long run average cost curve. It is quite common to have short run diminishing returns and long run economies of scale, particularly in the public utilities.

# •ANSWERS•

## Using Key Terms
### Across
1.  factors of production
5.  fixed costs
7.  total cost
9.  unit labor cost
10. law of diminishing returns
12. efficiency
13. average variable cost
15. economic cost
16. marginal physical product
19. production function
20. productivity
21. short run

### Down
2.  average total cost
3.  opportunity cost
4.  economies of scale
6.  constant returns to scale
8.  average fixed cost
11. variable costs
14. marginal cost
17. profit
18. long run

## True or False

1.  F   The production function represents the maximum output that can be obtained from a given mix of inputs, i.e. technical efficiency.
2.  T
3.  T
4.  F   The total cost at a zero level of output is fixed costs.

5. T
6. F   The difference is the opportunity costs of resources that are not given an explicit payment.
7. T
8. F   Rising AVC (MC) will eventually overcome falling AFC and cause the ATC to increase.
9. F   Economies of scale is a long-run phenomenon. The law of diminishing returns does not apply in the long run because there are no fixed inputs in the long run.
10. T

## Multiple Choice

| | | | | | | | | | |
|---|---|---|---|---|---|---|---|---|---|
| 1. | c | 5. | d | 9. | a | 13. | d | 17. | b |
| 2. | b | 6. | a | 10. | d | 14. | d | 18. | a |
| 3. | a | 7. | c | 11. | a | 15. | a | 19. | d |
| 4. | d | 8. | b | 12. | b | 16. | c | 20. | c |

## Problems and Applications

## *Exercise 1*

1. See Table 6.2 Answer, column 2.

### Table 6.2 Answer

| (1) | (2) | (3) |
|---|---|---|
| 0 | 0 | --- |
| 1 | 20 | 20 |
| 2 | 46 | 26 |
| 3 | 64 | 18 |
| 4 | 72 | 8 |
| 5 | 78 | 6 |
| 6 | 81 | 3 |
| 7 | 80 | - 1 |

2. **Figure 6.1 Answer**

3.  See Table 6.2 Answer, column 3.

4.  **Figure 6.2 Answer**

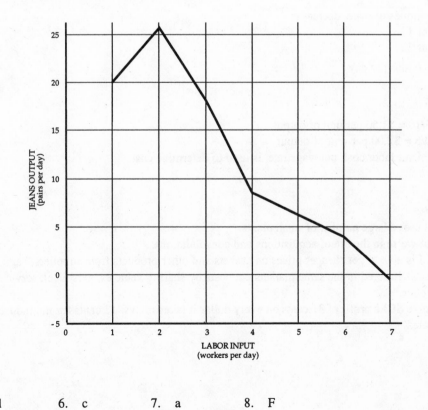

5.  d          6.  c          7.  a          8.  F

## Exercise 2

1. **Table 6.3 Answer**

| Rate of Output | Fixed Cost | Variable Cost | Total Cost | Average Total Cost | Marginal Cost |
|---|---|---|---|---|---|
| 0 | $ 10 | $ 0 | $ 10 | -------- | ------- |
| 1 | 10 | 6 | 16 | $16.00 | $ 6 |
| 2 | 10 | 10 | 20 | 10.00 | 4 |
| 3 | 10 | 16 | 26 | 8.67 | 6 |
| 4 | 10 | 26 | 36 | 9.00 | 10 |
| 5 | 10 | 40 | 50 | 10.00 | 14 |
| 6 | 10 | 58 | 68 | 11.33 | 18 |

2. above
3. below

## Exercise 3

1. c
2. d
3. lease on the building, sewing machines, and testing and certification
4. $1,100
5. $3,600
6. $2,850
7. $4,050; The economic cost is greater because it includes the implicit cost of the building; the accounting cost does not.

## Exercise 4

1. economies of scale, decreases
2. Plant 1
3. Plant 3
4. 4 to 6 tons per day

## Exercise 5

1. $15/10 = $1.50 per unit of output
2. $10/5 = $2.00 per unit of output
3. F    Unit labor cost, not wage rate, is used to determine cost.
4. T

## Exercise 6

1. SCI uses a large number of small plants.
2. "But we're in the era of acquisitions and consolidations..."
3. "SCI is able to get cheaper prices on caskets and other products from suppliers," and "if funeral homes clustered in the same markets cut costs by sharing vehicles, personnel, services, and supplies."
4. "...give SCI a profit of 31 cents on every dollar it takes in...vs. 12 cents for the industry as a whole."

# CHAPTER 7

# The Competitive Firm

## Quick Review

The pursuit of profits is the motivating, driving force in the management of firms in the U.S. and other market economies. In this chapter we examine the profit motive and pay particular attention to how competitive firms answer the following questions:

- What are profits?
- What are the unique characteristics of competitive firms?
- How much output will a competitive firm produce?

To start with, firms are the suppliers of goods and services. Large and small firms alike want to earn profits. Profits are the difference between total revenue and total cost, and a profit-maximizing firm must consider how revenues and costs change when the rate of production changes. The profit-maximizing producer compares marginal cost with marginal revenue. As long as marginal revenue exceeds marginal cost, profits increase as the production rate increases. This additional profit gives the producer an incentive to speed up production. As the rate of production increases, however, marginal costs usually rise while prices remain constant or decline.

Why does increased production push up marginal costs? Marginal costs rise when crowding and waste occur as a result of the increased rate of production. Why does increased production lower prices and marginal revenue? The law of demand is at work.

At some rate of production, marginal cost will exceed marginal revenue. Further increases in production will then lower profits. Consequently, a firm achieves maximum profits at the production rate at which marginal cost equals marginal revenue $(MC = MR) = P$.

The manager can tell how total revenue will change in response to a change in price if he or she knows the price elasticity of demand. The response of total revenue to a change in price depends on the price elasticity of demand as indicated in the table below.

| If elasticity of demand is: | Then for a | |
|---|---|---|
| | Rise in price: | Decline in price: |
| Greater than 1 (elastic demand) | Total revenue falls | Total revenue rises |
| Equal to 1 (unit elasticity) | Total revenue remains the same | Total revenue remains the same |
| Less than 1 (inelastic) | Total revenue rises | Total revenue falls |

For competitive firms, demand is perfectly elastic. The demand curve is flat from the point of view of the firm, and the marginal revenue curve is equal to the demand curve. Because they possess no market power, competitive firms are price takers and simply respond to changes in the *market price*—increasing output when *MR* exceeds *MC* and decreasing output when *MC* exceeds *MR*.

A firm is faced with various types of costs. Fixed costs, which a firm cannot change in the short run, can be altered by the long-run investment decision. Production decisions, however, involve changes in variable costs, which can be manipulated in the short run by changing the rate of output. In the short run, a firm continues to operate as long as it can cover its variable costs. In the short run a firm *shuts down* if variable costs of production cannot be covered. In the long run a firm must cover all costs, both explicit and implicit, or exit from the market. This is the firm's investment decision.

For competitive firms, that part of the marginal cost curve that lies above the average variable cost curve is equivalent to its short-run supply curve. The supply curve shifts as a result of certain determinants which include the prices of resources, technology, taxes, expectations (about prices, technology, and so on), and the number of suppliers. A change in price causes a movement along the supply curve to a new quantity supplied but no change in the supply curve itself.

Economic and accounting ideas of profit and cost are different. Accountants recognize all costs that are paid an explicit wage. Economists recognize explicit costs, but they also identify other factors in the production of a good that are not paid an explicit wage. Because economists include implicit costs in assessing the costs of production, economic profits are smaller than accounting profits. If a firm earns zero economic profits, it is able to maintain its operations in the long run. In fact, there may be quite substantial accounting "profits" even when economic profits are zero!

Changes in tax laws can affect both the production decision (short run) and the investment decision (long run). The key to understanding how changes in taxes affect business decisions is to determine whether the tax is viewed by the firm as a variable cost (like the social security tax) or a fixed cost (like a lump sum tax or license fee).

## Learning Objectives

After reading Chapter 7 and doing the following exercises, you should:

1. Know the difference between economic profits and accounting profits, and how profits are maximized.
2. Be able to compute profits and relate them to prices, costs, and the price elasticity of demand.
3. Understand why competitive firms are "price takers" and recognize the differences between the firm's demand and the market demand.
4. Know the relationships among total, average, and marginal costs (or revenue).
5. Recognize the difference between long-run and short-run decisions.
6. Know the profit maximization rule and the importance of marginal revenue and marginal cost.
7. Understand graphically how a firm determines profit, price, and production rate in the short run.
8. Understand how the firm makes the "shutdown" decision and the long-run investment decision.
9. Know how changes in the determinants affect the market supply curve.
10. Understand how various taxes affect the firm's output decision.

## Using Key Terms

Fill in the puzzle on the opposite page with the appropriate term from the list of Key Terms at the end of the chapter in the text.

## *Across*

2.      The value of all resources used in production.
4.      Equal to $10 per day at all rates of output in Figure 7.6 in the text.
6.      The competitive _____ is summarized in Table 7.3 in the text.
7.      Equal to $13 at every output level in Figure 7.7 in the text.
9.      The opportunity cost of capital.
11.     The short-run _____ is equal to the marginal cost curve in Figure 7.10 in the text.
12.     Equal to $5 at the output rate of one bushel per hour in Figure 7.7 in the text.

13. The ability to alter the market price of a good or service.
14. The long-run decision to enter or exit an industry.
17. Ranges from perfect competition to monopoly in Figure 7.1 in the text.
18. Equal to $52 at an output rate of four bushels per day in Figure 7.7 in the text.
19. Costs of production that change when the rate of output changes.
20. A period of time long enough for all inputs to be varied.

## Down

1. A market in which no buyer or seller has market power.
3. The sole supplier of a good or service.
5. A firm that must take whatever price the market offers for the goods it produces.
6. The choice of a short-run rate of output by Farmer Kitt.
8. Total revenue minus total economic cost.
10. Occurs at a price of $5 in Figure 7.9 in the text.
15. The period in which the quantity of some inputs cannot be changed.
16. Eventually becomes zero in a competitive industry because of market entry.

## Puzzle 7.1

# True or False: *Circle your choice and explain why any false statements are incorrect.*

T  F  1. A firm should produce until the next unit produced would raise marginal costs above marginal revenues.

T  F  2. If the price of a good remains the same regardless of the rate of output that a firm produces, the demand curve faced by the firm is perfectly elastic.

T  F  3. For a competitive firm, the supply curve is that part of the marginal cost curve that is above the short-run average total cost curve.

T  F  4. Since a firm's goal is to maximize profits, it should expand production as long as it is making profits.

T  F  5. If a firm maximizes revenue, it is maximizing profit.

T  F  6. A firm can minimize its losses by continuing to produce in the short run when price is less than ATC but greater than AVC.

T  F  7. Normal profit is when a firm's revenues just cover its economic costs.

T  F  8. When businesses earn zero economic profit, they have no incentive to stay in business.

T  F  9. A change in the tax rate on corporate profits will affect the firm's investment decision.

T  F  10. Perfectly competitive firms face horizontal demand curves because they have no market power.

# Multiple Choice: *Select the correct answer.*

_____ 1. Whereas consumers try to maximize utility, economists assume that firms try to maximize:
   (a) Profits.
   (b) Revenues.
   (c) Sales.
   (d) Production in a given period of time, *ceteris paribus*.

_____ 2. Economic costs and economic profits are typically:
   (a) Greater and smaller, respectively, than their accounting counterparts.
   (b) Smaller and greater, respectively, than their accounting counterparts.
   (c) Both smaller than their accounting counterparts.
   (d) Both larger than their accounting counterparts.

_____ 3. When a producer can control the market price for the good it sells:
   (a) The producer is an entrepreneur.
   (b) The producer is certain to make a profit.
   (c) The producer has market power.
   (d) The producer is a perfectly competitive firm.

_____ 4. In which of the following types of markets does a single firm have the most market power?
   (a) Perfect competition.
   (b) Monopolistic competition.
   (c) Oligopoly.
   (d) Monopoly.

_____ 5. Normal profit implies that:
  (a)   Economic profit is zero.
  (b)   All factors employed are earning an amount equal to their opportunity costs.
  (c)   The factors employed are earning as much as they could in the best alternative employment.
  (d)   All of the above.

_____ 6. The market equilibrium price occurs where:
  (a)   Price equals the minimum of average variable cost.
  (b)   Market supply crosses market demand.
  (c)   A firm's marginal revenue equals marginal cost.
  (d)   A firm's marginal cost equals average cost.

_____ 7. A competitive firm:
  (a)   Has a large advertising budget.
  (b)   Has output so small relative to the market supply that is has no effect on market price.
  (c)   Can alter the market price of the good(s) it produces.
  (d)   Can raise price to increase profit.

_____ 8. If a perfectly competitive firm can sell 100 computers at $500 each, in order to sell one more computer, the firm:
  (a)   Must lower its price.
  (b)   Can raise its price.
  (c)   Can sell the 101$^{st}$ computer at $500.
  (d)   Cannot sell an additional computer at any price because the market is at equilibrium.

_____ 9. A competitive firm's profits are maximized where:
  (a)   Market supply crosses the firm's marginal cost.
  (b)   Price equals the minimum of total cost.
  (c)   Price equals marginal cost.
  (d)   Marginal cost equals total revenue.

_____ 10. If price is greater than marginal cost, a perfectly competitive firm should increase output because:
  (a)   Marginal costs are increasing.
  (b)   Additional units of output will add to the firm's profits (or reduce losses).
  (c)   The price they receive for their product is increasing.
  (d)   Total revenues would increase.

_____ 11. If a perfectly competitive firm wanted to maximize its total _revenues_, it would produce:
  (a)   The output where MC equals price.
  (b)   As much output as it is capable of producing.
  (c)   The output where the ATC curve is at a minimum.
  (d)   The output where the marginal cost curve is at a minimum.

_____ 12. Total profit is:
  (a)   $TR - TC$.
  (b)   $Q \times (P - ATC)$.
  (c)   $(P \times Q) - TC$.
  (d)   All of the above.

_____ 13. When price exceeds average variable cost but not average total cost, the firm should, in the short run:
  (a)   Shut down.
  (b)   Produce at the rate of output where price = MC.
  (c)   Minimize per-unit losses by producing at the rate of output where ATC is minimized.
  (d)   Raise the price it charges.

_____ 14. A firm should shut down (stop producing) whenever:
   (a)   Minimum average variable cost exceeds price.
   (b)   Minimum average total cost exceeds price.
   (c)   It is taking a loss.
   (d)   Marginal cost exceeds marginal revenue.

_____ 15. A firm that makes an investment decision views all factors of production as:
   (a)   Variable over the long run.
   (b)   Variable over the short run.
   (c)   Fixed over the long run.
   (d)   Fixed over the short run.

_____ 16. The marginal cost curve:
   (a)   Will be affected by changes in the cost of inputs.
   (b)   Will eventually slope upward to the right as output increases.
   (c)   Above the AVC is the short run supply curve for a competitive firm.
   (d)   All of the above.

_____ 17. The market supply curve is calculated by:
   (a)   Summing the quantities supplied of individual supply curves at each price.
   (b)   Averaging the quantities supplied of individual supply curves at each price.
   (c)   Summing the prices of individual supply curves at each price.
   (d)   Averaging the prices of individual supply curves.

_____ 18. The supply curve is upward-sloping, i.e. it takes a _higher_ price to induce greater production, because of:
   (a)   Increasing total costs.
   (b)   Increasing fixed costs.
   (c)   Increasing marginal costs.
   (d)   The decreasing skill level of additional workers.

_____ 19. Taxes affect average total cost and marginal cost curves as follows:
   (a)   Profit taxes affect neither, property taxes affect only average total cost, and payroll taxes affect both average and marginal costs.
   (b)   Payroll taxes affect neither, property taxes affect only average total cost, and profit taxes affect both average and marginal costs.
   (c)   Payroll taxes affect neither, property taxes affect only marginal cost, and profit taxes affect both average and marginal costs.
   (d)   Property taxes affect neither, payroll taxes affect only marginal cost, and profit taxes affect both average and marginal costs.

_____ 20. Which of the following would influence a firm's long-run decision making?
   (a)   An increase in property tax assessments.
   (b)   A charge on wages for unemployment and disability benefits.
   (c)   An increase in profit taxes.
   (d)   All of the above.

# Problems and Applications
## *Exercise 1*

This exercise uses total cost and total revenue to determine how much output a competitive firm should produce.

Refer to Figure 7.1 to answer questions 1-5.

### Figure 7.1

1. Profit is the difference between _____ and _____.

2. This firm earns a profit at all output levels between _____ and _____ units.

3. What is the profit maximizing rate of output for this firm? _____

4. This firm experiences losses at all rates of output below _____ units.

5. Total costs increase more rapidly after 90 units of output because of the law of
_____.

## *Exercise 2*

This exercise shows how the equilibrium price is determined in a competitive market and how the profit maximizing rate of output is determined in a perfectly competitive market.

1. Using the information in Table 7.2 draw the market demand curve for chicken eggs in Figure 7.2. Label the curve *D*.

## Table 7.2
## Market demand for eggs

| Quantity (millions of eggs per day) | Price (per dozen) |
|---|---|
| 2 | $ 1.00 |
| 4 | $ 0.50 |

## Figure 7.2
## Market demand and market supply curves

Quantity (millions of eggs per day)

2. Using the information in Table 7.3 draw the market supply curve for chicken eggs in Figure 7.2. Label the curve *S*.

## Table 7.3
## Market supply of eggs

| Quantity (millions of eggs per day) | Price (per dozen) |
|---|---|
| 4 | $ 1.00 |
| 2 | $ 0.50 |

3. Use the information in Table 7.4 to determine the marginal cost at each output level for an individual egg farmer.

## Table 7.4
## Production costs for an individual egg farmer

| Quantity (eggs per minute) | Total cost | Marginal cost |
|---|---|---|
| 0 | $ 4.00 | --------- |
| 1 | $ 4.20 | _____ |
| 2 | $ 4.65 | _____ |
| 3 | $ 5.40 | _____ |
| 4 | $ 6.50 | _____ |
| 5 | $ 7.90 | _____ |

4. Use the information in Table 7.4 to draw the marginal cost curve for the individual egg farmer in Figure 7.3.

## Figure 7.3
## Costs of egg production

5. Use the market equilibrium price from Figure 7.2 to draw a line at the price that the individual farmer faces in Figure 7.3.

6. For a competitive firm, MR always equals _____.

7. According to the profit-maximization rule, this egg farmer should produce _____ eggs per minute.

8. At an output level of 5 eggs per minute, for the individual farmer, MC is (greater, less) than price and the farmer should (increase, decrease) output in order to maximize profit.

111

# Exercise 3

This exercise provides practice in using graphs in a perfectly competitive market situation.

**Figure 7.4**
**Production costs**

1. Label the three curves given in Figure 7.4 for a firm in a perfectly competitive market situation.

2. What is the profit maximizing rate of output for this firm?

3. Shade the area that represents total profit at the profit maximizing rate of output.

# Exercise 4

This exercise gives you a chance to calculate total revenue, total profit, and marginal cost and to find the output that will yield maximum profit.

1. Fill in the blanks for the formulas below.
   (a) Price x quantity = _____
   (b) Change in total cost / change in output = _____
   (c) Total revenue - total cost = _____

2. After checking your answers for question 1, complete Table 7.5.

**Table 7.5**
**Cost and revenue data**

| Qty. | Price | Total revenue | Total cost | Profit | Marginal cost |
|------|-------|---------------|------------|--------|---------------|
| 0 | $7 | $_____ | $ 5.00 | $_____ | -------- |
| 1 | 7 | _____ | 7.00 | _____ | _____ |
| 2 | 7 | _____ | 11.00 | _____ | _____ |
| 3 | 7 | _____ | 18.00 | _____ | _____ |
| 4 | 7 | _____ | 27.00 | _____ | _____ |
| 5 | 7 | _____ | 39.00 | _____ | _____ |

3. In Figure 7.5, graph price and marginal cost.

## Figure 7.5

4. What is the profit maximizing level of output for this firm? _____

5. At an output level of 2 items this firm could (increase, decrease) profit by producing more.

## Exercise 5

This exercise focuses on the shutdown decision.

Refer to Figure 7.6 to answer questions 1-6.

## Figure 7.6

1. What is the profit-maximizing production rate for the firm if the price is $23? _____

2. What is the profit-maximizing production rate for the firm if the price is $15? _____

3. At a price of $12 this firm is earning a (profit, loss) and should (continue to produce, shut-down) because the price is greater than (ATC, AVC).

4. The shutdown price for a firm is any price below the minimum of the _____ curve.

5. At a price of $8 this firm will minimize losses by (continuing to produce, shutting down). In this case total revenues are (less, greater) than total variable costs.

6. The shutdown point for this firm occurs at a price of _____.

# Common Errors

The first statement in each "common error" below is incorrect. Each incorrect statement is followed by a corrected version and an explanation.

1. Higher prices yield greater profits. WRONG!

   The effect of price increases on total revenue depends on the elasticity of demand. RIGHT!

   The law of demand tells us that when prices rise, quantity falls; total revenues may actually decrease (remember the $4 ice cream cones). Costs also change; if they don't fall as quickly as total revenues, then *profits* fall.

2. Surpluses and shortages are determinants of demand and supply that shift demand and supply curves. WRONG!

   Surpluses and shortages often result from shifts of demand or supply curves, but they do not cause such shifts themselves. RIGHT!

   Surpluses or shortages may appear in a market if the market price does not adjust to the equilibrium price. If there is a shift in demand or supply, shortages or surpluses may temporarily result until the market price reaches its equilibrium. Nevertheless, expectations of future shortages and surpluses can affect current demand.

3. If a firm is taking a loss, it is not maximizing profits. WRONG!

   A firm may be maximizing profits even if it is making zero profits or taking a loss. RIGHT!

   Minimizing losses is essentially the same as maximizing profits. A firm is maximizing profits as long as there is nothing it can do to make larger profits. Remember, even if the firm is taking a loss, it will not shut down if it can cover variable costs.

4. A change in price changes the supply of goods produced by a firm. WRONG!

   A change in price changes the quantity of a good supplied by a firm in a given time period. RIGHT!

   *Be careful!* Economists differentiate between the terms "quantity supplied" and "supply." A change in the quantity supplied usually refers to a movement along a supply curve as a result of a change in price or production rate. A change in supply refers to a shift of the supply curve as a result of a change in technology, the price of a resource, or the number of sellers.

5. A firm should always increase the rate of production as long as it is making a profit. WRONG!

A profitable firm should increase production rates only as long as additional revenues from the increase in production exceed the additional associated costs. RIGHT!

If the increase in production rates generates more costs than revenue, the firm will be less profitable. In this case, continued expansion will ultimately result in zero profits.

# •ANSWERS•

## Using Key Terms

### *Across*
2. economic cost
4. fixed costs
6. profit maximization rule
7. marginal revenue
9. normal profit
11. supply curve
12. marginal cost
13. market power
14. investment decision
17. market structure
18. total revenue
19. variable costs
20. long run

### *Down*
1. perfect competition
3. monopoly
5. competitive firm
6. production decision
8. economic profit
10. shutdown point
15. short run
16. profit

## True or False

1. T
2. T
3. F The supply curve is that part of the marginal cost curve above the AVC curve.
4. F The firm should expand production as long as it is making a profit on *additional* units. A firm could produce an output greater than the profit-maximizing output but still have an profit.
5. F To maximize revenue, a firm would produce as much output as it possibly can. To maximize profit, the firm should produce the output where the difference between TR and TC is the greatest.

115

6. T
7. T
8. F    A firm that earns zero economic profits is covering all its economic costs, including a
         normal profit to the entrepreneur.   There is no better use for the firm's resources (i.e. it is
         earning exactly what it could earn in the next best option).
9. T
10. T

## Multiple Choice

| | | | |
|---|---|---|---|
| 1. a | 5. d | 9. c | 13. b | 17. a |
| 2. a | 6. b | 10. b | 14. a | 18. c |
| 3. c | 7. b | 11. b | 15. a | 19. a |
| 4. d | 8. c | 12. d | 16. d | 20. d |

## Problems and Applications

### Exercise 1

1.  total revenue, total cost
2.  90, 220
3.  160 units
4.  90
5.  diminishing returns

### Exercise 2

**Figure 7.2 Answer**

1. See Figure 7.2 answer.
2. See Figure 7.2 answer.

3.   **Table 7.4 Answer**

| Quantity | Marginal cost |
|---|---|
| 0 | $ ------ |
| 1 | 0.20 |
| 2 | 0.45 |
| 3 | 0.75 |
| 4 | 1.10 |
| 5 | 1.40 |

116

## Figure 7.3 Answer

Quantity (eggs per minute)

4. See Figure 7.3 answer.
5. See Figure 7.3 answer.

6. price
7. 3
8. greater, decrease

# Exercise 3

1. **Figure 7.4 Answer**

Quantity (items per hour)

2. 4 items per hour
3. See Figure 7.4 answer.

# Exercise 4

1. a.  total revenue
   b.  marginal cost
   c.  profit

117

2. **Table 7.5 Answer**

| Quantity | Total revenue | Profit | Marginal cost |
|---|---|---|---|
| 0 | $ 0.00 | $ -5.00 | ------- |
| 1 | 7.00 | + 0.00 | $ 2.00 |
| 2 | 14.00 | + 3.00 | 4.00 |
| 3 | 21.00 | + 3.00 | 7.00 |
| 4 | 28.00 | + 1.00 | 9.00 |
| 5 | 35.00 | - 4.00 | 12.00 |

3. **Figure 7.5 Answer**

4. 3 items per day
5. increase

## Exercise 5

1. 39 units
2. 31 units
3. loss, continue to produce, AVC
4. AVC
5. shutting down, less
6. $10

# CHAPTER 8

# Competitive Markets

## Quick Review

The purely competitive market provides the standard by which all other market structures are judged. Other markets are labeled efficient or inefficient, depending on how their long-run equilibrium price and output compare with what would be achieved in a competitive market.

The essence of a competitive market is that the actors are powerless to influence product prices and resource flows. They are powerless because such a market is characterized by (1) a product that is homogeneous, (2) a large number of very small buyers and sellers, (3) prices that are free of artificial restrictions, and (4) an absence of barriers to entry into or exit from the market.

In this chapter we consider three principal questions:

- How are prices determined in competitive markets?
- How does competition affect the profits of a firm or industry?
- What does society gain from market competition?

Of course, firms sometimes incur losses. In that case, the market has sent a signal that some firms should leave the market. Supply is thereby reduced, price rises, *ceteris paribus,* and long-run equilibrium is established at a higher price. Resources that left the market will move to higher-valued uses elsewhere. Society's efficient allocation of scarce resources owes as much to losses as it does to profits.

Firms in a competitive market are called "price takers." The price that they "take" is the equilibrium price, at which market supply equals market demand. Because each firm is so small relative to the market, each entrepreneur recognizes that he or she alone cannot influence the price of the product by altering his or her share of the total supply. The price dictated by the market becomes, therefore, the marginal revenue. Following the rules described earlier, entrepreneurs produce at that rate of production at which $MR = MC$. This is the best they can do.

Let's suppose that at the current market price, profits are above the normal rates of return earned by similar resources in alternative uses. Owners of those resources will enter the market, start new firms, and produce output. But by doing so they will increase the supply of the product and, *ceteris paribus,* drive down the market price (each firm's marginal revenue). The entry of firms will continue until the above-normal returns are eliminated. Thus, each firm is forced by the competition (or threat of competition) from other firms to operate efficiently. In other words, the producer is forced to the minimum average total cost ($ATC$) of producing goods.

When the long-run equilibrium is reached in a competitive market, several important conditions result. First, consumers are willing to pay an amount ($P$) for the last unit produced that is just equal to the amount required ($MC$) to get firms to produce it. Furthermore, $MC = $ minimum $LATC$, because if price were any higher, returns would be above average and new firms would enter the industry and drive the price down.

Consumers get what they want at the lowest possible price. The economy's resources are used most efficiently in perfectly competitive markets.

Examples of competitive markets are easy to find. Personal computers, agricultural products, VCRs, and so on are just a few. This chapter uses the story of the personal computer to illustrate how competitive markets work and how the consumer benefits as a result. We should expect to see the same process occur in the market for HDTVs very soon.

## Learning Objectives

After reading Chapter 8 and doing the following exercises, you should:

1. Know how the absence of market power relates to the shape of demand and supply curves from the point of view of buyers and sellers.
2. Be able to tell why the demand curve facing a competitive firm is flat.
3. Be able to list the characteristics of the competitive market structure and describe the role of competition in the U.S. economy.
4. Know how barriers to entry influence the competitive process.
5. Know the difference between the firm's demand curve and the market demand curve.
6. Know why above-normal profits disappear in competitive industries.
7. Understand how a competitive market structure affects prices, cost, output, and profits in the short and long run.
8. Be able to identify the signals for the entry and exit of firms.
9. Be able to show the effects of shifts of market demand or supply on individual demand or supply.
10. Describe how marginal cost pricing leads to efficiency in the allocation of resources.

## Using Key Terms

Fill in the puzzle on the opposite page with the appropriate term from the list of Key Terms at the end on the chapter in the text.

### *Across*

3. The choice of a short-run rate of output by catfish farmers.
4. The offer of goods at a price equal to their marginal cost.
6. Competitive markets promote _____ because price is driven down to the level of minimum average costs.
7. According to Table 8.2 in the text, firms will enter an industry if _____ exists.
8. A market in which no buyer or seller has market power.
10. Equal to $300 at an output rate of 600 computers per month in Table 8.1 in the text.
11. This curve shifts to the right in Figure 8.2 in the text as more firms enter the industry.
12. The rate of output at which price equals minimum AVC.
13. The price signal the consumer receives in a competitive market is an accurate reflection of _____.
14. Equal to marginal revenue at an output rate of 600 computers per month in Table 8.1 in the text.
15. Total cost divided by the quantity produced.
16. Determined by the intersection of market demand and market supply.
17. Allows for indirect communication between producers and consumers by way of market sales and purchases.

### *Down*

1. Occurs where price equals minimum ATC in Figure 8.6 in the text.
2. Occurs where price equals marginal cost in Figure 8.6 in the text.

5. Obstacles that make it difficult or impossible for new firms to enter an industry.
9. The decision to build, buy, or lease plant and equipment.

# Puzzle 8.1

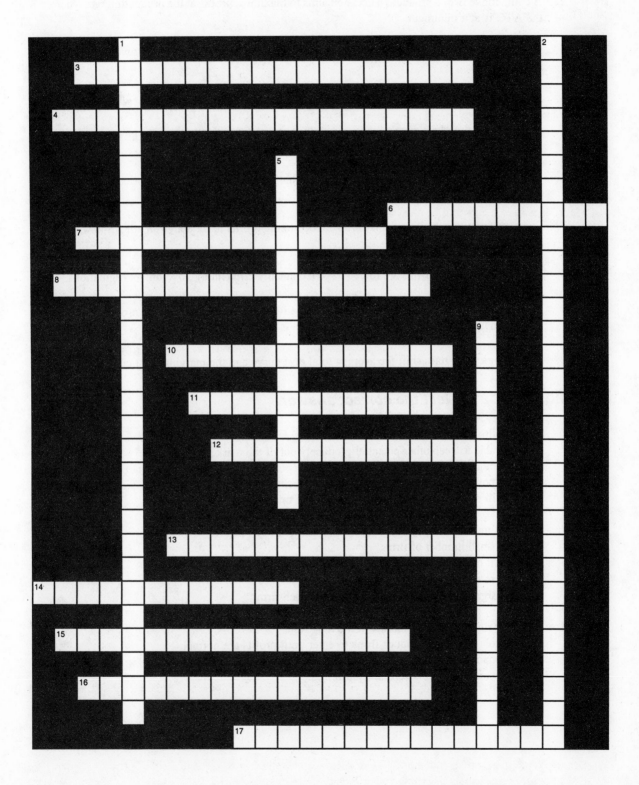

# True or False: *Circle your choice and explain why any false statements are incorrect.*

T  F  1.  The market supply curve is a horizontal summation of the *MC* curves above minimum *AVC* of the individual firms.

T  F  2.  A competitive firm's production decision aims to maximize profits at the production rate where the ATC is at a minimum.

T  F  3.  If a perfectly competitive firm were to raise its price above the market price, it would increase its total revenues.

T  F  4.  As long as an economic profit is available, a market will continue to attract new entrants.

T  F  5.  In competitive markets, economic losses are a signal to firms that better options are available for its resources.

T  F  6.  With marginal cost pricing, firms will produce the output where the market price equals the firm's MC.

T  F  7.  Since perfectly competitive firms earn zero economic profits in the long run, all firms will leave the industry.

T  F  8.  Perfectly competitive firms are forced to be technically efficient by government regulations.

T  F  9.  In the long-run equilibrium for a perfectly competitive market, the price of the product will equal the minimum marginal cost.

T  F  10.  Technological changes shift the average total cost curve and the marginal cost curve downward.

# Multiple Choice: *Select the correct answer.*

_____  1.  A competitive firm:
   (a)  Is able to keep other potential producers out of the market.
   (b)  Would like to keep other potential producers out of the market but cannot do so.
   (c)  Is powerless to alter its own rate of production.
   (d)  Will not care if more producers enter the market.

_____  2.  Which of the following is consistent with a competitive market?
   (a)  A small number of firms.
   (b)  Exit of small firms when profits are high for large firms.
   (c)  Zero economic profit in the long run.
   (d)  Marginal revenue lower than price for each firm.

_____  3.  In a perfectly competitive market in the long run:
   (a)  Economic profits induce firms to enter until profits are normal.
   (b)  Economic losses induce firms to exit until profits are normal.
   (c)  Economic profit is zero at equilibrium.
   (d)  All of the above.

4. The exit of firms from a market:
   (a) Shifts the market supply curve to the right.
   (b) Reduces profits of existing firms in a market.
   (c) Reduces the equilibrium output in the market.
   (d) All of the above.

5. Which of the following conditions is *not* characteristic of a perfectly competitive market?
   (a) There are many firms.
   (b) Products are homogeneous.
   (c) Barriers to enter the industry are low.
   (d) The market price is determined by an organization of sellers.

6. In a competitive market, if the market demand curve is tangent to the minimum point of the ATC curve, a firm may seek to earn economic profits by:
   (a) Producing at the rate of output where price equals demand.
   (b) Decreasing production costs through technological improvements.
   (c) Decreasing price.
   (d) Increasing price.

7. The entry of firms into a market:
   (a) Pushes the equilibrium price downward.
   (b) Reduces profits of existing firms in the market.
   (c) Shifts the market supply curve rightward.
   (d) All of the above.

8. The perfectly competitive market model is important because:
   (a) It characterizes most markets in the U.S. economy.
   (b) It shows how laissez faire can overcome market failures.
   (c) Many markets function much like the competitive model.
   (d) All of the above.

9. A competitive market promotes technical efficiency in the long run by pushing prices to the minimum of:
   (a) Short-run AVC.
   (b) Short-run MC.
   (c) Long-run ATC.
   (d) Long-run TC.

10. Which of the following conditions always characterizes a firm that is in short-run competitive equilibrium where profits are maximized?
    (a) Price equals minimum average total cost.
    (b) Price equals marginal cost.
    (c) There are no economic profits.
    (d) All of the above characterize such a firm.

11. The market supply curve will shift as a result of all of the following *except:*
    (a) Changes in technology.
    (b) Changes in the number of supplying firms.
    (c) Changes in expectations about making profits in an industry.
    (d) Changes in the current income of buyers.

12. In a competitive market where firms are incurring losses, which of the following should be expected as the industry moves to long-run equilibrium, *ceteris paribus?*
    (a) A higher price and fewer firms.
    (b) A lower price and fewer firms.
    (c) A higher price and more firms.
    (d) A lower price and more firms.

13. In long-run competitive equilibrium, price equals:
    (a) The minimum of the long-run average total cost curve.
    (b) The minimum of the long-run average variable cost curve.
    (c) Long-run marginal cost.
    (d) All of the above.

14. In which of the following cases would a firm enter a market?
    (a) P = short-run ATC.
    (b) P > long-run ATC.
    (c) P < short-run ATC.
    (d) P < long-run ATC.

15. The constant quest for profits in competitive markets results in:
    (a) Zero economic profits in the long run.
    (b) The production of goods and services that consumers demand.
    (c) Product and technological innovation.
    (d) All of the above are correct.

16. When economic profits exist in the market for a particular product, this is a signal to producers that:
    (a) Consumers would like more scarce resources devoted to the production of this product.
    (b) That the market is oversupplied with this product.
    (c) The best mix of goods and services are being produced with society's scarce resources.
    (d) Price is at the minimum of the ATC curve.

17. In a competitive market where firms are experiencing economic losses, which of the following would not be expected?
    (a) A decrease in MR for the remaining firms.
    (b) A decrease in market supply.
    (c) An increase in total revenue for the remaining firms.
    (d) An increase in output for the remaining firms.

18. Economic losses are a signal to producers:
    (a) That they are using resources in the most efficient way.
    (b) That they are not using resources in the best way.
    (c) That consumer demand is being satisfied.
    (d) That consumers are content with the allocation of resources.

19. When a computer firm is producing an output where the price is greater than the MC, then from society's standpoint:
    (a) The firm is producing too much because society is giving up more to produce additional computers than the computers are worth.
    (b) The firm is producing too much because society would be willing to give up more alternative goods in order to get additional computers.
    (c) The firm is producing too little because society is giving up more to produce additional computers than the computers are worth.
    (d) The firm is producing too little because society would be willing to give up more alternative goods in order to get additional computers.

_____ 20. Marginal cost pricing in competitive markets results in:
  (a) Economic efficiency.
  (b) Output being produced where price equals the opportunity cost of the last unit being produced.
  (c) Necessary information for consumers to make rational choices between alternative goods and services.
  (d) All of the above are correct.

# Problems and Applications

## Exercise 1

This exercise focuses on the market supply curve and how a competitive industry adjusts to long-run equilibrium.

Assume the HDTV industry is a competitive market and initially there are economic profits in the industry.

1. The lure of economic profits will cause (more, less) firms to enter the industry over time which will cause the market supply curve to _____.

2. Market price is determined by the intersection of _____
_____.

3. If the market supply shifts to the right, _ceteris paribus_, market price will (increase, decrease).

4. As long as new producers enter the market, market output will (expand, contract) and economic profits will (increase, decrease).

5. Economic profits will approach _____ for this industry in the long run.

6. In long-run competitive equilibrium, price will be equal to minimum _____.

## Exercise 2

This exercise uses information from a table to determine revenues, costs, and profits.

Use Table 8.1 to answer questions 1-9.

### Table 8.1

| Output | Price | Total revenue | Total cost | Total profit | Marginal revenue | Marginal cost | Average total cost |
|--------|-------|---------------|------------|--------------|------------------|---------------|--------------------|
| 0 | ---- | ---- | $10 | _____ | ---- | ---- | ---- |
| 1 | $13 | _____ | 15 | _____ | _____ | _____ | _____ |
| 2 | 13 | _____ | 22 | _____ | _____ | _____ | _____ |
| 3 | 13 | _____ | 31 | _____ | _____ | _____ | _____ |
| 4 | 13 | _____ | 44 | _____ | _____ | _____ | _____ |
| 5 | 13 | _____ | 61 | _____ | _____ | _____ | _____ |

125

1. It is obvious that Table 8.1 refers to a perfectly competitive firm because _____ is constant regardless of the level of output.

2. The fixed cost for this firm is equal to _____.

3. Calculate total revenue, total profit, marginal revenue, marginal cost, and average total cost for this firm.

4. What is the profit maximizing rate of output for this firm? _____

5. The short-run competitive equilibrium occurs where _____.

6. The long-run competitive equilibrium occurs where _____.

7. The minimum for average total cost for this firm is _____. This amount is (greater, less) than the current market price so this firm is operating in the (short, long) run.

8. In this case, firms will _____ the industry because economic _____ exist.

9. What happens to price as new firms enter the market? _____

## Exercise 3

When the hand-held calculator was invented in the 1970s, the market responded in competitive fashion. This exercise focuses on the adjustments made in a competitive market in both the short run and the long run.

Figure 8.1 presents the cost curves that are relevant to a firm's production decision, and Figure 8.2 shows the market demand and supply curves for the calculator market. Use Figures 8.1 and 8.2 and the knowledge of cost curves that you have gained from the text to answer questions 1-10.

### Figure 8.1
### Firm

### Figure 8.2
### Market (all firms)

1. If the market demand and supply curves are $S_1$ and $D_1$, the market equilibrium price will be:
   (a) $P_1$.
   (b) $P_2$.
   (c) $P_3$.
   (d) $P_4$.

2. Suppose the demand for calculators shifts to $D_4$. This shift might be caused by:
   (a) An increase in the number of consumers.
   (b) An increase in consumers' incomes.
   (c) A rise in the price of a substitute good.
   (d) All of the above.

3. If the demand curve is at $D_4$, the quantity supplied by the *firm* will be:
   (a) $q_1$.
   (b) $q_2$.
   (c) $q_3$.
   (d) $q_4$.

4. Suppose a recession results in a shift in the demand curve for calculators to $D_1$. Then the *firm* will produce:
   (a) $q_1$.
   (b) $q_2$.
   (c) $q_3$.
   (d) $q_4$.

5. In the short run, the firm will continue to produce some output until demand changes enough to drive price below:
   (a) $P_1$.
   (b) $P_2$.
   (c) $P_3$.
   (d) $P_4$.

6. At prices below $P_1$, the firm will shut down (produce no output) because:
   (a) Its loss will be less than if it produces at any level of output.
   (b) Its loss will be limited to its fixed costs.
   (c) Total revenue is less than total variable cost.
   (d) All of the above are the case.

7. The fact that the quantity supplied by the firm changes whenever the market price changes indicates that:
   (a) The firm is a price setter.
   (b) The firm is a price taker.
   (c) The firm has monopoly power.
   (d) The firm has no control over the quantity it produces.

8. Since the firm will not produce any output if the market price falls below $P_1$:
   (a) The firm's supply curve is that part of the *MC* curve above the minimum point on the *ATC* curve.
   (b) The average variable cost curve is the firm's supply curve.
   (c) The average total cost curve is the firm's supply curve.
   (d) The firm's supply curve is that part of its marginal cost curve that lies above its average variable cost curve.

9. If the price is $P_3$, and the demand curve is $D_3$ in the long run:
   (a) Returns to the firm are below average, and firms will leave the industry.
   (b) Returns are above average, and new firms will have an incentive to enter the market.
   (c) Returns are about average, and there is no incentive for firms to move into or out of the industry.
   (d) We really can't say without more information.

10. Long-run competitive equilibrium occurs at a price of:
    (a) $P_1$.
    (b) $P_2$.
    (c) $P_3$.
    (d) $P_4$.

## Exercise 4

Many newspapers provide information from competitive markets, such as the want ads, market prices, and advertising.

Reread the article in the text entitled "Fish Farms Fall Prey to Excess." Then quote the words that give an example of each of the following types of information which can help verify that a market is really competitive.

1. *Structural characteristics*. What phrases indicate that large numbers of farmers are involved?
   _____.

2. *Conduct*. What passage(s) indicate entry into or exit from the catfish market? _____
   _____

3. *Performance*. What passage(s) indicate information about prices, profits, or quantity of output that is consistent with the performance in a competitive market? _____
   _____
   _____

4. *Market boundaries*. On the basis of information in the article only, which of the following best characterizes the market boundaries of the catfish market? It appears to be strictly:
   (a) A local market.
   (b) A regional market.
   (c) A national market.
   (d) An international market.

5. What passage provides a clue about the extent of the market boundaries? _____
   _____

## Common Errors

The first statement in each "common error" below is incorrect. Each incorrect statement is followed by a corrected version and an explanation.

1. The demand curve for a competitive market is flat. WRONG!

   The demand curve for a competitive firm is flat. RIGHT!

The error above results from failure to distinguish between the market and the firm. Review Exercise 3 if this distinction is not clear.

2. Competitive firms do not make profits. WRONG!

Competitive firms can make economic profits in the short run. RIGHT!

In the long run, firms enter an industry and compete away economic profits. In the short run, a change in demand or supply may cause price to change and may bestow temporary economic profits on a firm. In the personal computer example in the text, technological changes shifted the supply curve and provided temporary profits.

*Be careful!* Always distinguish between short-run profit-maximizing production rates and price levels and long-run equilibrium production rates and price levels. While industries have a tendency to move toward long-run equilibrium, they may never reach it because of shocks that buffet a market.

3. Since competitive firms make zero profits in the long run, they cannot pay their stockholders and so they should shut down. WRONG!

Since competitive firms make zero economic profits in the long run, they are able to pay all factors of production, including the entrepreneurs, to keep the firms in existence. RIGHT!

*Be careful!* Keep the accounting and economic definitions of such words as "profit" separate and distinct. Keep movements along the supply curve (firms increase production rates) separate from shifts of the supply curve (firms enter or exit). Avoid confusing short-run responses (increasing production rates in existing plants) with long-run responses (entry or exit).

# •ANSWERS•

## Using Key Terms
### *Across*
3. production decision
4. marginal cost pricing
6. efficiency
7. economic profit
8. competitive market
10. profit per unit
11. market supply
12. shutdown point
13. opportunity cost
14. marginal cost
15. average total cost
16. equilibrium price
17. market mechanism

### *Down*
1. long-run competitive equilibrium
2. short-run competitive equilibrium
5. barriers to entry
9. investment decision

# True or False

1. T
2. F  The firm maximizes profits at the output rate where price (MR) = MC.
3. F  Total revenues would decrease to zero because the firm could not sell any output at a price above the market price.
4. T
5. T
6. T
7. F  Zero economic profits are an indication that there is no better use for a firm's resources. As a result, once economic profits reach zero, there is no further exit (or entry).
8. F  Competition forces perfectly competitive firms to be technically efficient.
9. F  The price of the product will equal the minimum ATC.
10. T

# Multiple Choice

| | | | | |
|---|---|---|---|---|
| 1. b | 5. d | 9. c | 13. a | 17. a |
| 2. c | 6. b | 10. b | 14. b | 18. b |
| 3. d | 7. d | 11. d | 15. d | 19. d |
| 4. c | 8. c | 12. a | 16. a | 20. d |

# Problems and Applications

## Exercise 1

1. more, shift to the right
2. market supply and market demand
3. decrease
4. expand, decrease
5. zero
6. ATC

## Exercise 2

1. price
2. $10
3. **Table 8.1 Answer**

| Output | Price | Total revenue | Total cost | Total profit | Marginal revenue | Marginal cost | Average total cost |
|---|---|---|---|---|---|---|---|
| 0 | ---- | ---- | $10 | $-10 | ---- | ---- | ---- |
| 1 | $13 | $13 | 15 | -2 | $13 | $5 | $15.00 |
| 2 | 13 | 26 | 22 | 4 | 13 | 7 | 11.00 |
| 3 | 13 | 39 | 31 | 8 | 13 | 9 | 10.33 |
| 4 | 13 | 52 | 44 | 8 | 13 | 13 | 11.00 |
| 5 | 13 | 65 | 61 | 4 | 13 | 17 | 12.20 |

4. 4 units of output
5. p=MC
6. p=MC=minimum ATC
7. $10.33, less, short
8. enter, profits
9. decreases

## Exercise 3

| 1. a | 3. d | 5. a | 7. b | 9. b |
|------|------|------|------|------|
| 2. d | 4. a | 6. d | 8. d | 10. b |

## Exercise 4

1. "estimated that half of the state's 300 growers"
2. "luring cotton farmers such as Redditt, who converted almost 200 acres of his land into ponds" and "about as many as one-third could go bankrupt"
3. "Catfish are selling for about 60 cents a pound, but producing a pound of catfish costs about 65 cents"; "But when so many farmers produced so many fish, the dam burst and panic selling began"; "Prices have been in a free fall for months."
4. c
5. "The economies of large regions of Arkansas, Louisiana, Texas, Alabama and Mississippi have become intertwined."

# CHAPTER 9
# Monopoly

## Quick Review

In this chapter we are concerned with monopoly—a market structure at the other end of the spectrum from a competitive market. In the former there is a single producer. The latter, as we learned in the previous chapter, has a large number of producers.

Let's focus on the following questions:

- What price will a monopolist charge?
- How much output will the monopolist produce?
- Are consumers better or worse off when only one firm controls an entire market?

The key to each of these questions rests with market power. Market power is the ability to influence significantly the market price of goods and services. The extreme case of market power is monopoly. The demand curve facing the monopolist and the market demand curve are identical. To sell larger quantities of output in a given time period, a monopoly must lower the price of its product. Such price reductions cause marginal revenue and price to diverge. A firm without market power has no such problem; it may sell as much output as it desires at the prevailing market price.

Like all profit-maximizing firms, a monopolist will produce that rate of output at which marginal revenue equals marginal cost. The monopolist will attain a higher level of profit than a competitive firm because of its ability to equate marginal revenue and marginal cost. By contrast, a competitive firm ends up equating marginal cost and price. In addition, monopolists are sometimes able to charge different prices to different buyers (a practice called "price discrimination") and extract high prices and profits even when market demand is relatively elastic.

The higher profits earned by a monopolist are sure to attract the envy of other entrepreneurs. A market-power position and its related profits are maintained only if barriers to entry keep others out of the market.

Monopolists charge a price which is higher than marginal cost. They also fail to fully utilize available resources. Finally, monopolists do not necessarily pick the least-cost production process. By contrast, competitive firms are compelled by the market to achieve these economic objectives in order to survive.

The principal arguments in favor of market power focus on the alleged ability of large firms to pursue long-term research and development, on the incentives implicit in the opportunity to attain market power, and on the greater efficiency that larger firms may attain. The first two arguments are weakened by the fact that competitive firms are under much greater pressure to innovate and can stay ahead in the profit game only if they do so. Nevertheless, larger firms may be able to achieve economies of scale—lower minimum average costs brought about by a larger scale of plant—and thus may be considered desirable on the grounds of efficiency. A firm with economies of scale over the entire range of market output is called a natural monopoly. Larger firms are not necessarily more efficient, however, since either constant returns to scale or even diseconomies of scale may arise as firm size increases. Few firms are natural monopolies.

Recently economists have investigated the restraining power of potential competition in markets where the barriers to entry are not too high. This idea is included in the concept of "contestable markets."

Because monopolies have so many adverse impacts on the economy, governments at all levels have been empowered to prevent or regulate the concentration of market power. The Sherman Act, the Clayton Act, and the Federal Trade Commission Act form the legal foundation for antitrust activities.

## Learning Objectives

After reading Chapter 9 and doing the following exercises, you should:

1. Know the meaning of market power.
2. Know why a monopolist has market power and a downward-sloping demand curve and why price and marginal revenue diverge.
3. Be able to show the relationship between the market demand and individual demand curve for a monopolist.
4. Know the difference between marginal cost pricing for a competitive firm and profit maximization for a monopoly.
5. Be able to determine a monopolist's most profitable rate of production.
6. Be able to show why a monopoly typically results in higher profits, less output, and higher prices than would occur in a competitive market.
7. Be able to contrast the long-run results in a competitive market with that of a monopoly.
8. Be able to describe the advantages and disadvantages of monopoly versus competition.
9. Be able to distinguish price discrimination from other types of pricing.
10. Be able to distinguish economies of scale from constant returns to scale and diseconomies of scale.
11. Understand why a natural monopoly occurs.
12. Know how and why antitrust policy is used to control monopoly.
13. Understand the idea of "contestable" markets.

## Using Key Terms

Fill in the puzzle on the opposite page with the appropriate term from the list of Key Terms at the end of the chapter in the text.

### *Across*

2. This curve lies below the demand curve at every point except the first in Figure 9.2 in the text.
7. Used to determine that the most profitable rate of production is four bushels per hour in Figure 9.3 in the text.
9. The ability to alter the market price of a good or service.
10. An industry in which one firm can achieve economies of scale over the entire range of market supply.
11. Total cost divided by the quantity produced in a given time period.
12. Government intervention to alter market structure or prevent abuse of market power.
13. For a monopolist, this short-run choice is made by locating the intersection of marginal cost and marginal revenue.

### *Down*

1. The sale of an identical good at different prices to different consumers by a single seller.
2. The market structure that Pepsi accuses Coke of trying to duplicate in the article titled "Pepsi Takes Coke to Court" in the text.
3. The percentage change in quantity demanded divided by the percentage change in price.
4. According to the article "Foxy Soviets Pelt the West" in the text, the Soviet Union erected _____ by not letting live sables leave the country.
5. Gives one producer an advantage over several smaller producers and acts as a barrier to entry.

6. An imperfectly competitive industry which is restrained by potential competition.
8. The pricing method characteristic of competitive markets but not a monopoly.

## Puzzle 9.1

# True or False: *Circle your choice and explain why any false statements are incorrect.*

T F 1. Since a competitive firm can sell unlimited quantities of output at the prevailing price, it can affect the market price of a good or service.

T F 2. The monopolist has a flat (i.e. horizontal) demand curve because of high barriers to entry.

T F 3. The demand curve for the monopolist is exactly the same as the market demand curve.

T F 4. Monopolists maximize profits at the output level at which price equals marginal cost.

T F 5. Since both monopolists and competitive firms maximize profits at the output level at which marginal revenue equals marginal cost, monopolists and competitive markets with the same marginal cost curves and market demand curves will produce the same output.

T F 6. In the long run, a monopolist can continue to earn economic profits.

T F 7. Monopolists have an advantage over competitive markets in receiving the full benefit of research and development efforts.

T F 8. Price discrimination can occur because of the differences in the demand curves among buyers.

T F 9. The theory of contestable markets focuses on market structure rather than market behavior.

T F 10. A natural monopoly experiences economies of scale over the entire range of market output.

# Multiple Choice: *Select the correct answer.*

_____ 1. Which of the following is the result of a monopolist's market power?
   (a)   It faces a downward-sloping demand curve.
   (b)   When it produces an extra unit of output, it must lower its price on all of its units.
   (c)   Its marginal revenue curve is below its demand curve.
   (d)   All of the above are results.

_____ 2. For a monopolist, the demand curve facing the firm is:
   (a)   The same as for the perfectly competitive firm.
   (b)   The same as the market-demand curve.
   (c)   Always below marginal revenue.
   (d)   Perfectly elastic.

_____ 3. When a monopolist sells an additional unit of output, the marginal revenue will be lower than the price because:
   (a)   The price of all the units sold will have to be lowered in order to sell the additional unit.
   (b)   The monopolist faces a flat (horizontal) demand curve for its product.
   (c)   Costs increase as more output is produced.
   (d)   Economies of scale exist for monopolists.

_____ 4. Which of the following is most likely *not* a monopolist?
   (a)   The only doctor in a small community.
   (b)   A large soft-drink firm such as Coca-Cola.
   (c)   The electric power company in your area.
   (d)   The water company in your area.

_____ 5. Which of the following rules will always be satisfied when a firm has maximized profit?
  (a) P = lowest level of long-run average costs.
  (b) P = MC.
  (c) MR = MC.
  (d) P = ATC.

_____ 6. In a monopoly and perfect competition, a firm should expand production when:
  (a) Price is below marginal cost.
  (b) Price is above marginal cost.
  (c) Marginal revenue is below marginal cost.
  (d) Marginal revenue is above marginal cost.

_____ 7. The supply curve for a monopolist:
  (a) Slopes upward.
  (b) Is the same as the marginal cost curve.
  (c) Is the same as the marginal revenue curve.
  (d) Doesn't exist.

_____ 8. If a monopolist finds that demand for its product is inelastic, it can:
  (a) Increase total revenue by lowering price.
  (b) Increase total revenue by raising price.
  (c) Reduce total costs by lowering prices.
  (d) Reduce total costs by raising production rates.

_____ 9. Which of the following does not act as a barrier to entry into a monopoly market?
  (a) Profits of the monopolist.
  (b) Government regulation.
  (c) Patents.
  (d) Difficulty of obtaining resources.

_____ 10. A monopolist with many plants produces less than would be produced if all of the plants were competing with one another in a competitive market:
  (a) Because the market demand curve is perfectly inelastic for the monopolistic firm but not for the competitive firms.
  (b) Because the market demand curve slopes downward for the monopolistic market and for the competitive market.
  (c) Because the marginal revenue curve is below the demand curve for the monopolistic firm but not for the competitive firms.
  (d) Because profit is maximized where MR = MC for the monopolistic firm but not for the competitive firms.

_____ 11. The price charged by a profit-maximizing monopolist in the long run occurs:
  (a) At the minimum of the long-run average cost curve.
  (b) Where P = MR = MC.
  (c) At a price on the demand curve above the intersection where MR = MC.
  (d) At a price on the long-run average cost curve below the point where MR = MC.

_____ 12. When a monopoly continues to make above-normal profits in the long run, you can be sure that:
  (a) It produces more efficiently than a competitive market can.
  (b) Barriers to entry prevent other firms from competing away the above-normal profits.
  (c) There is a conspiracy between the government and the monopolist to maintain high prices.
  (d) It has an inelastic demand curve, which gives it greater revenues at every price.

_____ 13. If a monopoly used marginal cost pricing to determine its output and price, which of the following statements would be true?
   (a) The monopolist would not be maximizing its profits.
   (b) The monopolist would produce a higher level of output than it would if it was maximizing its profits.
   (c) The monopolist would produce the optimal level of output from the consumer's standpoint.
   (d) All of the above would be true.

_____ 14. The allocatively efficient output for a firm is the output where:
   (a) MC=MR.
   (b) The ATC is at a minimum.
   (c) The AVC is at a minimum.
   (d) MC=Demand.

_____ 15. Price discrimination allows a producer to:
   (a) Reap the highest possible average price for the quantity sold.
   (b) Increase the elasticity of consumer demand.
   (c) Minimize marginal costs.
   (d) Decrease total costs.

_____ 16. A family doctor charges patients for a particular service on the basis of what the patient can afford to pay. Which type of pricing is being used?
   (a) Monopoly pricing (price making).
   (b) Competitive pricing (price taking).
   (c) Price discrimination.
   (d) P=MR.

_____ 17. The argument that concentration of market power enhances research and development efforts may be weak because:
   (a) Monopolies cannot afford basic research.
   (b) A monopoly may have no clear incentive to pursue new research and development.
   (c) No one has attempted to gather any empirical evidence.
   (d) No existing monopoly has a research and development program.

_____ 18. According to the theory of contestable markets, monopoly may *not* be a problem if:
   (a) The structure of a market is competitive.
   (b) Firms can exit from the market.
   (c) Antitrust regulations are enforced.
   (d) Potential competition exists.

_____ 19. The primary purpose of anti-trust policy in the United States is to:
   (a) Issue patents.
   (b) Encourage competition.
   (c) Limit foreign competition.
   (d) Regulate monopolies.

_____ 20. Which of the following was the first to prohibit conspiracies in restraint of trade?
   (a) The Sherman Act.
   (b) The Clayton Act.
   (c) The Federal Trade Commission Act.
   (d) The Gramm-Rudman Act.

## Problems and Applications

### *Exercise 1*

This exercise provides practice in calculating total revenue and marginal revenue, and shows the relationship between marginal revenue and demand.

1. Use the information given in Table 9.1 to calculate total revenue and marginal revenue.

### Table 9.1  Revenue data

|   | Quantity | Price | Total Revenue | Marginal Revenue |
|---|---|---|---|---|
| A | 0 | $12.00 | $ _____ | ------- |
| B | 1 | 11.00 | _____ | $ _____ |
| C | 2 | 10.00 | _____ | _____ |
| D | 3 | 9.00 | _____ | _____ |
| E | 4 | 8.00 | _____ | _____ |
| F | 5 | 7.00 | _____ | _____ |
| G | 6 | 6.00 | _____ | _____ |

2. Use the information from Table 9.1 to graph the demand curve and the marginal revenue curve in Figure 9.1. Label each curve and label the points (B through G) on the demand curve.

### Figure 9.1  Demand and marginal revenue curves

3. For a monopoly, price is determined from the _____ curve, directly above the point where _____ .

4.  For a monopoly, marginal revenue is always (greater, less) than price, after the first unit, because the firm must (raise, lower) its price to sell additional output.

## Exercise 2

This exercise reviews costs and revenues and provides further experience with profit maximization.

Figure 9.2 represents cost curves for a monopolist. Use Figure 9.2 to answer questions 1-4.

### Figure 9.2  Cost curves and profit maximization

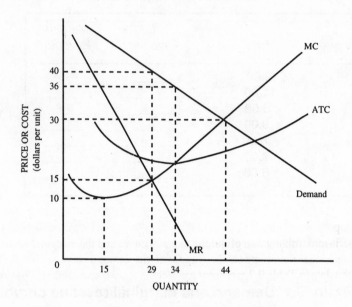

1.  What is the profit-maximizing rate of output for the monopolist in Figure 9.2? _____

2.  What price will the monopolist charge in Figure 9.2? _____

3.  This monopolist (is, is not) earning an economic profit because, at the profit-maximizing rate of output in Figure 9.2, ATC is (above, below) the demand curve.

4.  Now assume the curves in Figure 9.2 represent a perfectly competitive market. What is the profit-maximizing rate of output? _____ What price will the firms charge at this output? _____ How do price and output compare to the profit-maximizing rate of output and price for a monopolist?
    _____

## Exercise 3

This exercise emphasizes the relationship between costs and revenues for a monopolist and determination of profit maximization.

1.  Use the data in Table 9.2 to calculate total revenue, marginal revenue, and marginal cost for a monopolist.

## Table 9.2 Revenue and cost data

| Quantity | Price | Total revenue | Marginal revenue | Total cost | Marginal cost |
|---|---|---|---|---|---|
| 0 | $14 | $_____ | ---- | $13 | ---- |
| 1 | 13 | _____ | $_____ | 15 | $_____ |
| 2 | 12 | _____ | _____ | 18 | _____ |
| 3 | 11 | _____ | _____ | 23 | _____ |
| 4 | 10 | _____ | _____ | 30 | _____ |
| 5 | 9 | _____ | _____ | 39 | _____ |
| 6 | 8 | _____ | _____ | 51 | _____ |

2.  For a monopolist, the profit-maximizing rate of output occurs where marginal revenue equals _____.

3.  In this case, the profit-maximizing rate of output is _____ units.

4.  At the profit-maximizing rate of output, the monopolist will charge _____ for the product.

5.  At the profit-maximizing rate of output, this monopolist earns a profit of _____.

6.  In order to sell one additional unit, the monopolist would have to (decrease, increase, make no change in) price.

7.  Since this monopolist is earning a profit, the ATC curve must be (above, below, equal to) the demand curve at the profit-maximizing rate of output.

8.  Now suppose the data in Table 9.2 represent a perfectly competitive market. The profit-maximizing rate of output occurs where marginal cost equals _____.

9.  In this case, the profit-maximizing rate of output would be _____ units at a price of _____.

10. At the competitive profit-maximizing rate of output, profits equal _____.

11. Compared to a perfectly competitive markets, a monopoly charges a (higher, lower) price, produces a (higher, lower) output, and earns a (greater, smaller) profit.

## Exercise 4

Reread the article titled "New Competition May Mean Bad News for CNN" and then answer the following questions.

1.  What phrase indicates that CNN has monopoly power in the 24-hour news market? _____
_____

2.  What barriers to entry have kept other networks from competing with CNN? _____
_____

3.  Why are competitors trying to overcome the barriers to entry? _____
_____

# Common Errors

The first statement in each "common error" below is incorrect. Each incorrect statement is followed by a corrected version and an explanation.

1. Monopolists have supply curves. WRONG!

   Monopolists have marginal cost curves, but not supply curves. RIGHT!

   The marginal cost indicates the quantity that a competitive firm will supply at a given price. (*Remember*: Price equals marginal cost for the profit maximizing competitive firm.) But we cannot tell what a monopolist will supply at a given price by looking at the marginal cost curve. We need to know marginal revenue and therefore the demand curve before we can tell what quantity the firm will supply. (*Remember*: Marginal cost equals marginal revenue when profits are maximized.)

   *Be careful!* Do not label the marginal cost curve of a monopolist (or any noncompetitive firm) as a "supply" curve in your diagrams.

2. When there are economies of scale, a firm can simply increase production rates in the short run and unit costs will decline. WRONG!

   When there are economies of scale, a firm can choose a plant size designed for increased production rates at lower unit costs. RIGHT!

   Economies of scale are not realized through production decisions in the short run. They are realized through investment decisions, by the choice of an optimal-sized plant for higher production rates. Scale refers to plant size or capacity, not to production rates within a plant of a given size. Think of economies of scale in terms of investment decisions concerning choices of optimal capacity for the long run, not production decisions concerning the lowest cost production in the short run.

# •ANSWERS•

## Using Key Terms
### Across
2. marginal revenue
7. profit maximization rule
9. market power
10. natural monopoly
11. average total cost
12. antitrust
13. production decision

### Down
1. price discrimination
2. monopoly
3. price elasticity of demand
4. barriers to entry
5. economies of scale
6. contestable market
8. marginal cost pricing

# True or False

1. F  A competitive firm has no control over the market price because it is such a tiny part of the relatively huge market. Because it is relatively insignificant, it can sell as much as it wants at the market price.
2. F  The monopolist typically has a relatively inelastic demand curve because of barriers to entry, i.e. few substitutes.
3. T
4. F  Monopolists maximize profits where MR = MC.
5. F  Monopolists will tend to produce less than the output that would be produced in a competitive market because the MR curve is below the demand curve for the monopolist.
6. T
7. T
8. T
9. F  The theory focuses on behavior rather than structure, i.e. not how many producers exist in a market but how many could potentially exist.
10. T

# Multiple Choice

| | | | | |
|---|---|---|---|---|
| 1. d | 5. c | 9. a | 13. d | 17. b |
| 2. b | 6. d | 10. c | 14. d | 18. d |
| 3. a | 7. d | 11. c | 15. a | 19. b |
| 4. b | 8. b | 12. b | 16. c | 20. a |

# *Exercise 1*

1. **Table 9.1 Answer**

| Quantity | Total revenue | Marginal revenue |
|---|---|---|
| 0 | $ 0.00 | ----- |
| 1 | 11.00 | $ 11.00 |
| 2 | 20.00 | 9.00 |
| 3 | 27.00 | 7.00 |
| 4 | 32.00 | 5.00 |
| 5 | 35.00 | 3.00 |
| 6 | 36.00 | 1.00 |

2. **Figure 9.1 Answer**

3.  demand, MC = MR
4.  less, lower

## *Exercise 2*

1.  29 units
2.  $40
3.  is, below
4.  44 units, $30, price is less and output is greater for the perfectly competitive firm

## *Exercise 3*

1. **Table 9.2 Answer**

| Quantity | Price | Total revenue | Marginal revenue | Total cost | Marginal cost |
|----------|-------|---------------|------------------|------------|---------------|
| 0 | $14 | $ 0 | ---- | $13 | ---- |
| 1 | 13 | 13 | $ 13 | 15 | $ 2 |
| 2 | 12 | 24 | 11 | 18 | 3 |
| 3 | 11 | 33 | 9 | 23 | 5 |
| 4 | 10 | 40 | 7 | 30 | 7 |
| 5 | 9 | 45 | 5 | 39 | 9 |
| 6 | 8 | 48 | 3 | 51 | 12 |

2.  marginal cost
3.  4

144

4. $10
5. $10
6. decrease
7. below
8. price
9. 5, $9
10. $6
11. higher, lower, greater

## Exercise 4

1. "... with the market to itself ... "
2. "... huge distribution hurdles caused by lack of space on crowded cable systems ... "
3. "Last year ... CNN ... generated about $227 million in operating profit for Turner Broadcasting System Inc."

# CHAPTER 10
# Oligopoly

## Quick Review

This chapter takes up the following questions:

- What determines how much market power a firm has?
- How do firms in an oligopoly set prices and output?
- What problems does an oligopoly have in maintaining price and profit?

There are many gradations of market power, running from perfect competition on one end to monopoly on the other. The market power of the firms in each market structure ranges from very weak to very strong along the continuum. The determinants of market power, that is, the extent to which the firm can influence market outcomes, are determined by the number of producers, the size of each firm, barriers to entry, and the availability of substitute products.

Market power is commonly measured by calculating concentration ratios: the proportion of total market output produced by the four largest domestic producers. The concentration ratio is very high in industries such as autos, long-distance telephone services, and diapers, and nonexistent in competitive markets such as wheat or catfish farming. Concentration ratios can be misleading since they deal with national markets and ignore power in local markets and do not take account of the competition from foreign producers.

An oligopoly is a market structure consisting of a few interdependent firms referred to as oligopolists. It is frequently argued that oligopoly behavior can be understood by utilizing a kinked demand curve. The argument is that once an acceptable price, output, and market shares are established, firms are reluctant to change price because they fear that their rivals will follow any price decrease, but will not follow any price increase. In either case, little would be accomplished if a firm changes its price. This leads to a demand curve which is flatter above the equilibrium price and steeper below. The kink imparts a vertical section to the marginal revenue curve, which means that firms, while still using the profit-maximizing rule, will maintain both price and output in the face of moderate increases in marginal costs.

Because of the small number of firms involved in an oligopoly, it is obvious that they have, potentially, a shared monopoly and should they behave as such, could reap monopoly profits as a group. To do this, they must somehow band together to choose the monopoly price and output and find a way to ensure that each oligopolist is satisfied with the firm's share of the market. The possibilities for doing so seem limited only by the imagination of the persons involved. Schemes involving price fixing, price leadership, and direct allocation of market shares have all been tried and firms have been frequently prosecuted because of the illegal nature of such schemes.

Barriers to entry are the key to maintaining monopoly profits in the long run. Patents, control of a distribution system, government regulation, nonprice competition, even the cost of switching suppliers (because of retraining which may be required) can all serve as barriers to entry. Market power contributes to market failure when it results in significant misallocation of resources; thus society's concern is with the behavior of firms. Antitrust laws—the Sherman Act, the Clayton Act and the Federal Trade Commission Act—explicitly forbid many of the practices described in this chapter. Oligopolists may be very powerful and mount costly defenses in antitrust suits. Some contend that they are being prosecuted for being successful. Since resources of the antitrust agencies are limited, they must choose which cases should be prosecuted. To do so, they use a numerical measure called the Herfindahl-Hirshman Index (HHI). Since 1992, the Justice Department has examined existing market structure and entry barriers. Low barriers to entry may mean the market is contestable even though it is very concentrated!

## Learning Objectives

After reading Chapter 10 and doing the following exercises, you should:

1. Be able to describe the continuum of market structures.
2. Understand the implications of market power for the optimal mix of the economy's output.
3. Know the determinants of market power.
4. Be able to calculate and interpret concentration ratios and the Herfindahl-Hirshman Index.
5. Be aware of some of the economy's most concentrated industries.
6. Know how market structure affects market behavior and market outcomes.
7. Understand and be able to describe the kinked demand curve model of oligopoly.
8. Know the difference between the long-run market outcomes resulting from perfectly competitive markets and oligopoly.
9. Understand the setting in which game theory is useful in studying business decision making.
10. Be able to describe the coordination problem inherent in the shared-monopoly idea of oligopoly.
11. Know some techniques which oligopolists have used to implement coordination and enforcement of market shares.
12. Be able to list and describe several barriers to entry.
13. Know three prominent antitrust laws and their major provisions.
14. Be able to determine whether an antitrust case should be prosecuted using the HHI.

## Using Key Terms

Fill in the puzzle on the opposite page with the appropriate term from the list of Key Terms at the end of the chapter in the text.

### *Across*

1.  The number and relative size of firms in an industry.
4.  Trans World Airlines, Delta Air Lines, and Northwest Airlines were accused of using this tactic in an *In the News* article in the text.
7.  Government intervention to prevent the abuse of market power.
8.  One way a firm can establish the market price for all firms in the industry.
9.  A measure of industry concentration that accounts for the number of firms and the size of each.
11. One of the dominant firms in an oligopoly.
15. Used by a firm to make its product appear different and superior to other products.
16. The curve drawn with a gap in Figure 10.6 in the text.
17. Obstacles that help to keep potential competitors out of an industry.
18. A market structure with high barriers to entry, substantial market power, and a few firms.

### *Down*

2.  A group of firms with an explicit agreement to fix prices and output shares.
3.  Firms produce at the rate of output where MR=MC.

5.   An imperfectly competitive industry subject to potential entry if prices or profits increase.
6.   The study of how decisions are made when strategic interaction exists.
10.  The proportion of total industry output produced by the largest firms.
12.  Occurs when market power leads to resource misallocation or greater inequity.
13.  The percentage of total market output produced by a firm.
14.  An explicit agreement among producers regarding the price at which a good is to be sold.

## Puzzle 10.1

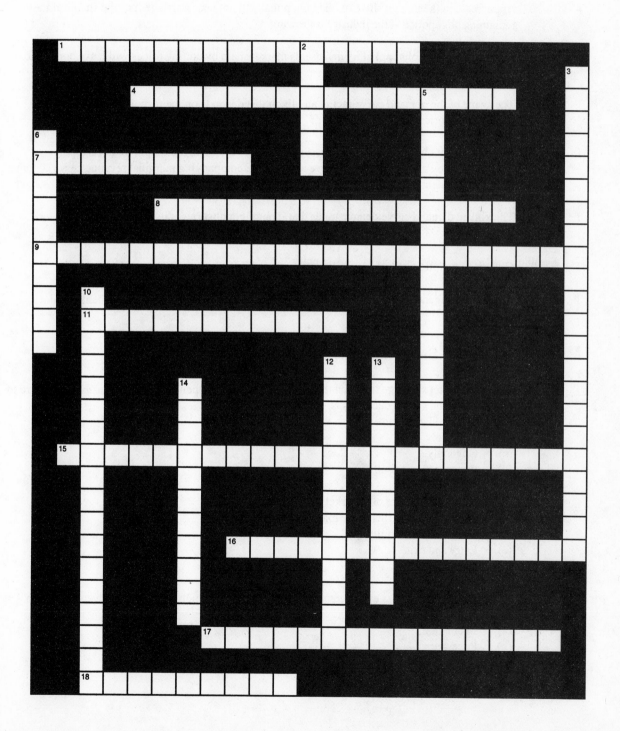

# True or False: *Circle your choice and explain why any false statements are incorrect.*

T  F  1.  Firms are divided into specific market structures based on their ability to earn a profit.

T  F  2.  In imperfect competition, individual firms do not have direct influence on the market price of a particular product.

T  F  3.  Firms in an oligopoly market are highly independent because of their relatively small number.

T  F  4.  An increase in the market share of one oligopolist will not necessarily reduce the shares of the remaining oligopolists if the industry is growing.

T  F  5.  An attempt by one oligopolist to increase its market share by cutting prices will leave competitors unaffected.

T  F  6.  The shape of the demand curve facing an oligopolist depends on the responses of its rivals to a change in the price of its own output.

T  F  7.  The reason that changes in marginal cost may have no effect on the output of an oligopoly characterized by a kinked demand curve is that the accompanying marginal revenue curve contains a vertical segment or gap.

T  F  8.  The kinked demand curve demonstrates that if an oligopolist raises its price, it is likely to lose market share.

T  F  9.  One type of explicit price fixing is known as price leadership.

T  F  10.  The antitrust agencies prohibit certain structural characteristics of a market, not behavioral characteristics.

# Multiple Choice: *Select the correct answer.*

_____  1.  The only market structure in which there is significant interdependence among firms with regard to their pricing and output decisions is:
(a)  Monopolistic competition.
(b)  Monopoly.
(c)  Oligopoly.
(d)  Perfect competition.

_____  2.  Structural characteristics of a market include:
(a)  The number of firms in the market.
(b)  Long run profitability.
(c)  Entry and exit.
(d)  Pricing behavior.

_____  3.  Which of the following is evidence of the interdependence which characterizes the relationship among oligopolists?
(a)  Retaliation.
(b)  Price wars.
(c)  Gamesmanship.
(d)  All of the above.

_____ 4. Characteristics of an oligopolistic market include:
    (a) Tacit collusion.
    (b) High barriers to entry.
    (c) High concentration ratios.
    (d) All of the above.

_____ 5. A kinked demand curve indicates that rival oligopolists match:
    (a) All price changes.
    (b) No price changes.
    (c) Price reductions but not price increases.
    (d) Price increases but not price reductions.

_____ 6. The gap in the marginal revenue curve of an oligopolist is caused by:
    (a) The existence of two alternative demand curves that apply to the oligopolist, depending on whether it raises prices or lowers prices.
    (b) The failure of the marginal cost curve to intersect the demand curve at the profit-maximizing level.
    (c) The ability of oligopolists to make above-normal profits if they cooperate with each other.
    (d) All of the above.

_____ 7. Because of the gap in the marginal revenue curve, when the marginal cost curve rises, the kinked demand curve oligopolist may have an incentive to:
    (a) Speed up production and lower prices—behavior that leads to greater profits.
    (b) Maintain both production rates and prices—behavior that leads to lower profits but not necessarily to losses.
    (c) Lower production rates and maintain prices—actions that raise profits by counteracting cost increases.
    (d) Speed up production rates and maintain prices—actions that result in losses.

_____ 8. If an oligopolist is going to change its price or output, its concern is:
    (a) The response of consumers.
    (b) The possiblity of losing market share.
    (c) Gamesmanship practiced by its competitors.
    (d) All of the above are concerns.

_____ 9. If a firm is producing at the kink in its demand curve and increases its price, according to the kinked-demand model:
    (a) It will gain market share.
    (b) It will lose market share to the firms that do not follow the price increase.
    (c) Its market share will not be affected.
    (d) It will not gain market share but it will definitely increase profits.

_____ 10. Which of the following is an explanation of why oligopolists have an incentive to collude?
    (a) The demand for each firm's product would be kinked.
    (b) Each firm would face a perfectly inelastic demand for its product.
    (c) Each firm would face a relatively inelastic demand for its product rather than a relatively elastic demand when firms raise prices independently.
    (d) The market demand curve would become perfectly inelastic.

_____ 11. Game theory is:
    (a) The study of price fixing and collusion.
    (b) The study of how decisions are made when interdependence between firms exists.
    (c) An explanation of how oligopolists become monopolists.
    (d) Only useful in perfectly competitive markets.

_____ 12. Oligopolists will maximize total market profits at the rate of output where:
   (a)   MR = MC for the largest firms.
   (b)   MR = MC for the average firm.
   (c)   MR = MC for the marginal firm.
   (d)   The market's MC equals the market's MR.

_____ 13. Open and explicit agreements concerning pricing and output shares transform an oligopoly into a:
   (a)   Monopoly.
   (b)   Cartel.
   (c)   Differentiated oligopoly.
   (d)   Perfectly competitive firm.

_____ 14. Price leadership:
   (a)   Typically results in greater price stability in oligopolistic markets.
   (b)   Is observed in oligopolistic markets.
   (c)   Permits oligopolistic firms in a given market to coordinate market-wide price changes without formal collusion.
   (d)   All of the above.

_____ 15. For an oligopoly, above-normal profit cannot be maintained in the long run unless:
   (a)   A cartel is formed.
   (b)   Barriers to entry exist.
   (c)   A firm has a high concentration ratio.
   (d)   The market is contestable.

_____ 16. An example of nonprice competition in the automobile market is:
   (a)   Advertising.
   (b)   Availability of service on weekends.
   (c)   Providing financing for the purchase of an automobile.
   (d)   All of the above.

_____ 17. Imperfectly competitive firms use nonprice competition to:
   (a)   Shift the demand curve leftward.
   (b)   Differentiate their product.
   (c)   Shift the supply curve upward.
   (d)   Threaten potential entry.

_____ 18. Market power leads to market failure when it results in:
   (a)   Decreased market output.
   (b)   Increased market prices.
   (c)   Long lasting, above normal economic profits.
   (d)   All of the above.

_____ 19. Which of the following are problems associated with pursuing anti-trust policy based on the behavior of firms rather than the structure of a market?
   (a)   It is more expensive to investigate behavior rather than structure.
   (b)   It is more difficult to prove anti-competitive behavior.
   (c)   The general absence of public awareness and interest in the problem of collusion.
   (d)   All of the above are problems.

_____ 20. The 1992 and 1996 anti-trust guidelines adopted by the Justice Department and the Federal Trade Commission:
   (a)   Moved anti-trust focus away from a strict reliance on structural criteria.
   (b)   Increased the focus on market contestability.
   (c)   Allowed a consideration of potential greater efficiencies when mergers and acquisitions occur.
   (d)   All of the above are correct.

## Problems and Applications

## *Exercise 1*

This exercise shows how to compute concentration ratios and market shares for an industry.

1.  Market share is:
   (a)   The percentage of total market output produced by the largest firms (usually the four largest).
   (b)   The percentage of total market output produced by the largest firm.
   (c)   The percentage of total market output produced by a given firm.
   (d)   A type of stock issued by the firms in a market.

2.  Concentration usually refers to:
   (a)   The percentage of total market output produced by the four largest domestic firms.
   (b)   The percentage of total market output produced by any four large domestic firms.
   (c)   The percentage of total market output produced by a given domestic firm.
   (d)   The percentage of total market output produced by the four largest domestic or foreign firms.

3.  Table 10.1 gives the sales of the top four firms (A, B, C, D) in a market. Calculate the total sales for the top four firms and total sales for the market. Then, using this information, compute the market share for each firm separately, and then the market share for the "Top four firms" and the market share for "All other firms."

### Table 10.1
### Sales and market shares of top four firms, by company

| Firm | Sales (millions of dollars per year) | Market share |
|------|--------------------------------------|--------------|
| A | $  60 | _____% |
| B | 40 | _____ |
| C | 30 | _____ |
| D | 20 | _____ |
|  |  |  |
| Top four firms | $_____ | _____% |
| All other firms | 50 | _____% |
| All firms | $_____ | 100  % |

4.  T   F   The sum of the market shares of the top four firms is the same as the four-firm concentration ratio.

# Exercise 2

This exercise illustrates the differences between using the concentration ratio and the Herfindahl-Hirshman Index to measure market power. It also will help you complete a problem in the text.

Table 10.2 presents the market shares for two separate markets. Each market has only four firms.

## Table 10.2
## Market shares for calculating concentration ratios and the Herfindahl-Hirshman Index

| First market | | Second market | |
|---|---|---|---|
| Firm | Market share | Firm | Market share |
| A | 25% | E | 97% |
| B | 25% | F | 1% |
| C | 25% | G | 1% |
| D | 25% | H | 1% |

1. The four-firm concentration ratio for the first market is _____ and for the second market is _____ .

2. The Herfindahl-Hirshman Index for the first market is _____ and for the second market is _____ .

3. Would you expect the market power exerted in the two markets to be the same? _____ Why or why not? _____
_____

4. According to the Justice Department guidelines:
   (a) Mergers would be permitted in both markets.
   (b) A merger would be permitted only in the first market.
   (c) A merger would be permitted only in the second market.
   (d) Mergers would not be permitted in either market.

## Exercise 3

This exercise reviews costs and revenues and provides further experience with profit maximization.

Figure 10.1 represents cost curves for an oligopolist. Use Figure 10.1 to answer questions 1-4.

## Figure 10.1

1.  What is the profit-maximizing rate of output for the oligopolist in Figure 10.1? _____

2.  What price will the oligopolist charge in Figure 10.1? _____

3.  If the MC curve shifts up by a small amount, $4 or less, the profit maximizing oligopolist will (increase, decrease, not change) price because of the gap in the (MR, demand) curve.

4.  The demand curve for the oligopolist is kinked because rival oligopolists will match price (increases, reductions) but not price (increases, reductions).

## Exercise 4

The media often provide information about the strategies, both successful and unsuccessful, employed by oligopolists as they attempt to compete in the marketplace. By using one of the articles in the text, this exercise will show you what to look for.

Reread the article in the text entitled "Pop Culture: RC Goes For the Youth Market" and then answer the following questions.

1.  What is the concentration ratio in the U.S. soft drink market? _____

2.  What was the Royal Crown strategy in the 1980s? What phrase indicates the result? _____
    _____

3.  What is the new Royal Crown strategy? What is their target? _____
    _____

4.  What barriers to entry exist in the soft drink market? _____
    _____

5.  Calculate an HHI on the basis of the information in the pie chart in the article. _____

6.  Would game theory be useful in analyzing behavior in this market? Why? _____
    _____

# Common Errors

The first statement in each "common error" below is incorrect. Each incorrect statement is followed by a corrected version and an explanation.

1.  The concentration ratio accurately measures market power. WRONG!

    The concentration ratio is a rough, simple measure of market power. RIGHT!

    Information on availability of substitutes, the appropriate market, the relative size of firms in the market, and barriers to entry must be known before we can determine whether market power exists. Concentration ratios are usually computed for the nation as a whole, but many industries are characterized by local or regional markets. Also, any given market may produce a variety of different products, each with a unique concentration ratio. The concentration ratio gives no idea of barriers to entry that may exist, nor does it give any idea whether a market contains one dominant firm or several equally large firms.

2.  American industry consists mostly of monopolies. WRONG!

    There are only a few monopolies in the U.S. economy. RIGHT!

    The text has shown that many U.S. markets are imperfectly competitive, but concentration ratios of 100 percent are rare. Monopolies are most likely to occur in the utility industries, which are then heavily regulated by government.

3.  All large firms have market power. WRONG!

    The largest firms in concentrated markets are *likely* to have market power. RIGHT!

    Control of a market is more important than actual firm size in determining market power. Relative size as measured by concentration is more important than absolute size as measured by sales. For example, while conglomerates may be very large, they may play only small roles in many different markets and have no ability to influence prices in any of them.

4.  Oligopolists have unlimited power to raise prices and curtail production to make large profits. WRONG!

    Oligopolists' ability to raise prices is limited by demand and their competitive rivalry. RIGHT!

    The demand for oligopolists' products is limited by foreign competition, availability of substitutes, and potential entry by other firms. Such markets as the railroad-car market, the market for rifles, and the auto market contain only a few large firms, but they are limited by potential competition from other countries or at home.

Furthermore, there is no guarantee that oligopolists will cooperate with each other. Oligopolists may use their market power cooperatively through collusion, price leadership, or indirect means of supporting prices above competitive levels. Such cooperative activity *may* lead to profits in the long run as well as in the short run. Changes in demand and costs, however, can force oligopolists to take losses or even to fail. Most importantly, oligopolists may not cooperate with each other. They may conduct price wars and engage in nonprice competition in order to erode each other's market share. Such conduct often leads to instability and substantial losses.

5.  Oligopolistic firms compete with each other. MISLEADING!

    Oligopolies are often characterized by competitive rivalry. RIGHT!

    When firms have market power, they become aware of their interdependence. The often warlike or conspiratorial conduct—rivalry—that occurs is quite different from the conduct of competitive firms. Since no competitive firm can affect market prices, no one firm sees any other as a threat, nor is there any possibility of colluding to fix prices. True competition is often marked on the one hand by independent behavior of the competing firms and on the other by cooperation to hold down costs. For example, while farmers rarely succeed in increasing the prices of farm products by cooperative efforts, they may share the use of farm equipment with neighboring farmers to lower costs. There is certainly no reason for one farmer to engage in a price war with another farmer, since both represent such a small part of the market.

# •ANSWERS•

## Using Key Terms
### Across
1.  market structure
4.  predatory pricing
7.  antitrust
8.  price leadership
9.  Herfindahl-Hirshman Index
11. oligopolist
15. product differentiation
16. marginal revenue
17. barriers to entry
18. oligopoly

### Down
2.  cartel
3.  profit maximization rule
5.  contestable market
6.  game theory
10. concentration ratio
12. market failure
13. market share
14. price fixing

## True or False

| | | |
|---|---|---|
| 1. | F | The division is based on market power. |
| 2. | F | Firms do have varying degrees of control over the market price in imperfect competition. |
| 3. | T | |
| 4. | F | Market share is a percentage measure. If one firm's percentage share of the market increases, other firms must experience a reduction in market share. |
| 5. | F | Oligopolists are interdependent, i.e. a change in one firm's price or output will affect its competitors. |
| 6. | T | |
| 7. | T | |
| 8. | T | |
| 9. | F | Price leadership is an example of tacit collusion, not explicit price fixing. |
| 10. | F | Anti-trust policy prohibits anti-competitive behavior. |

## Multiple Choice

| | | | | | | | | | | |
|---|---|---|---|---|---|---|---|---|---|---|
| 1. | c | 5. | c | 9. | b | 13. | b | 17. | b |
| 2. | a | 6. | a | 10. | c | 14. | d | 18. | d |
| 3. | d | 7. | b | 11. | b | 15. | b | 19. | d |
| 4. | d | 8. | d | 12. | d | 16. | d | 20. | d |

## Problems and Applications

## Exercise 1

1. c
2. a
3. **Table 10.1 Answer**

| Firm | Sales | Market share |
|---|---|---|
| A | $ 60 | 30% |
| B | 40 | 20 |
| C | 30 | 15 |
| D | 20 | 10 |
| Top four firms | $150 | 75% |
| All other firms | 50 | 25% |
| All firms | $200 | 100% |

4. T

## Exercise 2

1. 100 percent; 100 percent
2. 2,500 (= $25^2 + 25^2 + 25^2 + 25^2$); 9,412 (= $97^2 + 1^2 + 1^2 + 1^2$)
3. No. The second market would exhibit much more market power since firm E is the dominant firm and would effectively determine the price. By contrast, market power would be more diffused among the four equally sized firms in the first market.
4. d  Both markets have a Herfindahl-Hirshman Index above 1800.

## Exercise 3

1. 76 units
2. $37
3. not change, MR
4. reductions, increases

## Exercise 4

1. The four firm concentration ratio is 92.6%, the sum of the shares of the four largest producers.
2. The strategy was, apparently, not to spend on advertising. The result was ". . . we lost a whole generation of cola drinkers . . . ."
3. Their new strategy is to spend $15 million on advertising, the largest amount in their history, and to toss out a ". . . bunch of beverages targeted toward younger drinkers."
4. The article indicates that Pepsi and Coke ". . . have huge amounts of marketing muscle, financial resources, experience and bottling agreements, . . ." which will deter new entrants.
5. Based on the information in the pie chart, the HHI is 3117.5
   ($41.5^2 + 32.3^2 + 16.9^2 + 7.4^2 = 3117.5$)
6. Very likely, since Coke and Pepsi dominate the soft drink market. There are numerous opportunities for moves and countermoves by these oligopolists, and this is where game theory is very useful.

CHAPTER 11

# Monopolistic Competition

## Quick Review

Monopolistic competition is a type of market that we see frequently in malls, downtown shops, and among other small businesses. Studying monopolistic competition will allow us to understand the effects of advertising and customer loyalty. The following questions will help us understand monopolistic competition:

- What are the unique features of monopolistic competition?
- How are market outcomes affected by this market structure?
- What are the long-run consequences of different market structures?

Each market structure can be identified by its structural characteristics. A market characterized as "monopolistic competition" has many firms and each firm has some market power; that is, each firm also has a downward-sloping demand curve for its product or service. The firms are relatively independent because modest changes in price or output have no noticeable effect on the sales of any other firm. The barriers to entry are also characteristically low. Though some of the firms in monopolistically competitive industries are household names (IBM, Goodyear, Starbucks), their market power is constrained. Concentration ratios in these industries are relatively low and even then the firms must often contend with significant competition from foreign entrants.

The market power possessed by monopolistically competitive firms is the direct result of product differentiation. Advertising is very important in creating brand loyalty. This gives the firm demand curve a downward slope. Firms in monopolistic competition use the same profit-maximizing rule ($MC = MR$) as firms in other markets. In the short run firms may earn economic profits, but low barriers to entry permit the entry of new firms with the consequent erosion of those profits. In the long run only normal profits can be earned. Because the demand curves of the firms slope downward, the long-run equilibrium will be one in which $P = LATC$, but will occur at a point to the left of the minimum of the $LATC$ curve. Thus there is production inefficiency ($P >$ min $LATC$) and allocative inefficiency because the wrong mix of output is produced.

Firms in monopolistic competition spend tremendous amounts on advertising aimed at increasing demand and hopefully reducing the price elasticity of demand for their output. Other forms of nonprice competition are also used. In the process, the consumer's opportunity to choose between more service and lower prices frequently vanishes. The presumption follows that nonprice competition leads to a less desirable use of society's resources. We can expect, however, that this type of *behavior* will persist as long as imperfectly competitive market *structures* exist.

## Learning Objectives

After reading Chapter 11 and doing the following exercises, you should:

1. Be able to describe structural characteristics of monopolistic competition.
2. Know how firms in monopolistic competition achieve their market power.
3. Know why the demand curve faced by the firms in monopolistically competitive markets is downward-sloping.
4. Be able to tell why monopolistically competitive firms use the $MC = MR$ rule in making the production decision.
5. Be able to describe the process by which the economic profits are eroded away by the entry of new firms.
6. Be able to explain why the long-run equilibrium in monopolistic competition suffers from production *and* allocative inefficiency.
7. Understand the difference between price competition and nonprice competition and how it may lead to an undesirable use of resources.

## Using Key Terms

Fill in the puzzle on the opposite page with the appropriate term from the list of Key Terms at the end of the chapter in the text.

### *Across*

3. Features that make one product appear different from competing products in the same market.
5. Obstacles that make it difficult or impossible for new firms to enter a market.
6. The ability to alter the market price of a good or service.
7. The choice of the short-run rate of output.
8. The offer of goods at prices equal to their marginal cost.

### *Down*

1. A market in which firms produce a similar product but each maintains some independent control of price.
2. The proportion of total industry output produced by the largest firms.
4. The difference between total revenue and total economic costs.

## True or False: *Circle your choice and explain why any false statements are incorrect.*

T  F  1.  A monopolistically competitive firm confronts a downward-sloping demand curve and, as a result, has some market power.

T  F  2.  In monopolistic competition, changes in the output or price of any single firm will have no significant influence on the sales of other firms.

T  F  3.  In monopolistic competition, each firm competes with other firms offering identical substitutes.

T  F  4.  When marginal costs rise, monopolistically competitive firms do not change output or price.

T  F  5.  For a monopolistically competitive firm, low barriers to entry tend to push economic profits toward zero in the long run.

T  F  6.  As new firms enter a monopolistically competitive industry, the demand curve for individual firms will shift to the right.

T  F  7.  The monopolistically competitive firm charges prices at the minimum of the long-run average total cost curve in the long run.

T  F  8.  Monopolistic competition tends to be less efficient than a perfectly competitive industry because the price is always above the minimum ATC.

T  F  9.  Monopolistic competition results in allocative efficiency.

T  F  10.  Advertising plays a role in reducing the importance of substitute goods in determining market power.

## Multiple Choice: *Select the correct answer.*

_____  1.  One of the main differences between oligopoly and monopolistic competition is:
  (a)  The amount of advertising that firms do.
  (b)  The amount of nonprice competition that occurs.
  (c)  The degree of interdependence among firms.
  (d)  That the profit maximizing output level occurs where MR = MC.

_____  2.  One of the main similarities of perfect competition and monopolistic competition is:
  (a)  That in the long run, price equals average total cost and marginal revenue equals marginal cost.
  (b)  The amount of product differentiation.
  (c)  The point on the long-run average total cost curve at which firms maximize profits.
  (d)  All of the above.

_____  3.  A major difference between monopoly and monopolistic competition is:
  (a)  One maximizes profits by setting MR equal to MC, and the other does not.
  (b)  The number of firms.
  (c)  One type of firm has market power, and the other does not.
  (d)  One has a downward-sloping demand curve, and the other does not.

_____ 4. In monopolistic competition:
   (a) Firms have market power.
   (b) Entry is easy.
   (c) A firm's demand curve is downward-sloping.
   (d) All of the above.

_____ 5. "Product differentiation" refers to:
   (a) Different prices for the same product in a certain market.
   (b) The selling of identical products in different markets.
   (c) Features that make one product appear different from competing products in the same market.
   (d) The charging of different prices for the same product in different markets.

_____ 6. A monopolistically competitive firm maximizes profits or minimizes losses in the long run by producing where:
   (a) MR = MC.
   (b) The demand curve is tangent to the long-run average total cost curve.
   (c) P = ATC.
   (d) All of the above.

_____ 7. If more firms enter a monopolistically competitive market, we would expect:
   (a) The demand curves facing existing firms to shift to the left and become more price inelastic.
   (b) The demand curves facing existing firms to shift to the left and no change in price elasticity.
   (c) The demand curves facing existing firms to shift to the left and become more price elastic.
   (d) The demand curves facing existing firms to shift to the right and no change in price elasticity.

_____ 8. Exit from a market characterized by monopolistic competition:
   (a) Is rare because firms have market power.
   (b) Occurs frequently because barriers to entry are high.
   (c) Occurs when a firm's demand is below its long-run average cost curve at all levels of output.
   (d) Results from economies of scale.

_____ 9. Entry into a market characterized by monopolistic competition:
   (a) Is rare because firms have market power.
   (b) Is frequent because barriers to entry are low.
   (c) Occurs when a firm's demand is below its long-run average cost curve at all levels of output.
   (d) Results from economies of scale.

_____ 10. Firms in a monopolistically competitive market will:
   (a) Produce efficiently.
   (b) Make zero economic profits in the long run.
   (c) Use the profit-maximizing rule TC = TR.
   (d) All of the above.

_____ 11. Compared to marginal cost pricing, a monopolistically competitive firm will:
   (a) Produce a lower output and charge a higher price.
   (b) Produce a greater output and charge a higher price.
   (c) Produce a lower output and charge a lower price.
   (d) Produce a greater output and charge a lower price

_____ 12.  Monopolistically competitive firms are productively inefficient because long-run equilibrium occurs at an output rate where:
(a)  MC is greater than MR.
(b)  Price is greater than MC.
(c)  ATC is greater than the minimum ATC.
(d)  Diseconomies of scale exist.

_____ 13.  In monopolistic competition there is allocative inefficiency because:
(a)  Price is greater than the minimum ATC.
(b)  Production is not at the minimum ATC.
(c)  Of excess capacity.
(d)  Price is greater than MC.

_____ 14.  A monopolistically competitive firm can raise its price somewhat without fear of great change in unit sales because of:
(a)  Brand loyalty.
(b)  Economies of scale.
(c)  Perfectly elastic demand.
(d)  Large market shares of firms in the market.

_____ 15.  Advertising is:
(a)  An efficient form of competition.
(b)  Less important than price competition in oligopolistic and monopolistic competition.
(c)  A major component of competition in perfectly competitive markets.
(d)  A form of nonprice competition.

_____ 16.  When a monopolistically competitive firm advertises, it is attempting to increase:
(a)  The demand and decrease the price elasticity of demand for its product.
(b)  The demand and increase the price elasticity of demand for its product.
(c)  Long-run profits.
(d)  Market demand.

Select the letter of the diagram representing long-run equilibrium in Figure 11.1 that best matches the type of market named in questions 17-20. Use each diagram *only once*.

## Figure 11.1 Long-run cost curves

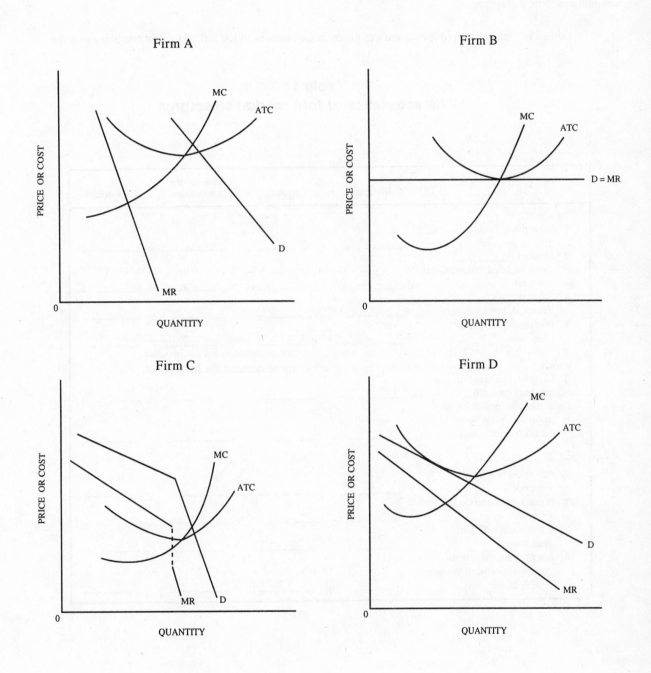

_____ 17. Perfect competition.

_____ 18. Oligopoly.

_____ 19. Monopolistic competition.

_____ 20. Monopoly.

# Problems and Applications

## Exercise 1

This exercise contrasts monopoly, oligopoly, monopolistic competition, and competition, and summarizes their differences.

In Table 11.1 select the appropriate answer given in parentheses at the left and fill in the blanks on the right.

**Table 11.1**
**Characteristics of four market structures**

| | Monopoly | Oligopoly | Monopolistic competition | Competition |
|---|---|---|---|---|
| *Characteristic* | | | | |
| 1. How many firms are there? (many, few, one) | _____ | _____ | _____ | _____ |
| 2. Product is_____ . (standardized, differentiated, unique) | _____ | _____ | _____ | _____ |
| 3. Entry is _____ . (blocked, impeded, easy) | _____ | _____ | _____ | _____ |
| 4. Is there market power? (yes, no) | _____ | _____ | _____ | _____ |
| *Conduct* | | | | |
| 5. Do firms use marginal cost pricing? (yes, no) | _____ | _____ | _____ | _____ |
| 6. Is there the possibility of collusion, price leadership, or price wars? (yes, no) | _____ | _____ | _____ | _____ |
| *Performance (long run)* | | | | |
| 7. Are prices too high? (yes, no) | _____ | _____ | _____ | _____ |
| 8. Is market production too low? (yes, no) | _____ | _____ | _____ | _____ |
| 9. Is the market efficient? (yes, no) | _____ | _____ | _____ | _____ |
| 10. Are profits greater than normal expected in the long run? (yes, no) | _____ | _____ | _____ | _____ |

## Exercise 2

This exercise examines the characteristics of monopolistic competition using a graph.

Use Figure 11.2 to answer questions 1-6.

### Figure 11.2

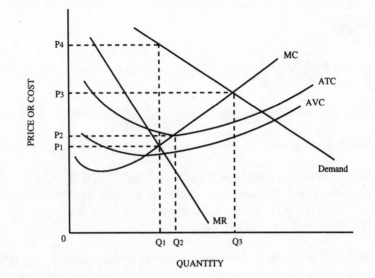

1. The profit-maximizing rate of output for a monopolistically competitive firm occurs where
   _____.

2. According to Figure 11.2, the profit-maximizing rate of output is _____ units and the price is
   _____.

3. Does Figure 11.2 represent a short run or a long run situation? _____

4. This firm is earning a (profit, loss) because at the profit-maximizing output level, the demand
   curve is above the _____ curve.

5. In the long run, the average total cost curve will be tangent to the _____ curve and
   economic profits will be _____.

6. A perfectly competitive firm would maximize profits at an output of _____ and a price of _____.

## Exercise 3

This exercise will use one of the articles in the text to show what kind of information to look for to determine whether a market is characterized by monopolistic competition.

Reread the article entitled "JNCO Jeans: Teen Cool." Then answer the following questions.

1. What phrase gives information about the number of firms competing in the jeans market?
   _____

2. How do the firms differentiate their products?_____
   _____

3. Through its advertising campaigns and by sponsoring extreme athletes, JNCO hoped to establish _____ for its product.

4. In the jeans market there is evidence of:
   (a) Nonprice competition.
   (b) Easy entry.
   (c) Product differentiation.
   (d) All of the above.

# Common Errors

The first statement in each "common error" below is incorrect. Each incorrect statement is followed by a corrected version and an explanation.

1. Monopolies that face competition are monopolistically competitive. WRONG!

   Monopolistically competitive firms are nearly competitive, but they have brand loyalty. RIGHT!

   Do not be misled by the terminology "monopolistic." This type of industry is essentially competitive except that firms have some customer loyalty. That gives them a little ("monopolistic") pricing flexibility and a downward-sloping demand curve. But they still make zero profit in the long run, just like competitive firms.

2. There are only a few firms in a monopolistically competitive market. WRONG!

   There are many firms in a monopolistically competitive market. RIGHT!

   Again don't let the word "monopolistic" fool you. Firms can easily enter or exit from a monopolistically competitive market. Each firm is likely to have excess capacity—which suggests there may be too many firms in a monopolistically competitive market. The restaurant business is a good example of a monopolistically competitive market.

3. Because price equals average cost in the long run in a monopolistically competitive firm, such firms must be efficient. WRONG!

   Because price equals average cost in the long run in a monopolistically competitive firm, profits are zero in the long run, but the firm is inefficient. RIGHT!

   Long-run profits are normal (zero economic profits) because competition forces prices to equal long-run average cost. The firm does not reach the *lowest* long-run average cost level, however, and so it is inefficient. The firm's demand curve touches the long-run average cost curve, but not at its lowest point.

# •ANSWERS•

## Using Key Terms
### Across
3. product differentiation
5. barriers to entry
6. market power
7. production decision
8. marginal cost pricing

## Down

1. monopolistic competition
2. concentration ratio
4. economic profit

## True or False

1. T
2. T
3. F   In monopolistic competition, each firm offers slightly different products.
4. F   The MR curve for monopolistically competitive firms does not have a vertical segment because there is no significant interdependence between firms. As a consequence, a shift in MC will result in an intersection between MC and MR at a new output level.
5. T
6. F   As new firms enter, individual firms will experience a decrease in the number of customers resulting in a shift in demand to the left.
7. F   A monopolistically competitive firm will charge a price above the minimum ATC because of product differentiation.
8. T
9. F   A monopolistically competitive firm will produce less than the allocatively efficient output level because of a downward sloping demand curve facing each firm.
10. T

## Multiple Choice

| | | | | |
|---|---|---|---|---|
| 1. c | 5. c | 9. b | 13. d | 17. b |
| 2. a | 6. d | 10. b | 14. a | 18. c |
| 3. b | 7. c | 11. a | 15. d | 19. d |
| 4. d | 8. c | 12. c | 16. a | 20. a |

## Problems and Applications

## Exercise 1

### Table 11.1 Answer

| | Monopoly | Oligopoly | Monopolistic competition | Competition |
|---|---|---|---|---|
| 1. | one | few | many | many |
| 2. | unique | standardized or differentiatiated | differentiated | standardized |
| 3. | blocked | impeded | impeded or easy | easy |
| 4. | yes | yes | yes | no |
| 5. | no | no | no | yes |
| 6. | no | yes | no | no |
| 7. | yes | yes | yes | no |
| 8. | yes | yes | yes | no |
| 9. | no | no | no | yes |
| 10. | yes | yes | no | no |

171

## Exercise 2

1. MC=MR
2. $Q_1$, $P_4$
3. short run
4. profit. ATC
5. demand, zero
6. $Q_3$, $P_3$

## Exercise 3

1. ". . . throngs of competitors from trying to steal a share of the market."
2. ". . . with distinctive stitching and hot ad campaigns."
3. brand loyalty
4. d

# C H A P T E R  12

# (De)Regulation of Business

## Quick Review

Perfectly competitive markets provide a model for economic efficiency. However, the strict requirements for the model to operate are seldom encountered in the real world. Free markets thus may fail to provide optimal answers to the WHAT, HOW, and FOR WHOM questions, and government may intervene in hopes of making things better. But, devising the appropriate social and economic regulations is difficult. Optimal intervention, an elusive concept at best, is required or intervention might make things worse! During the early 1970s many economists and government officials came to the conclusion that regulation of the economy had gone too far and that in fact considerable *deregulation* was required to redress this "government failure." However, the development of services like the Information Superhighway may require some form of government intervention in some parts while crying out for deregulation in others.

This chapter considers government's role in the marketplace by discussing the following questions:

- When is government regulation necessary?
- What form should that regulation take?
- When is it appropriate to deregulate an industry?

Historically, economists and politicians have recognized many reasons why an industry should be regulated. "Market failure" means that the market provides an inadequate output mix. Sources of market failure include natural monopoly, market power, externalities, public goods, and the inequitable distribution of income.

The existence of any one of these failures prevents the market from providing satisfactory answers to the economic problem. To improve market outcomes where market failure occurs, governments intervene in several ways. Most frequently the intervention takes the form of antitrust activity, economic and social regulation, public-sector production, taxation, or subsidies.

The clearest case for intervention is in "natural monopolies," where a market is best served by a single firm because it alone can capture continuous economies of scale. In regulating natural monopolies, regulators may pursue three basic, but potentially conflicting goals including price efficiency, production efficiency, and equity. Finding the right combination of policy levers—such as regulating price, output, or profit—is a very difficult job and the risks of regulating badly are unfortunately quite high.

In addition, it has become increasingly clear that regulation itself may impose significant opportunity costs on the economy. Resources are used in devising and administering regulations. The firms in a regulated market use resources to comply with (or get around!) regulations. In addition to these administrative and compliance costs, efficiency costs that result from bad decisions, incomplete information, and so on may worsen the mix of output; moreover, their effects may be compounded over time!

Because many industries are viewed as operating in suboptimal fashion, the process of deregulation has begun. Railroads, trucking, telephone service, and airlines are industries in which deregulation has basically been completed. However, there are still many industries that are regulated and even some where regulation has increased, as in the health industry. Moreover, some cable TV was deregulated in 1986 with arguably unsatisfactory results and modified reregulation was required in 1992.

In markets as dynamic as telecommunications, traditional industry boundaries become blurred. The market once dominated by telephone companies now includes cable TV, satellite services, electric utilities, etc. Much effort now goes into breaking down barriers to entry for new participants. The Telecommunications Act of 1995 required the Baby Bells to improve access to their own local telephone markets before they could have permission to enter new markets like those for video and data services. The scope for error in designing regulations is enormous and even good regulation may quickly be outdated by the pace of technological advance.

The question to be answered is always, "Do the benefits of the regulation exceed the cost of regulation?" These are questions which must be evaluated on an industry-by-industry basis. Deregulation in practice seems to have served the consumer well. Prices are lower and output greater in the deregulated markets.

## Learning Objectives

After reading Chapter 12 and doing the following exercises, you should:

1. Know several sources of market failure and several techniques of intervention.
2. Be able to distinguish social regulation from economic regulation.
3. Be able to demonstrate natural monopoly graphically and verbally.
4. Understand economies of scale.
5. Understand the potential conflict among the goals of price efficiency, production efficiency, and equity.
6. Know the difficulties associated with regulating the price, output, or profits of natural monopolies.
7. Understand the difficulty of devising regulations and why second-best solutions are a realistic goal.
8. Be able to distinguish between administrative, compliance, and efficiency costs of regulation.
9. Know the history of regulation and deregulation in the U.S. economy, and be able to cite some results of deregulation.

## Using Key Terms

Fill in the puzzle on the opposite page with the appropriate term from the list of Key Terms at the end of the chapter in the text.

### Across
3. The market structure in Figure 12.1 in the text.
5. An imperfectly competitive industry subject to potential entry if prices or profits increase.
6. The doctrine of nonintervention by government.
8. Occurs when the market mechanism results in a suboptimal outcome.
9. Obstacles that make it difficult or impossible for new firms to enter a market.
10. The decrease in minimum average costs because of an increase in the size of plant and equipment.
12. Equal to total revenue minus total economic profit.
13. The goods and services that must be given up in order to obtain something else.
14. A form of nonprice competition to make a product appear different from competing products.

### Down
1. Government intervention that fails to improve economic outcomes.
2. The use of high prices and profits on one product to subsidize low prices on another product.
4. The offer of goods at prices equal to their marginal cost.
7. Government intervention to alter the behavior of firms.
11. Laws to prevent the abuse of market power.

# Puzzle 12.1

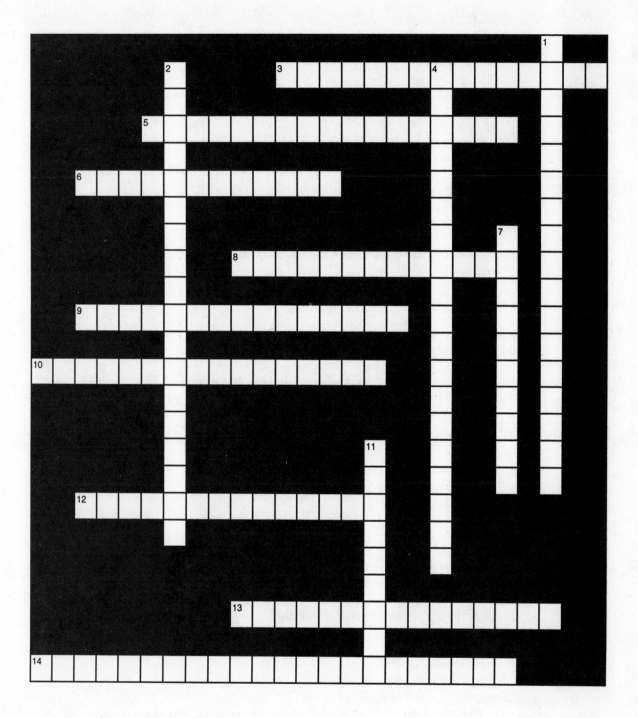

## True or False: *Circle your choice and explain why any false statements are incorrect.*

T  F  1.  Economic regulation focuses on prices, production, and the conditions for industry entry or exit.

T  F  2.  The argument for regulation is that markets can generate imperfect outcomes, and the argument for deregulation is that government sometimes worsens market outcomes

T  F  3.  Deregulation implies that government failure is worse than the market failure that regulation is designed to correct.

T  F  4.  Since social regulation is concerned with workplace safety, discrimination, and other undesirable outcomes, it does not affect prices or output.

T  F  5.  Unregulated natural monopolies produce optimal rates of output.

T  F  6.  Price regulation of a natural monopoly does not require a subsidy.

T  F  7.  Regulated monopolies that are allowed a specific profit rate have an incentive to hold down costs.

T  F  8.  Eliminating the economic profit of a natural monopolist can be justified on the basis of society's equity goal.

T  F  9.  Recent experiences with deregulation in the cable TV and telephone industries imply that all regulation should end.

T  F  10.  The marginal benefits of regulation should exceed the marginal costs of regulation if additional regulations are to be imposed.

## Multiple Choice: *Select the correct answer.*

_____  1.  Which of the following is an example of government failure?
   (a)   Over regulation resulting in wasted resources.
   (b)   Public goods.
   (c)   Externalities.
   (d)   All of the above.

_____  2.  Which of the following is an example of market failure?
   (a)   Inequities in the output mix and the distribution of income.
   (b)   Natural monopoly.
   (c)   Under production, from society's perspective.
   (d)   All of the above.

_____  3.  If government failure did not exist:
   (a)   Laissez faire would apply to all markets.
   (b)   Deregulation would be unnecessary.
   (c)   The invisible hand would be the most efficient and equitable way to run the economy.
   (d)   All markets would be regulated.

_____ 4.  Government can intervene in the structure or behavior of a market. Which of the following correctly distinguishes between antitrust and regulation?
(a)   Antitrust focuses on both, while regulation focuses mostly on behavior.
(b)   Antitrust focuses on both, while regulation focuses mostly on structure.
(c)   Regulation focuses on both, while antitrust focuses mostly on behavior.
(d)   Regulation focuses on both, while antitrust focuses mostly on structure.

_____ 5.  Economic regulation focuses on:
(a)   Prices in a market.
(b)   Production by the market.
(c)   Conditions under which firms enter and exit from an industry.
(d)   All of the above.

_____ 6.  To produce at the greatest possible allocative efficiency, a natural monopoly:
(a)   Should be allowed to maximize profit without government interference.
(b)   Sets price equal to average cost.
(c)   Must be subsidized by the government to overcome losses if $P = MC$.
(d)   Produces where $MC = ATC$.

_____ 7.  Which of the following problems results from output regulation of a natural monopoly?
(a)   Losses and bankruptcy for the natural monopoly.
(b)   Loss of quality.
(c)   Excess output.
(d)   All of the above.

_____ 8.  If the government regulated a natural monopolist to achieve price efficiency without subsidies or price discrimination, the monopolist would:
(a)   Earn economic profits.
(b)   Earn only normal profits.
(c)   Have no incentive to stay in the market.
(d)   Earn less of a profit than before, but still earn a profit.

_____ 9.  Which of the following problems results from profit regulation of a natural monopoly?
(a)   Production does not occur at a socially optimal rate.
(b)   The firm has no incentive to strive for efficiency.
(c)   There is an incentive to "pad costs".
(d)   All of the above are problems.

_____ 10.  The economic cost of a manufacturer's complying with an "air bag" law would be:
(a)   The additional money required to buy an automobile with an air bag.
(b)   The resources that were used to produce the air bag.
(c)   The best alternative goods and services forgone when the air bag is produced.
(d)   All of the above.

_____ 11.  The basic issue in regulatory policy is:
(a)   Whether or not the benefits of government regulation exceed the costs.
(b)   How to achieve second-best solutions in all markets.
(c)   How to eliminate all natural monopolies.
(d)   How to achieve profit regulation in all industries.

_____ 12.  Second-best solutions:
(a)   Are options that should never be implemented.
(b)   Reflect the realistic choices that society must make between imperfect markets and imperfect government intervention.
(c)   Are not consistent with utility maximization in the "real world."
(d)   Will always have cost greater than benefits.

_____ 13. When market outcomes are improved after government regulation is enforced:
   (a)   Technical efficiency is being achieved.
   (b)   The net effect of government intervention on society in this case has been beneficial.
   (c)   Government intervention still may not be justified if the economic costs of regulation are too high.
   (d)   All of the above are correct.

_____ 14. When there is market failure:
   (a)   Government intervention is always beneficial.
   (b)   A laissez-faire approach is the best policy.
   (c)   Government intervention is beneficial only in the case of natural monopolies.
   (d)   Government intervention is beneficial only when the marginal benefit of intervention exceeds its marginal cost.

_____ 15. The first major regulatory target in the United States was:
   (a)   Airlines.
   (b)   Railroads.
   (c)   Trucking firms.
   (d)   Telephone companies.

_____ 16. Deregulation of the trucking industry led to:
   (a)   A reduction in most truck rates.
   (b)   A significant increase in the number of trucking firms.
   (c)   The elimination of monopoly profits and increased quantity and variety of service.
   (d)   All of the above.

_____ 17. As a consequence of the deregulation of the telephone industry:
   (a)   Many telephone companies have abandoned the market.
   (b)   Long-distance phone rates have increased sharply.
   (c)   Local telephone rates have risen in the absence of cross-subsidization of local costs from long-distance profits.
   (d)   Long-distance users now subsidize local users of phone service to a greater extent than before deregulation.

_____ 18. The inefficiency of regulation of interstate airlines was revealed by:
   (a)   The absence of nonprice competition among interstate airlines.
   (b)   The long history of losses and bankruptcies among major regulated airlines.
   (c)   The regulatory practice of allowing unrestricted entry into interstate markets.
   (d)   Fares that were as much as 60 percent higher on interstate routes than on comparable (unregulated) intrastate routes.

_____ 19. Deregulation of the airline industry has been followed by:
   (a)   Lower fares on shorter, less-traveled routes.
   (b)   Increased concentration in the airline industry.
   (c)   Higher average cost of service by surviving airlines.
   (d)   Reduced competition in most airline markets.

_____ 20. The electric utility industry became a target for deregulation when:
   (a)   The cost of constructing nuclear power plants declined.
   (b)   New technology allowed the transmission of power from region to region with insignificant power loss.
   (c)   Local utility companies began behaving like monopolies.
   (d)   All of the above.

# Problems and Applications

## Exercise 1

This exercise provides practice in identifying market imperfections, finding an appropriate form of government intervention, and recognizing the possible side effects of government intervention.

Table 12.1 lists market imperfections, means for the government to intervene, and some of the side effects of government policy.

### Table 12.1
### Market imperfections, government interventions, and side effects

| Market imperfections | Means of government intervention | Side effects of government policy |
|---|---|---|
| I. Externalities<br>II. Inequities<br>III. Natural monopoly<br>IV. Nonexclusive goods<br>V. Market power<br>VI. Lack of information about tastes, costs, or prices<br>VII. Lack of information about profitability or technology | A. Taxes, subsidies, or transfers<br>B. Regulation of prices, output, or entry<br>C. Antitrust activity<br>D. Provision of information<br>E. Production of goods by the government | 1. Inefficiency (unnecessarily high costs)<br>2. Shortages or surpluses<br>3. Lack of quality<br>4. Inefficient government bureaucracy<br>5. Dynamic inefficiencies |

1. For each of the situations described in Table 12.2, choose the roman numeral(s) for each market imperfection that applies, the letter(s) that represent appropriate action by the government, and the number(s) that indicate possible side effects of government involvement.

# Table 12.2
# Market imperfections and government intervention

| Situation | Market imperfection | Government intervention | Possible side effects of government policy |
|---|---|---|---|
| 1. Because of severe balance-of-trade deficits, the United States needs to export more goods abroad. If not, foreign exchange markets will be increasingly disrupted. However, many small American companies do not know enough about foreign markets to become exporters of goods and services. | _____ | _____ | _____ |
| 2. It is not economical to have firms compete to provide sewage facilities for residential areas. Each house needs only one set of pipes and it is most efficient to attach all pipes from houses to one major sewer conduit. | _____ | _____ | _____ |
| 3. Many workers at a firm find they are becoming nauseated in the workplace. Futhermore, the cancer rate among the employees appears to be very high. They cannot get management to study the problem because the firm can simply fire them and hire new employees. | _____ | _____ | _____ |
| 4. Farmers are willing to use the latest techniques for growing crops. However, they have difficulty determining what the newest techniques are by themselves and the market does not undertake the continuous research process necessary to develop them. | _____ | _____ | _____ |
| 5. If the farmers do not change continually to the latest disease-resistant seed varieties, it is likely that there will be a disastrous spread of disease that will threaten the economy's food supply. However, new varieties of grain are expensive to develop, and the private market would not undertake the continuous research process necessary to develop them. | _____ | _____ | _____ |
| 6. At the beginning of World War II, the United States found that it was cut off from important suppliers of rubber, sugar, and hemp by the Japanese. The private market had not kept enough inventories of these goods on hand in case of war. | _____ | _____ | _____ |
| 7. The St. Joe Mineral Company dumped taconite tailings filled with asbestos into the Great Lakes. While St. Joe suffered no bad side effects from this activity, many people who used the lakes began to suffer such effects. | _____ | _____ | _____ |
| 8. Many older people are poor and as they age and become weaker are beset by various problems and cannot take care of themselves adequately. Private charities do not do enough to maintain a standard of care that society as a whole considers desirable. | _____ | _____ | _____ |
| 9. It is very costly to run electrical lines into a house; thus, it is not economical to put more than one set of electric lines into a home. Electrical services are most economically provided by only one firm. | _____ | _____ | _____ |
| 10. General Electric and Westinghouse decided to coordinate their activities and conspired to set the price of electronic equipment on which they were bidding. | _____ | _____ | _____ |

## Exercise 2

This exercise emphasizes the characteristics of a natural monopoly using a graph.

Use Figure 12.1 to answer questions 1-6.

## Figure 12.1

1. Label the ATC curve, the MC curve, the MR curve, and the demand curve in Figure 12.1.

2. What is the profit-maximizing price and output level for the unregulated natural monopolist in Figure 12.1?

3. At the unregulated output level, the natural monopolist (will, will not) earn an economic profit.

4. Regulation designed to achieve price efficiency would result in a price of _____ and an output level of _____.

5. At the output level in question 4, the natural monopoly will earn a (profit, loss) because ATC is (greater, less) than the price.

6. Profit regulation for the natural monopoly would result in a price of _____ and an output level of _____.

## Exercise 3

This exercise focuses on market failure and government intervention.

Reread the In the News article "Calif. Consumers Can Choose Power Company" in the text.

1. What passage indicates increased government intervention in the electricity market?

   _____

2. Which of the following forms of market failure justified government intervention?
   (a) Externalities
   (b) Public good
   (c) Natural monopoly
   (d) Inequity

3. Which phrase indicates the benefit of deregulation?_____

4. How are power companies responding to the deregulation?_____

## Common Errors

The first statement in each "common error" below is incorrect. Each incorrect statement is followed by a corrected version and an explanation.

1. Once regulations are in place and enforced, the cost to society is zero. WRONG!

   Regulations impose costs of their own. RIGHT!

   The often-heard phrase "there ought to be a law" implies what is meant here. It seems that the law solves the problem but causes no problems itself. This is an inadequate assessment. It costs society a great deal in the way of opportunity costs to devise, administer, and comply with regulations. In addition, once a regulation is in place, it's very, very difficult to remove because bureaucratic machinery works very slowly. As an example, in the early days of the energy crisis, trucks were allowed to carry freight from point $A$ to point $B$, but not allowed to haul anything back from point $B$ to point $A$. Regulations have costs all their own!

2. The government can aid competition by helping competitors in a market to survive. WRONG!

   The government interferes with free entry and exit when helping competitors survive, and this interferes with competition. RIGHT!

   When the government prevents exit from the market, it is interfering with the contestability of the market. By not allowing inefficient firms to exit from the market, the government makes it more difficult for the more efficient firms to enter the market. Barriers to exit lead to barriers to entry, which interfere with the competitive process.

## •ANSWERS•

## Using Key Terms
### Across
3. natural monopoly
5. contestable market
6. laissez faire
8. market failure
9. barriers to entry
10. economies of scale
12. economic profit
13. opportunity cost
14. product differentiation

### Down
1. government failure
2. cross subsidization
4. marginal cost pricing
7. regulation
11. antitrust

# True or False

1. T
2. T
3. T
4. F Complying with social regulations, e.g. workplace safety, can involve significant costs. As a result, prices and output can be significantly affected.
5. F Unregulated natural monopolies tend to produce less than optimal levels of output.
6. F Price regulation occurs where MC = demand which is below the firm's ATC, making a subsidy necessary.
7. F When a firm is allowed a specific profit rate, it has no incentive to keep costs in check.
8. T
9. F The regulation of natural monopolies can improve outcomes.
10. T

# Multiple Choice

| | | | | | | | | | |
|---|---|---|---|---|---|---|---|---|---|
| 1. | a | 5. | d | 9. | d | 13. | c | 17. | c |
| 2. | d | 6. | c | 10. | c | 14. | d | 18. | d |
| 3. | b | 7. | b | 11. | a | 15. | b | 19. | b |
| 4. | a | 8. | c | 12. | b | 16. | d | 20. | b |

# Problems and Applications

## Exercise 1

1. **Table 12.2 Answer**

| Situation | Market imperfections | Government interventions | Possible side effects of government policy |
|---|---|---|---|
| 1. | VI, VII | D | 1, 4 |
| 2. | III, V | B or E | 1, 2, 3, 4, 5 |
| 3. | I, IV | B, D | 1, 2, 3, 4, 5 |
| 4. | VI, VII | D | 1, 4, 5 |
| 5. | I, III, IV, VI, VII | A, D, E | 1, 3, 4, 5 |
| 6. | I, IV | A, E | 2, 4, 5 |
| 7. | I | A or B | 1, 2, 4, 5 |
| 8. | II, IV | A | 1, 4, 5 |
| 9. | III, V | B | 1, 2, 3, 4, 5 |
| 10. | V | C | 1, 2, 4, 5 |

183

## Exercise 2

1. **Figure 12.1 Answer**

2. $P_1, Q_1$
3. will
4. $P_3, Q_3$
5. loss, greater
6. $P_2, Q_2$

## Exercise 3

1. "So far, 16 states have laws to deregulate electricity." ". . . the Clinton administration proposed legislation for nationwide competition by 2003."
2. c
3. ". . . the average family could save $232 a year."
4. They are advertising in an effort to segment the market.

# CHAPTER 13

# Environmental Protection

## Quick Review

Nearly everyone is concerned about the environment and agrees that we ought to protect it. It wasn't always that way. Until the 1960s the problems associated with polluting the environment were not widely understood and certainly did not attract the attention they do today. Of course, a clean environment is only one of the things we want, and as with nearly everything else we desire, there is the cost of obtaining it. In this chapter we consider four questions that are crucial to understanding environmental protection and the least costly ways of obtaining the optimal amount of it:

- How do (unregulated) markets encourage pollution?
- What are the costs of greater environmental protection?
- How much of our (scarce) resources should be allocated to environmental protection?
- How can government policy best ensure an "optimal" environment?

Today we are well aware of many kinds of pollution: problems associated with the earth's ozone layer and global warming, other forms of air pollution, water pollution, and noise pollution, just to name a few.

One wonders why producers pollute (although we all contribute to the problem in one way or another). The answer lies in market incentives. In making production decisions, producers will choose the profit-maximizing rate of output and attempt to produce it at the lowest possible cost—even if by doing so they push some real costs onto society as a whole. When they are successful in pushing these costs onto third parties, we say that an "externality" has been created. It represents a divergence between social cost (the full resource cost of an economic activity) and private costs (those borne directly by the producer or the consumer of a good).

The solutions to the pollution problem lie in two basic areas: (1) using market incentives and (2) bypassing the market and using direct controls. We shouldn't lose sight of the fact that a pollution-free economy would be very difficult and expensive to achieve. Resources would have to be reallocated to fight pollution and would have to be taken away from the production of other goods and services that we also desire. Prices and patterns of employment would change. That partly explains *why we do not desire to eliminate all pollution.* Indeed, the optimal rate of pollution would be one at which the marginal costs of cleaning up the environment is equal to the value of the marginal benefits from cleaning it up.

The Clean Air Act and its amendments of 1990 moved the economy away from the direct-regulation (command and control) approach which specified mandatory pollution reductions *and* the specific technologies for achieving them. This approach, while effective in achieving pollution reduction goals, did not do so at the lowest possible cost. Government agencies are now moving toward market-based systems which achieve given reductions at lower costs and also provide incentives for new, more cost-efficient technologies to be developed. The system relies on a market for "pollution credits" on the Chicago Board of Trade. Those with the highest marginal costs of pollution reduction are the buyers; those with the lowest marginal costs are the sellers. Both parties gain, as does society, because the total resource cost of reducing pollution is reduced.

185

# Learning Objectives

After reading Chapter 13 and doing the following exercises, you should:

1. Know the principal types and sources of pollution.
2. Understand how to apply the notion of opportunity cost to the pollution problem.
3. Understand how market forces influence the production and efficiency decisions for the producer.
4. Be able to distinguish between private costs and social costs.
5. Understand the term "externality," and how externalities arise.
6. Be able to show how taxes, emission charges, marketable pollution rights, and effluent charges can be used to control pollution.
7. Be able to show how regulation can be used to control pollution.
8. Understand the international dimensions of the pollution problem.
9. Understand how the optimal rate of pollution is determined and know why it is *not* zero.
10. Know the theory behind the Clean Air Act and its amendments.
11. Understand the rationale for the market for pollution credits.


# Using Key Terms

Fill in the puzzle on the opposite page with the appropriate term from the list of Key Terms at the end of the chapter in the text.

## *Across*
1. A fee imposed on polluters based on the quantity of pollution.
5. Occurs when government intervention fails to improve economic outcomes.
9. The most desired goods and services that are given up in order to obtain something else.
10. Costs or benefits of a market activity borne by a third party.

## *Down*
2. Occurs when the marginal social benefit of pollution control equals its marginal social cost.
3. The total costs of all resources used in an economic activity.
4. The choice of a short run rate of output using existing plant and equipment.
6. The choice of a production process that minimizes costs for any rate of output.
7. Occurs when the market mechanism results in a suboptimal outcome.
8. The resource costs borne by the specific producer.

# Puzzle 13.1

187

# True or False: *Circle your choice and explain why any false statements are incorrect.*

T  F  1.  Pollution abatement imposes opportunity costs on society.

T  F  2.  Pollution results from the flawed response of producers to market incentives.

T  F  3.  Firms that are able to push part of their costs onto society by polluting will produce a greater output of their product than society desires.

T  F  4.  Externalities are a measure of the divergence between social costs and private costs.

T  F  5.  When externalities exist, firms will not allocate their resources to maximize social welfare.

T  F  6.  Direct government regulation is generally preferable to alteration of market incentives in correcting pollution problems.

T  F  7.  Marketable pollution permits rely on government regulation, not market incentives, to reduce the level of pollution.

T  F  8.  The optimal rate of pollution will be attained when the total benefits received from lowering the pollution level are equal to the total costs that must be incurred to achieve it.

T  F  9.  The problem of pollution applies to market economies where the market fails as a result of externalities, but is not a problem in command economies without markets.

T  F  10.  The greenhouse problem is evidence of market failure in both the United States and other countries.

# Multiple Choice: *Select the correct answer.*

_____  1.  In making the production decision, polluting firms equate:
(a)  Marginal social cost with marginal social benefits.
(b)  Marginal revenue and private marginal costs.
(c)  Marginal social cost and marginal revenue.
(d)  Marginal private costs and marginal social costs.

_____  2.  Social costs:
(a)  Are less than private costs.
(b)  Include private costs.
(c)  Are unrelated to private costs.
(d)  Are always borne by the producer.

_____  3.  When social costs and private costs of consumption and production diverge, then inevitably:
(a)  Producers have an incentive to produce too little.
(b)  Consumers have an incentive to consume too little.
(c)  Both producers and consumers have an incentive to produce and consume too much.
(d)  External costs are zero.

_____ 4. When external costs result from the production of some good, the output level of that good tends to be:
(a) Larger than is desirable.
(b) Smaller than is desirable.
(c) Neither too small nor too large.
(d) Too small if the private costs exceed the external costs.

_____ 5. The market will overproduce goods that have external costs because:
(a) Producers experience lower costs than society.
(b) Producers experience higher costs than society.
(c) The government is not able to produce these goods.
(d) Producers cannot keep these goods from consumers who do not pay so they have to produce greater amounts.

_____ 6. A firm that dumps its waste products into our waterways will be:
(a) Paying the full cost of production.
(b) Paying more than the full cost of production.
(c) Able to sell its product at a lower price than if it cleaned up its wastes.
(d) Internalizing externalities.

_____ 7. Other things being equal, if a perfectly competitive firm is forced to switch to a more expensive, nonpolluting production process:
(a) The average cost curve will shift downward.
(b) The profit-maximizing level of output will be increased.
(c) The marginal cost curve will shift downward or to the right.
(d) Total profits will decrease.

_____ 8. When firms are allowed to pollute the environment without bearing the costs of polluting, then:
(a) Their marginal cost curve is too low.
(b) Their average variable cost curve is too low.
(c) Their average total cost curve is too low.
(d) All of the above.

_____ 9. Solution to the pollution-abatement problem involves:
(a) Eliminating the divergence between internalized private costs and social costs.
(b) Compelling firms to internalize all costs resulting from their production.
(c) Forcing polluters to pay all social costs.
(d) Doing all of the above.

_____ 10. If emission charges were affixed to all production and consumption activities:
(a) The relative price of highly polluting activities would increase.
(b) People would stop producing and consuming.
(c) Pollution would be eliminated.
(d) There would be no redistribution of income.

_____ 11. The purpose of an emission charge is to:
(a) Increase the difference between social and private costs.
(b) Internalize externalities.
(c) Reduce the socially optimal rate of output.
(d) Externalize the costs of pollution.

_____ 12. The primary purpose of tradable pollution permits is to:
   (a)   Reduce, but not eliminate, the level of pollution.
   (b)   Reduce the cost of pollution control.
   (c)   Reduce both the level of pollution and the cost of pollution control.
   (d)   Completely eliminate pollution.

_____ 13. The 1990 Clean Air Act relied on which of the following strategies to clean up the environment?
   (a)   Marketable pollution permits.
   (b)   "Command and control" approach to regulation.
   (c)   Subsidizing new pollution-control technologies.
   (d)   All of the above.

_____ 14. When there are external costs of production, then the social optimum occurs where marginal revenue equals:
   (a)   Private marginal cost.
   (b)   Social marginal cost.
   (c)   The minimum of the average cost curve.
   (d)   Social marginal benefit.

_____ 15. An optimal amount of pollution can be described as:
   (a)   The minimal amount technically possible.
   (b)   The amount that would result when polluting firms spend revenues on pollution-control equipment until they earn only normal profits.
   (c)   The amount for which a $1 increase in pollution-control expenditures creates $1 in additional social welfare.
   (d)   Zero.

_____ 16. The marginal benefit of reducing pollution:
   (a)   Rises as the environment gets cleaner.
   (b)   Falls as the environment gets cleaner.
   (c)   Is constant.
   (d)   Is not an issue in determining the optimal rate of pollution.

_____ 17. The pursuit of a pollution-free environment is:
   (a)   The morally correct strategy and costs should not be a consideration.
   (b)   Probably not in society's best interests, in view of the extremely high opportunity costs.
   (c)   The economically correct strategy.
   (d)   The economically correct strategy as long as benefits accrue to society.

_____ 18. In cost-benefit analysis, the government should intervene as long as:
   (a)   Government corrects market failures without incurring resources costs.
   (b)   The value of government failure exceeds the value of market failure.
   (c)   Government's improvement of market outcomes exceeds costs of government intervention.
   (d)   Government corrects market failures in spite of government failure.

_____ 19. The costs of pollution control will:
   (a)   Always be borne entirely by the polluting producer.
   (b)   Always be passed on completely to the consumer.
   (c)   Be distributed between producer and consumer depending on factors like the price elasticity of demand.
   (d)   Be borne entirely by the taxpayers in the United States.

20. When human lives are involved, a cost-benefit ratio:
   (a) Should have no bearing on decision making.
   (b) Must be considered because it provides a measure of the opportunity costs of government policies.
   (c) Is useless because human lives cannot be measured in dollars and cents.
   (d) Is an indication that a policy should be implemented if it is a very high value.

# Problems and Applications

## *Exercise 1*

This exercise shows how to compute the optimal rate of pollution and will help with a problem in the text.

Table 13.1 indicates various levels of pollution that might be experienced in a lake near your home. It also contains information concerning the value of damages imposed on society by the pollution and the cost to society of cleaning the lake to particular levels. For example, the lake could be made pollution-free with an expenditure of $280,000. The question is: "Is it worth it?" Complete questions 1-7 to find out.

## Table 13.1
## Annual value of damages associated with polluted water and costs of reducing pollution

| (1)<br>Quantity of pollution (units of waste material per 100 cubic feet of water) | (2)<br>Monetary value of damages (thousands of dollars) | (3)<br>Marginal benefits of pollution abatement (thousands of dollars) | (4)<br>Costs of treating polluted water (thousands of dollars) | (5)<br>Marginal cost of pollution abatement (thousands of dollars) |
|---|---|---|---|---|
| 6 | $140 | $   --- | $  0 | $   --- |
| 5 | 100 | 40 | 5 | 5 |
| 4 | 70 | _____ | 15 | _____ |
| 3 | 45 | _____ | 30 | _____ |
| 2 | 25 | _____ | 50 | _____ |
| 1 | 10 | _____ | 100 | _____ |
| 0 | 0 | _____ | 280 | _____ |

1. Assume that without any controls, polluters will annually impose $140,000 of damages on the lake's users by generating 6 units of waste for every 100 cubic feet of water. To clean out the sixth unit of pollutants (that is, lower the quantity of pollution from 6 units to 5) costs $5,000. The value of the benefits gained is $40,000. Complete the rest of column 3.

2. Complete column 5 in Table 13.1 in the same way. The first calculation has been done for you.

3. Should the annual level of pollution be reduced from 6 units to 5? _____

4. Which of the following reasons explains why annual pollution should (or should not) be reduced from 6 to 5 units of pollution?
   (a) The optimal rate of pollution has been reached.
   (b) The marginal social benefits exceed the marginal social cost from reducing the pollution.
   (c) The marginal social costs exceed the marginal social benefits from reducing the pollution.

5. Should pollution be reduced annually from 5 units to 4? _____

6. What is the optimal rate of pollution? _____

7. Which of the following reasons explains why the lake should not be made free of pollution?
   (a) The optimal rate of pollution has been reached when the lake is free of pollution.
   (b) The marginal social costs incurred in eliminating the pollution would exceed the total social benefits achieved.
   (c) The marginal social costs incurred in eliminating all of the pollution would be less than the marginal social benefits achieved.
   (d) None of the above are the case.

## Exercise 2

This exercise shows how externalities affect third parties. This exercise will help you complete the problems in the text.

A chemical plant and a plastics factory are located adjacent to the same stream. The chemical plant is located upstream. The downstream plastics factory requires pure water for its production process. Its basic supply is the stream that runs past both firms.

**Figure 13.1**
**Markets for plastics and chemicals**

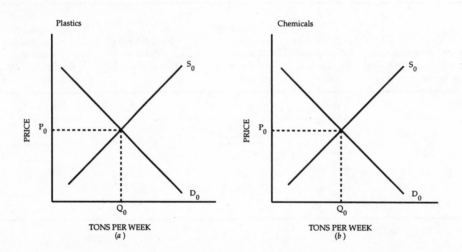

In Figure 13.1, diagrams $a$ and $b$, $S_0$ and $D_0$ represent the supply and demand for plastics and chemicals, respectively. Assume that the economy is initially competitive and resources are allocated efficiently. Equilibrium price and quantity are $P_0$ and $Q_0$ in each case. But then the chemical producer decides to dump waste products into the stream rather than dispose of them with the costly process that had been used.

1. In Figure 13.1 diagram $b$, draw in a new supply curve for chemicals after the dumping in the stream begins. Label it $S_1$. (*Hint:* There are many ways to draw the curve.)

2. The pollution from the chemical plant forces the plastics manufacturer to use a costly water-purifying system. Draw a new supply curve for plastics in Figure 13.1 diagram $a$. Label it $S_1$. (There are many ways to draw this curve correctly.)

192

3. The effect of the decision to pollute on the quantity of chemicals sold is the same as if:
   (a) A new, improved technology were discovered.
   (b) Wages to its labor force were reduced.
   (c) The Social Security tax on employers had been abolished.
   (d) All of the above were the case.

4. As a result of the chemical plant's polluting activities:
   (a) The price of chemicals has risen.
   (b) The price of chemicals has fallen.
   (c) The price of plastics has not changed.
   (d) None of the above is the case.

5. As a result of the chemical plant's activities:
   (a) More chemicals are produced and sold than society desires.
   (b) More labor is used to produce chemicals than society desires.
   (c) More capital inputs are used to produce chemicals than society desires.
   (d) All of the above are the case.

6. The effect of the chemical firm's pollution is to:
   (a) Raise the price of plastics and reduce the quantity sold.
   (b) Lower the price of plastics and increase the quantity sold.
   (c) Raise the price of plastics and increase the quantity sold.
   (d) Do none of the above.

7. The impact of the pollution on the plastics industry in this example is, *ceteris paribus*, to:
   (a) Reduce the output of plastics below the level that society desires.
   (b) Reduce the employment possibilities in the plastics industry.
   (c) Raise the price of products made with plastics.
   (d) Do all of the above.

# Exercise 3

This exercise shows the difference between private marginal costs and social marginal costs.

1. An iron-producing firm mines iron ore. Assume the iron ore industry is competitive. Table 13.2 depicts the private costs and social costs of the firm's iron production at each daily production rate. Complete Table 13.2.

## Table 13.2 Costs of producing iron

| Production rate (tons per day) | Total private cost (dollars per day) | Private marginal cost (dollars per ton) | Total social cost (dollars per day) | Social marginal cost (dollars per ton) |
|---|---|---|---|---|
| 0 | $ 0 | $ --- | $ 0 | $ --- |
| 1 | 40 | _____ | 80 | _____ |
| 2 | 90 | _____ | 170 | _____ |
| 3 | 150 | _____ | 270 | _____ |
| 4 | 220 | _____ | 380 | _____ |
| 5 | 300 | _____ | 500 | _____ |
| 6 | 390 | _____ | 630 | _____ |
| 7 | 490 | _____ | 770 | _____ |
| 8 | 600 | _____ | 920 | _____ |
| 9 | 720 | _____ | 1,080 | _____ |
| 10 | 850 | _____ | 1,250 | _____ |
| 11 | 990 | _____ | 1,430 | _____ |
| 12 | 1,140 | _____ | 1,620 | _____ |

2.  In Figure 13.2, the price of the iron in the competitive market is $140 per ton. Draw the private marginal cost curve and label it *PMC*. Draw the social marginal cost curve and label it *SMC*. Label the demand curve "Demand."

**Figure 13.2**

3.  What is the profit-maximizing production rate for the firm if it considers only its private costs?
    (a)    5 tons per day.
    (b)    7 tons per day.
    (c)    9 tons per day.
    (d)    11 tons per day.

4.  What is the profit-maximizing production rate if the firm is required to pay all social costs?
    (a)    5 tons per day.
    (b)    7 tons per day.
    (c)    9 tons per day.
    (d)    11 tons per day.

5.  How much should the pollution (emission) fee be in order to induce the iron-producing firm to produce the socially optimal rate of output?
    (a)    $4 per ton.
    (b)    $40 per ton.
    (c)    $100 per ton.
    (d)    $50 per ton.

# Exercise 4

The effects of pollution have become an increasingly important topic in the media. This exercise will use one of the articles in the text to show the kind of information to look for to identify the effects of pollution.

Reread the In the News article entitled "Dirty Air Can Shorten Your Life." Then answer the following questions.

1. What are the three general sources of pollution mentioned in the article?_____
   _____

2. What phrase tells you that EPA standards do not guarantee healthy air to breathe?_____
   _____

3. How is the author implicitly measuring the cost of pollution in affected areas?_____
   _____

4. What phrase indicates that the effects of breathing polluted air are like those associated with smoking cigarettes?_____

5. The effect of new and tougher standards on the polluting industries by the monitoring agency would cause the MC and ATC curves to shift (upward, downward)?

# Common Errors

The first statement in each "common error" below is incorrect. Each incorrect statement is followed by a corrected version and an explanation.

1. We should eliminate all pollution. WRONG!

   There is an optimal rate at which pollution can take place given the limited resources of our economy. RIGHT!

   Eliminating pollution involves some significant costs. Would it be practical to make sure that every cigarette butt on campus was picked up—even those that might have been flipped into the bushes? No, because the additional costs necessary to achieve a 100 percent pollution-free environment would exceed the additional benefits of doing so. We stop short of that 100 percent pollution-free level—at the point where the marginal social benefits equal the marginal social costs. It would be inefficient to do otherwise.

2. If business firms have a social conscience, they won't pollute. WRONG!

   Even if business firms have a social conscience, there will still be pollution. RIGHT!

   Firms produce goods and services to make profits. In so doing, they serve the rest of society by providing the goods and services society wants and jobs for millions of workers in the process. To avoid polluting, the firms would have to raise their own costs beyond what society could support, and firms would close down or never exist.

# •ANSWERS•

## Using Key Terms
### Across
1. emission charge
5. government failure
9. opportunity cost
10. externalities

### Down
2. optimal rate of pollution
3. social costs
4. production decision
6. efficiency decision
7. market failure
8. private costs

## True or False

1.     T
2.     F    Pollution is the result of the rational responses of producers to market incentives (i.e. private costs).
3.     T
4.     T
5.     T
6.     F    Market incentives are typically more efficient than direct government regulation.
7.     F    Pollution permits rely on market incentives.
8.     F    The optimal rate of pollution is attained when marginal benefits are equal to marginal costs.
9.     F    Pollution also occurs as a result of government failure when government planners place a low priority on environmental quality.
10.    F    It is an indication of both market and government failure.

## Multiple Choice

| | | | | |
|---|---|---|---|---|
| 1. b | 5. a | 9. d | 13. a | 17. b |
| 2. b | 6. c | 10. a | 14. b | 18. c |
| 3. c | 7. d | 11. b | 15. c | 19. c |
| 4. a | 8. d | 12. b | 16. b | 20. b |

# Problems and Applications

## *Exercise 1*

1. See Table 13.1 Answer, column 3.

**Table 13.1 Answer**

| Quantity of pollution | (3) Marginal benefits | (5) Marginal cost |
|---|---|---|
| 6 | $ --- | $ --- |
| 5 | 40 | 5 |
| 4 | 30 | 10 |
| 3 | 25 | 15 |
| 2 | 20 | 20 |
| 1 | 15 | 50 |
| 0 | 10 | 180 |

2. See Table 13.1 Answer, column 5.
3. Yes, because the marginal benefits are worth $40,000 annually, while the marginal costs are only $5,000 annually.
4. b
5. yes
6. when pollution has been reduced to 2 parts per 100 cubic feet of water annually.
7. c

## *Exercise 2*

1. See Figure 13.1 Answer, diagram *b*, line $S_1$.

**Figure 13.1 Answer**

2. See Figure 13.1 Answer, diagram *a*, line $S_1$.

3. d    4. b    5. d    6. a    7. d

# Exercise 3

1. **Table 13.2 Answer**

| Production rate | Private marginal cost | Social marginal cost |
|---|---|---|
| 0 | $ --- | $ --- |
| 1 | 40 | 80 |
| 2 | 50 | 90 |
| 3 | 60 | 100 |
| 4 | 70 | 110 |
| 5 | 80 | 120 |
| 6 | 90 | 130 |
| 7 | 100 | 140 |
| 8 | 110 | 150 |
| 9 | 120 | 160 |
| 10 | 130 | 170 |
| 11 | 140 | 180 |
| 12 | 150 | 190 |

2. **Figure 13.2 Answer**

3. d          4. b          5. b

# Exercise 4

1. Large particles, small particles, gases.

2. ". . . this form of pollution is killing citizens even in areas that meet Environmental Protection Agency air quality standards. . ."

3. By estimating the probability of premature death due to breathing polluted air.

4. ". . . run a risk of premature death about one sixth as great as if they'd been smoking for 25 years."

5. upward

CHAPTER 14
# The Farm Problem

## Quick Review

This chapter discusses the "farm problem." Even the title indicates the need for a solution. The federal government has been working on the problem since the 1930s and the programs they've put in place now cost taxpayers upwards of $15 billion annually. Many voters view this crazy quilt of policies as a good example of government failure! The questions that arise in examining the problem are:

- Why are farm prices and profits so unstable?
- Why has the farm sector shrunk so much?
- How do government farm programs affect farm output, prices, and income?

In answer to the first question, farming has always been an uncertain occupation at best, and there have been many farm depressions. The farm depression of the early 1980s was the worst on record. Real farm income was actually lower in 1983 than in 1933! The problems now seem more deep-seated and intractable than before, and the impact of changes taking place will be felt for a long, long time. Some go so far as to say that traditional farming is dead.

On the supply side there have always been the forces of nature to deal with. Sudden droughts, freezes, or blights have always raised havoc with supply. On the demand side, both price and income elasticities are perverse. A low income elasticity (low sensitivity of the demand for agricultural goods to changes in income) causes domestic demand to grow slowly. Political considerations have prevented the expansion of export markets, and the period in which the dollar was strong only made exporting more difficult.

As if this weren't enough, tremendous productivity advances, which would be welcome in most other markets, have resulted in much lower prices and farm incomes because the price elasticity of market demand is low (low sensitivity of the quantity demanded of agricultural goods to changes in price). In addition, the producers in this competitive market are beset by the same problems that hampered firms in many other sectors and brought even giant firms to their knees. Farming is now dominated by huge farms, which must contend with foreign competition, high interest rates, and unanticipated fluctuations in the prices of other inputs. The results have been falling land prices, a continuous decline of the farm population, farms lost, and the destruction of a way of life.

Well-intentioned government policy has produced perverse results. The price-support programs encourage production of products already in surplus, raise prices to consumers, and distort the allocation of resources. Direct income-support programs seem to provide more income to those who need it least and set-aside programs pay people for not producing. Deficiency payments encouraged farmers to subdivide their farms to circumvent a provision which limited the payment to $50,000 for a single farm. The dairy termination program reduced the size of the dairy herd, and the price of dairy products rose. Nothing seems to work well.

Farmers say they want parity, not charity, and continue to call for price supports to reestablish the *relative* purchasing power that farm commodities commanded some seventy years ago. The Reagan administration moved in the opposite direction with the Farm Security Act of 1985 arguing that farmers must be made more responsive to market forces. For example, supporting dairy prices at artificially high levels and then giving away the surplus strikes many as government run amok once again. Subsequent legislation continued the inexorable trend.

Farm-support legislation must be renewed every five years, and the 1990 legislation took additional steps to free farmers from government target prices and selling (rather than accumulating) surpluses. The 1995 legislation, entitled the "Freedom to Farm Act," established a gradual phase-out of support prices and set-asides for major commodities. As a result of the Asian crisis farm prices fell in 1997 and 1998 and farmers demanded more federal aid.

## Learning Objectives

After reading Chapter 14 and doing the following exercises, you should:

1. Know the dimensions and nature of the farm problem.
2. Understand the role of income and price elasticities in the farm problem.
3. Be able to relate the farm problem to forces on both the supply side and demand side of the market.
4. Understand the impact of supply- and demand-induced changes in prices of inputs on farm decision-making and profits.
5. Be able to describe several types of farm policies and their effects on the farming economy.
6. Be able to describe the causes and dimensions of the two great farm depressions.
7. Understand the direction and rationale of the Freedom to Farm Act of 1995.

## Using Key Terms

Fill in the puzzle on the opposite page with the appropriate term from the list of Key Terms at the end of the chapter in the text.

### *Across*

1. Income transfer paid to farmers for the difference between target and market prices.
3. Total revenue minus total economic costs.
7. Percentage change in quantity demanded divided by the percentage change in price.
10. The ability to change the market price of a good or service.
11. The implicit price paid by the government for surplus crops taken as collateral.
12. Land withdrawn from farm production in an effort to increase crop prices.

### *Down*

2. Percentage change in quantity demanded divided by percentage change in income.
4. The relative price of farm products from 1910-1914.
5. An incentive to engage in undesirable behavior.
6. Obstacles that make it difficult or impossible for new producers to enter a market.
8. Equal to $q_2$ minus $q_D$ at a price of $p_f$ in Figure 14.4 in the text.
9. Total revenue minus total cost.

# Puzzle 14.1

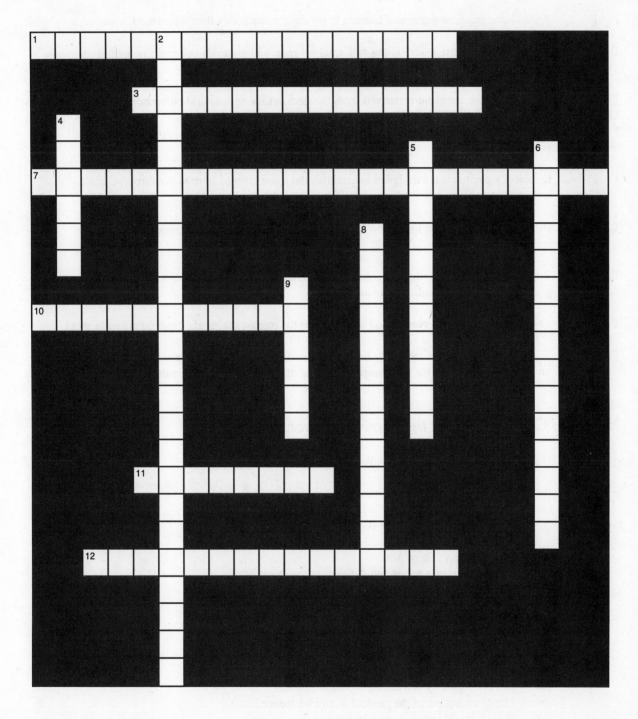

## True or False: *Circle your choice and explain why any false statements are incorrect.*

T  F  1.  Because there are 2 million farms in the U.S., individual farmers have some market power.

T  F  2.  Agricultural price-supports lead farmers to produce more goods than consumers want.

T  F  3.  When prices for farm commodities fall, total revenue will go down because the market demand for farm commodities is price inelastic.

T  F  4.  The demand for farmland is derived from the demand for agricultural commodities.

T  F  5.  Price supports have lowered the price of farm products, increased consumption, and reduced production.

T  F  6.  Deficiency payments are designed to establish the same ratio of farm to nonfarm income as would parity prices.

T  F  7.  Direct income payments to farmers are less efficient at raising farm incomes than are price-support programs.

T  F  8.  When a large crop is produced by American farmers, farmers receive higher incomes because the price elasticity for agricultural products is low.

T  F  9.  The intent of the 1996 Freedom to Farm Act was to increase the level of federal aid to farmers.

T  F  10.  When the government continually bails out farmers during economic crises, rather than relying on the farmers themselves to manage their risks, the government has created a "moral hazard."

## Multiple Choice: *Select the correct answer.*

_____  1.  If an agricultural market is perfectly competitive, then:
  (a)  A farmer is a price taker.
  (b)  A farmer uses price discrimination.
  (c)  The market demand curve is perfectly elastic.
  (d)  Each firm's demand curve is perfectly inelastic.

_____  2.  The 1996 Freedom to Farm Act:
  (a)  Eliminated target prices and deficiency payments.
  (b)  Focused on stabilizing farm incomes rather than farm prices.
  (c)  Eliminated many restrictions on acreage set-asides.
  (d)  All of the above.

_____  3.  Which of the following would result from a price-support program when the support price is set above the equilibrium price?
  (a)  The price paid by consumers would be higher.
  (b)  The consumption of the product would be reduced.
  (c)  Output would increase, *ceteris paribus*.
  (d)  All of the above would result.

4. When government subsidizes the purchase of irrigation water by farmers, the result is:
   (a) Higher marginal costs of production.
   (b) Lower fixed costs to farmers.
   (c) Increased output because marginal costs are lower.
   (d) Higher fixed costs to farmers.

5. Which of the following programs will raise farm incomes without generating market distortions?
   (a) Set-aside programs.
   (b) Direct income-support programs.
   (c) Import restrictions.
   (d) All of the above.

6. The primary intent of the 1996 Freedom to Farm Act was to:
   (a) Make farmers more dependent on market forces.
   (b) Increase prices paid to farmers.
   (c) Increase set-aside acreage.
   (d) All of the above.

7. Which of the following is consistent with farming as a competitive market?
   (a) A small number of firms.
   (b) Marginal revenue lower than price for each firm.
   (c) Exit of small firms when profits are high for large firms.
   (d) Zero economic profit in the long run.

8. When effective price floors are set for an agricultural market:
   (a) Quantity demanded will be less than the equilibrium quantity, and price will be greater than the equilibrium price.
   (b) Quantity demanded will be less than the equilibrium quantity, and price will be less than the equilibrium price.
   (c) Quantity demanded will be greater than the equilibrium quantity, and price will be greater than the equilibrium price.
   (d) Quantity demanded will be greater than the equilibrium quantity, and price will be less than the equilibrium price.

9. The surplus induced by farm price-support programs can be eliminated by all of the following *except*:
   (a) Export sales.
   (b) Reduced demand.
   (c) Government purchases and stockpiling.
   (d) Supply restrictions.

10. What impact did the "Asian crisis" have on U.S. agriculture beginning in 1998?
    (a) Decreased farm exports to Asia.
    (b) A decrease in grain prices.
    (c) A decrease in employment in the U.S. farm equipment industry.
    (d) All of the above.

11. Which of the following is *not* generally a characteristic of agriculture?
    (a) Ease of entry and exit.
    (b) Market power.
    (c) Homogeneous products.
    (d) Artificial restraints on prices.

_____ 12. Individual farmers view the demand curve they face for agricultural commodities as very price elastic, and:
   (a) They are correct even though the market demand curve tends to be quite inelastic.
   (b) They are correct, and the market demand curve is quite elastic as well.
   (c) They are incorrect because the market demand curve tends to be price inelastic.
   (d) They are incorrect because price and quantity demanded are inversely related in the product market.

_____ 13. Which of the following characterizes the price and income elasticities for farm products?
   (a) When prices fall, consumers respond by buying a great deal more; when income increases, consumers respond by buying less.
   (b) When prices and income fall, consumers respond by buying less.
   (c) When prices fall, farmers get less revenue; when income rises, consumers do not change purchases much.
   (d) All of the above are characteristic.

_____ 14. The government creates a "moral hazard" when it:
   (a) Encourages the type of behavior that leads to an undesirable allocation of resources.
   (b) Ignores the plight of a group suffering economic depravation, e.g. farmers during the third farm depression.
   (c) Passes laws it knows can't be enforced.
   (d) Doesn't provide the same level of moral leadership that it expects from U.S. citizens.

_____ 15. If the price of corn falls by 20 percent on world markets, causing American corn consumption to increase by 5 percent, _ceteris paribus_, the absolute value of the price elasticity of demand for corn in the United States would be:
   (a) 0.25.
   (b) 0.5.
   (c) 4.0.
   (d) 25.0.

_____ 16. The relationship between farm and nonfarm prices which existed during the period 1910 to 1914 has come to be known as:
   (a) The payment-in-kind program.
   (b) The farm parity price.
   (c) The target price.
   (d) Price supports.

_____ 17. A program of deficiency payments is best classified as a federal:
   (a) Price-support program.
   (b) Income-support program.
   (c) Farm cost subsidy.
   (d) Acreage set-aside.

_____ 18. If the market price of wheat is below the government's "loan rate":
   (a) The Commodity Credit Corporation lends the farmer an amount equal to the loan rate times the farmer's wheat output and takes the farmer's wheat crop as collateral.
   (b) The wheat farmer defaults on the loan but keeps the crop; the CCC keeps the money.
   (c) The wheat farmer, in effect, "buys" the crop from the CCC.
   (d) All of the above.

_____ 19. An advantage of set-aside programs over price-support programs is that they:
   (a) Reduce the price of agricultural goods.
   (b) Transfer more income to farmers.
   (c) Raise the price of agricultural production but do not lead to a surplus of output.
   (d) Affect the demand side as well as the supply side of the farm problem.

_____ 20. Which of the following agricultural programs reduces agricultural output, rather than increasing it?
   (a)   Direct income-support programs.
   (b)   Farm cost subsidies.
   (c)   Marketing orders.
   (d)   Export sales.

# Problems and Applications

## Exercise 1

This exercise shows the impact of farm subsidies on the market and consumers.

Figure 14.1 represents the agricultural market. Use this figure to answer questions 1-6.

## Figure 14.1

1. Without government intervention, the price of farm goods is determined by the intersection of
   _____.

2. The equilibrium price is _____ and farmers supply farm goods equal to _____.

3. Individual farmers are price (makers, takers) and will always produce the level of output where price equals _____.

4. Government price supports would (increase, decrease) the price of farm goods and cause price to move to _____.

5. At the new price farmers would supply farm goods equal to _____.

6. The price support caused a (shortage, surplus) of output in the agricultural market equal to the distance _____.

# Exercise 2

Articles about agriculture often provide information about shortages or surpluses. This exercise will use one of the articles in the textbook to show the kind of information to look for to determine whether shortages or surpluses exist.

Reread the In the News article entitled "EU Farm Subsidies." Then answer the following questions.

1. The article indicates there are:
   (a)  Shortages.
   (b)  Surpluses.

2. What passage in the article indicates the existence of the shortage or surplus? _____
   _____

3. Which diagram in Figure 14.3 best represents the shortage or surplus mentioned in the article?
   _____

## Figure 14.3
## Shortages or surpluses

4. What phrase indicates the impact of the farm subsidies on consumers? _____
   _____

# Common Errors

The first statement in each "common error" below is incorrect. Each incorrect statement is followed by a corrected version and an explanation.

1. Advances in farm productivity should be accompanied by improved profitability. WRONG!

   Competition translates improved productivity into lower prices, which can cause lower profitability. RIGHT!

   The spectacular increases in farm productivity that have occurred in the past decades have resulted in lower prices and lower incomes. Increases in supply coupled with price-inelastic and slow-growing demand have lowered rather than raised net farm income. Yet competition forces the adoption of the newest techniques of scientific farming.

2. When farmers have a bumper crop because of good weather, they will receive high incomes. WRONG!

   When farmers have a bumper crop, their income is likely to fall to low levels. RIGHT!

Because the demand for farm goods is price inelastic, a large percentage increase in output will cause an even larger percentage reduction in price.

# •ANSWERS•

## Using Key Terms
### Across
1. deficiency payment
3. economic profit
7. price elasticity of demand
10. market power
11. loan rate
12. acreage set-aside

### Down
2. income elasticity of demand
4. parity
5. moral hazard
6. barriers to entry
8. market surplus
9. profit

## True or False

1. F The fact that there are so many farmers in the U.S. means that individual farmers have no market power.
2. T
3. T
4. T
5. F Price supports have raised the price of farm products, reduced consumption, and encouraged production.
6. F Deficiency payments are payments made to farmers to make up the difference between target and market prices. Target prices may or may not be designed to reach parity.
7. F Direct income payments are more efficient because they do not cause market distortions, e.g. surpluses.
8. T
9. F The primary intent of the 1996 Freedom to Farm Act was to wean farmers away from federal aid, i.e. make farmers more dependent on market forces.
10. T

## Multiple Choice

| | | | | | | | | |
|---|---|---|---|---|---|---|---|
| 1. a | 5. b | 9. b | 13. c | 17. b |
| 2. d | 6. a | 10. d | 14. a | 18. a |
| 3. d | 7. d | 11. b | 15. a | 19. c |
| 4. c | 8. a | 12. a | 16. b | 20. c |

# Problems and Applications

## Exercise 1

1. market supply and market demand
2. $P_1$, $Q_1$
3. takers, MC
4. increase, $P_2$
5. $Q_3$
6. surplus, $Q_3$-$Q_2$

## Exercise 2

1. b
2. The article says, ". . . governments also agree to purchase any surplus production."
3. diagram b (surplus)
4. "All this protection costs the average EU consumer over $200 a year."

# CHAPTER 15

# The Labor Market

## Quick Review

Most of us do not think of ourselves in the abstract as "inputs," or factors of production, but in the language of the circular flow of economic activity, that's what we are. In the circular-flow model there are markets for products and markets for factors of production. People are demanders in the product market but suppliers in the factor market. This chapter discusses the supply side of that market first and then looks at the demand side. It considers these questions:

- How do people decide how much time to spend working?
- What determines the wage rate an employer is willing to pay?
- Why are some workers paid so much and others so little?

Let's begin with the first question. People choose between leisure and the satisfaction of material needs. Given the institutional structure of our economy, material needs are satisfied mainly by working for income. When we work, however, we sacrifice leisure. Hence, the opportunity cost of goods and services obtained by working is the number of hours of leisure that must be sacrificed to earn the required income. Conversely, the opportunity cost of leisure is the amount of goods and services that cannot be bought because of the time not spent working. Psychological and social needs may also motivate people to work. These needs affect the utility of both leisure and the income gained from work.

The marginal utility of labor reflects the satisfaction to be gained from added income as well as any direct pleasure a job may provide. A worker compares the marginal utility of labor with that of leisure and chooses either more labor or more leisure, depending on which offers greater marginal utility.

The supply curve of labor reflects the tradeoff between material needs and leisure. People feel two conflicting emotions when they receive an increase in their wage. The substitution effect makes a person want to work more. (An hour of work is worth more in terms of goods and services that can be obtained; the opportunity cost of leisure has risen.) The income effect diminishes the need to work. (The same quantity of goods and services can be obtained with less labor after the wage increase.)

Usually these two effects result in an upward-sloping supply curve for labor; a wage increase encourages a person to work more hours. But if a person dislikes work or feels enough of his or her needs are already met, a higher wage may result in fewer hours worked, so that his or her supply curve bends backward. In this case the income effect overpowers the substitution effect.

The demand for labor depends on the demand for the goods that labor produces. The demand for labor is thus a derived demand; the marginal revenue product curve is a derived demand curve. It shows the additional revenue generated by an additional unit of labor. An employer will not want to pay a worker more than the extra revenue that the worker creates. Hence, the marginal revenue product curve sets an upper limit to wages.

The more labor a business employs, the less revenue each additional unit of labor brings to the firm.

This reflects the law of diminishing returns: employing more workers in a given firm implies that each worker has less plant and equipment with which to work. As a result, each worker's marginal product declines as more workers are hired. The other factors of production also experience diminishing returns.

The interaction of market demand and market supply determines the equilibrium market wage. When either the market supply or market demand curve shifts as a result of changes in its nonprice determinants, surpluses or shortages may result. The labor market adjusts just as a product market does. Shortages lead to wage increases; surpluses, to wage decreases.

Firms choose among factors on the basis of the increase in product that each extra factor generates for the input price. A profit-maximizing producer will always choose the most cost-efficient input, that is, the one with the highest ratio of marginal product to factor price (not necessarily the factor with the lowest price).

The marginal revenue product (*MRP*) is not the only means by which wage rates are determined, however. Wage rates also reflect market power, custom, discrimination, and the opportunity wage. In cases where *MRP* is difficult to measure, such as the salary of a CEO, the opportunity wage is used.

## Learning Objectives

After reading Chapter 15 and doing the following exercises, you should:

1. Understand the labor-supply curve and its nonprice determinants.
2. Be able to apply the law of diminishing marginal utility to the labor market.
3. Know how people determine the number of hours they want to work.
4. Be able to explain the shape of the labor-supply curve using the income and substitution effects of wages.
5. Know how to calculate the elasticity of the market supply of labor.
6. Understand why the demand for factors of production is derived from the demand for goods and services.
7. Be able to derive the marginal revenue product curve and know why it slopes downward.
8. Understand how market supply and market demand interact to determine market wage rates when their nonprice determinants change.
9. Understand cost efficiency and how the efficiency decision is made.
10. Know that the "opportunity wage" reflects a worker's productivity in his or her best alternative employment, *ceteris paribus*.

## Using Key Terms

Fill in the puzzle on the opposite page with the appropriate term from the list of Key Terms at the end of the chapter in the text.

### *Across*
1. The choice of a production process for any given rate of output.
7. Determined by the intersection of the market supply and market demand for labor.
13. The percentage change in quantity of labor supplied divided by the percentage change in wage rate.
14. The willingness and ability to work specific amounts of time at alternative wage rates.
15. A specific combination of resources used to produce a good or service.

### *Down*
2. The quantity of resources purchased by a firm depends on the firm's expected sales and output.
3. An increased wage rate causes people to work more hours.
4. The MPP of labor declines as the quantity of labor employed increases.
5. The change in total output because of one additional unit of input.
6. An increased wage rate allows people to reduce the hours worked without losing income.
8. The change in total revenue because of one additional unit of input.

9.    The total quantity of labor that workers are willing and able to supply at alternative wage rates.
10.    The MPP of an input divided by its price.
11.    The highest wage an individual would earn in his or her best alternative job.
12.    The quantity of labor employers are willing and able to hire at alternative wage rates.

# Puzzle 15.1

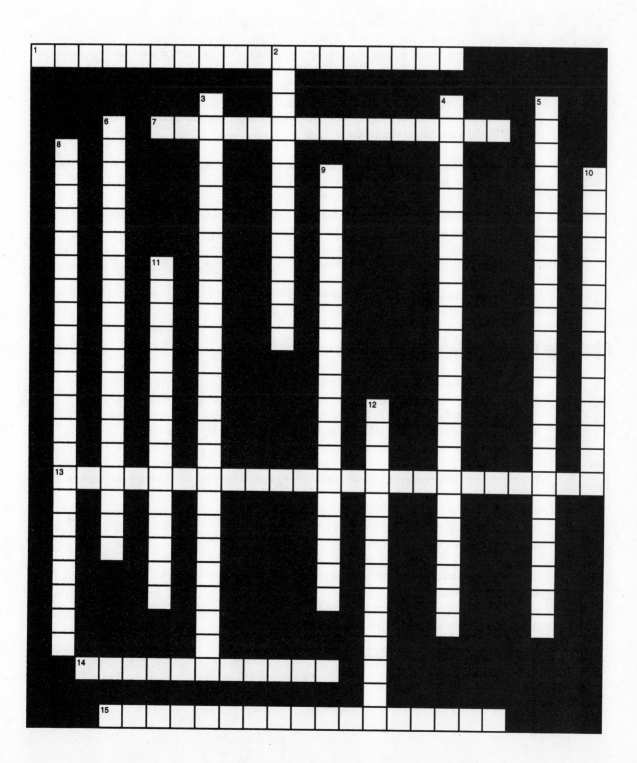

# True or False: *Circle your choice and explain why any false statements are incorrect.*

T   F   1.   The supply curve for labor bends backward when the income effect of wages exceeds the substitution effect of wages.

T   F   2.   The intersection of the labor market supply and market demand curves establishes the minimum wage.

T   F   3.   For wages to be higher without sacrificing jobs, productivity must decrease.

T   F   4.   The highest wage a firm is willing to pay labor is determined by the marginal revenue product.

T   F   5.   The value of additional income decreases as total income increases.

T   F   6.   The demand for labor is downward sloping because the larger the quantities of workers hired the less qualified the additional workers are.

T   F   7.   The concept of derived demand means that the demand for bricklayers, for example, is determined by the demand for new brick houses.

T   F   8.   The law of diminishing returns suggests that the fewer the number of workers employed, the more total output they can produce in a given time period, *ceteris paribus.*

T   F   9.   The marginal physical product curve is the labor-demand curve.

T   F   10.  If salary caps were placed on CEO wages below their opportunity wage, there would be a shortage of CEOs.

# Multiple Choice: *Select the correct answer.*

_____   1.   The number of hours that a worker is willing to work is determined by the trade-off between:
  (a)   Increasing marginal utility for income and decreasing marginal utility for leisure.
  (b)   Increasing marginal utility for leisure and decreasing marginal utility for income.
  (c)   Increasing total utility for leisure and decreasing total utility for income.
  (d)   Increasing marginal utility for both income and leisure.

_____   2.   The constraint that is *most* important in determining the tradeoff between leisure and work is:
  (a)   Income.
  (b)   Time.
  (c)   Available goods and services.
  (d)   Satisfaction from working.

_____   3.   If consumers wanted to increase wages and the number of jobs available for apple pickers, the best strategy would be to:
  (a)   Insist that the government establish a minimum wage for apple pickers.
  (b)   Boycott apples until wages increased.
  (c)   Buy more apples.
  (d)   Insist that the sellers raise the price of apples.

_____ 4. An upward-sloping labor-supply curve illustrates, *ceteris paribus*, that:
    (a)    The supply of labor and the wage rate are inversely related.
    (b)    The quantity supplied of labor and the hours of work per week are directly related.
    (c)    The quantity supplied of labor and the hours of work per week are inversely related.
    (d)    A greater quantity of labor would be supplied at higher wage rates.

_____ 5. The elasticity of labor supply does *not* depend on:
    (a)    The demand for labor.
    (b)    Income and wealth.
    (c)    The prices of consumer goods.
    (d)    Expectations for income or consumption.

_____ 6. A competitive firm should continue to hire workers until:
    (a)    The MRP is equal to demand.
    (b)    The MPP is equal to the number of workers hired.
    (c)    The MRP is equal to the market wage rate.
    (d)    The MRP is equal to zero.

_____ 7. Shifts of the labor-supply curve are caused by:
    (a)    Changes in tastes for jobs.
    (b)    Wage increases.
    (c)    Changes in the number of job vacancies.
    (d)    All of the above.

_____ 8. Which of the following policies is consistent with surpluses of labor in the labor market?
    (a)    Price supports in the product market.
    (b)    Minimum-wage legislation.
    (c)    Wage controls (ceilings).
    (d)    All of the above.

_____ 9. Which of the following helps explain why the wages received by two workers with different jobs are not the same?
    (a)    Differences in marginal revenue products at their respective jobs.
    (b)    The opportunity wages of the two workers differ.
    (c)    The prices of the products they produce differ.
    (d)    All of the above may contribute to the difference.

_____ 10. Which of the following is true about the equilibrium market wage?
    (a)    All workers are satisfied with the wage.
    (b)    All employers are satisfied with the wage.
    (c)    There is no unemployment in this market at the equilibrium wage.
    (d)    All of the above are correct.

_____ 11. At the market equilibrium wage:
    (a)    $MRP$ = wage rate.
    (b)    The ratio of the $MPP$ of each factor to the factor's price is the same for all factors.
    (c)    The market demand curve for labor intersects the market supply curve of labor.
    (d)    All of the above.

_____ 12. The cost efficiency of labor is equal to:
    (a)    The marginal cost of output.
    (b)    The $MPP$ of labor times the wage rate.
    (c)    The $MPP$ of labor divided by the wage rate.
    (d)    The $MRP$ of labor divided by the unit price of labor.

_____ 13. In order to calculate marginal revenue product, we need to know:
   (a)   The change in total output and the change in quantity of labor.
   (b)   The marginal physical product and the unit price of the factor.
   (c)   The marginal revenue and the amount of the product produced.
   (d)   The marginal revenue and the cost of the factor.

_____ 14. The diminishing returns to a factor may be due to:
   (a)   The declining utility of a good as we consume more of it.
   (b)   Crowding or overuse of other factors as production is increased.
   (c)   The decline in the demand curve for a product.
   (d)   The decline in the marginal revenue curve for a product.

_____ 15. The efficiency decision involves choosing the input combination or process:
   (a)   Which produces the greatest output.
   (b)   Which results in the lowest output per dollar of input.
   (c)   Which results in the greatest output for a given cost.
   (d)   Which has the lowest ratio of _MPP_ to input.

_____ 16. The marginal revenue product curve and marginal physical product curve have similar shapes:
   (a)   Because marginal revenue product depends on marginal physical product.
   (b)   Because the product demand curve slopes downward in accordance with the law of diminishing returns.
   (c)   Because the law of demand and the law of diminishing returns are due to the same economic behavior.
   (d)   For all of the above reasons.

_____ 17. Employment will definitely rise when:
   (a)   Productivity and wages rise.
   (b)   Productivity rises and wages fall.
   (c)   Productivity falls and wages rise.
   (d)   Productivity and wages fall.

_____ 18. A change in wages causes a:
   (a)   Shift in the marginal revenue product curve for labor.
   (b)   Shift in the marginal physical product curve for labor.
   (c)   Shift in the derived demand curve for labor.
   (d)   Movement along the labor-demand curve.

_____ 19. When the minimum wage is raised in a competitive market, ceteris paribus,:
   (a)   All workers are better off.
   (b)   All workers are worse off.
   (c)   Some workers are better off and some are worse off.
   (d)   Workers are not affected by a minimum wage increase, only by decreases.

_____ 20. "Opportunity wage" is defined as:
   (a)   The highest wage an individual would earn in his or her best alternative employment.
   (b)   The value of goods or services that an individual can purchase with the income earned by working 1 hour.
   (c)   The income equivalent of a volunteer worker.
   (d)   The income a worker loses when he or she quits a job.

# Problems and Applications

## Exercise 1

This exercise shows how to determine the supply of labor. It provides practice in graphing labor supply and examines backward-bending supply curves, the substitution effect, and the income effect.

Suppose you came to school without any means of support and your advisor suggests that you take a job at the school. Your only task is to correct true-false examinations (the professors give you all of the answers to the exams), add up the scores, and calculate each student's grade. You can work as many hours as you wish because opportunities are plentiful.

*Drawing Labor-Supply Curves*

If the work were offered to you on a volunteer basis, you would not work at all. But at $2 an hour you might work 1 hour per day—just to see how well your classmates are doing. Only at $4 an hour would it be worthwhile to work many hours—perhaps 4 hours per day. At $8 an hour you would work 6 hours per day and at $16 an hour you would make it a full-time job of 8 hours per day. But at $32 an hour you would decide to spend more time at leisure and work only 6 hours per day.

1.  Fill in column 2 of Table 15.1, your labor-supply schedule, using the information in the paragraph above.

### Table 15.1
### Supply of labor

| (1) Hourly wage (dollars per hour) | (2) Work effort (hours worked per day) | (3) Elasticity of supply |
|---|---|---|
| $ 0 | _____ | — |
| 2 | _____ | _____ |
| 4 | _____ | _____ |
| 8 | _____ | _____ |
| 16 | _____ | _____ |
| 32 | _____ | _____ |

2.  Graph the labor-supply curve in Figure 15.1. First label the axes for the graph and then draw the curve and label it. (The curve should pass through point *A*.)

# Figure 15.1

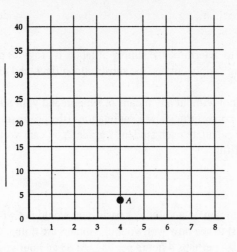

## *Backward-Bending Supply Curves*

3. On the backward-bending segment of a supply curve, wage and quantity supplied are:
   (a) Directly (positively) related.
   (b) Inversely related.
   (c) Related by a horizontal line.
   (d) Related by a vertical line.

4. Which of the following circumstances might explain a backward-bending supply curve such as the one you have drawn in Figure 15.1?
   (a) You want to make a certain amount of income, and you want to spend the rest of your time sleeping and watching videos.
   (b) Because of the increased income you receive from an increase in your wage, you can increase your leisure without losing any income.
   (c) The marginal utility of each extra dollar falls as income rises.
   (d) All of the above might explain such a curve.

## *Substitution and Income Effects*

5. An increase in wage rates:
   (a) Definitely increases hours worked through both the substitution and income effects.
   (b) Tends to increase hours worked through the substitution effect but may tend to decrease hours worked through the income effect.
   (c) Tends to increase hours worked through the substitution effect but definitely decreases hours worked through the income effect.
   (d) Tends to decrease hours worked through the substitution effect and may increase hours worked through the income effect.

6. On the backward-bending portion of the supply curve:
   (a) The income effect is greater than the substitution effect.
   (b) The substitution effect overpowers the income effect.
   (c) Both effects tend to decrease the quantity of labor supplied as a result of a wage increase.

7. In column 3 of Table 15.1, compute the elasticity of supply between each successive wage rate. Use the midpoint formula from the text.

# Exercise 2

This exercise illustrates the relationship between marginal physical product and marginal revenue product for a company producing bottled water.

1. T   F   The marginal physical product (MPP) measures the change in total output that occurs when one additional worker is hired.

2. Which of the following formulas would provide a correct calculation of the marginal physical product?
   (a) Quantity / labor
   (b) Change in quantity /labor
   (c) Change in quantity / change in labor
   (d) Change in total revenue /change in labor

3. Calculate total revenue, marginal revenue product, and marginal physical product for Table 15.2.

## Table 15.2.   Marginal physical product and marginal revenue product

| (1)<br>Labor<br>(workers<br>per hour) | (2)<br>Quantity<br>produced<br>(gallons<br>per hour) | (3)<br>Price<br>(dollars<br>per gallon) | (4)<br>Total revenue<br>(dollars per<br>hour) | (5)<br>Marginal<br>revenue<br>product<br>(dollars<br>per worker) | (6)<br>Marginal<br>physical<br>product<br>(gallons<br>per worker) |
|---|---|---|---|---|---|
| 0 | 0 | $1 | _____ | _____ | _____ |
| 1 | 15 | 1 | _____ | _____ | _____ |
| 2 | 27 | 1 | _____ | _____ | _____ |
| 3 | 36 | 1 | _____ | _____ | _____ |
| 4 | 42 | 1 | _____ | _____ | _____ |
| 5 | 45 | 1 | _____ | _____ | _____ |
| 6 | 46 | 1 | _____ | _____ | _____ |

_____ 4. The law of diminishing returns implies that:
   (a) The marginal revenue declines as additional labor is employed in a given production process.
   (b) The marginal revenue product declines as additional labor is employed in a given production process.
   (c) The marginal physical product of labor increases as additional labor is employed in a given production process.
   (d) None of the above.

5. T   F   There are diminishing returns to labor with increased production in Table 15.2.

# Exercise 3

This exercise provides experience in computing and graphing derived demand as well as determining the number of workers to hire.

1. You are the producer of a sports drink called EnerG, which sells for $1 per gallon. You have to pay $6 an hour for labor. Complete Table 15.3.

### Table 15.2  EnerG production, by labor hours

| (1)<br><br>Wage<br>(dollars<br>per hour) | (2)<br><br>Labor<br>(workers<br>per hour) | (3)<br>Quantity<br>produced<br>(gallons<br>per hour) | (4)<br>Price<br>(dollars<br>per<br>gallon) | (5)<br>Total<br>revenue<br>(dollars<br>per<br>gallon) | (6)<br>Marginal<br>revenue<br>product<br>(dollars<br>per worker) |
|---|---|---|---|---|---|
| 6 | 0 | 0 | $1 | $_____ | $_____ |
| 6 | 1 | 15 | 1 | _____ | _____ |
| 6 | 2 | 27 | 1 | _____ | _____ |
| 6 | 3 | 36 | 1 | _____ | _____ |
| 6 | 4 | 42 | 1 | _____ | _____ |
| 6 | 5 | 45 | 1 | _____ | _____ |
| 6 | 6 | 46 | 1 | _____ | _____ |

2. T   F   The demand curve for EnerG workers is found by plotting the marginal revenue product curve.

3. In Figure 15.2 draw the demand curve for labor from Table 15.3. Label it demand or MRP.

### Figure 15.2

4.  Draw a straight line at a wage of $6 in Figure 15.2 and label it wage rate.

5.  How many workers are you willing to hire to produce EnerG?
    (a)  0.
    (b)  1.
    (c)  2.
    (d)  3.
    (e)  4.
    (f)  5.
    (g)  6.

6.  How much EnerG will be produced per hour? _____

## Exercise 4

This exercise examines the impact of a minimum wage on a labor market.

### Figure 15.3

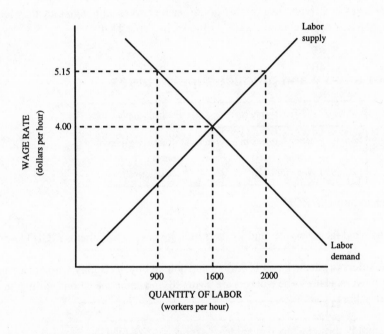

1.  Figure 15.3 shows the labor market for unskilled workers. The equilibrium wage rate occurs at _____ per hour and at a quantity of _____ workers.

2.  Now assume that the minimum wage is set at $5.15 per hour. The result of this government intervention is to create a (shortage, surplus) of labor.

3.  At the new minimum wage _____ workers keep their jobs and _____ workers lose their jobs.

4.  According to the article in the text titled "Clinton Wants Minimum Wage Up $1 by 2000", why does Clinton believe a minimum wage is important? _____

5.  An increase in labor productivity in Figure 15.3 would cause the labor (supply, demand) curve to shift to the (left, right).

221

# Common Errors

The first statement in each "common error" below is incorrect. Each incorrect statement is followed by a corrected version and an explanation.

1. People work because they have to. WRONG!

   Generally, people work in order to buy the goods and services they want. RIGHT!

   People have flexibility in choosing the conditions under which they will work. What they *choose* to do reflects their utility of leisure compared with their utility of the goods and services they can buy with their income from work. If their needs for goods were satisfied, they might not work at all.

2. The labor-supply curve is the same as the supply curve of the products that labor produces. WRONG!

   The labor-supply curve is a supply curve in a factor market, whereas a product supply curve applies to a product market. RIGHT!

   Supply curves in different markets are not the same curves, although they may look the same. The chief difference is found on the axes, as shown in Table 15.4.

## Table 15.4
## Axes of labor-supply and product-supply curves

| Axis | Labor-supply curve | Product supply curve |
|------|--------------------|-----------------------|
| *x*-axis | Labor services in a given time period | Output in a given time period |
| *y*-axis | Wage for labor | Price of a product |

3. Workers demand jobs. WRONG!

   Employers demand labor services and workers (employees) supply them. RIGHT!

   Demand refers to what a buyer is willing and able to buy. Certainly workers are not seeking to pay their employers. Rather, the workers are trying to find someone who is willing and able to pay them for their labor.

4. Employers employ those factors that are least expensive. WRONG!

   Employers want to employ those factors that are most cost-effective. RIGHT!

   If a factor is cheap, there may be a reason for it. It may not last long, may not work correctly, or may require heavier use of other factors of production—for example, maintenance workers. The marginal productivity of the cheap factor may therefore be low. An apparently more expensive factor might perform its proper function well and even save on the costs of other factors. The marginal productivity of the more expensive input would more than make up for its higher cost. Businesses would choose the more expensive factor of production.

5. Marginal revenue product is the same as marginal revenue. WRONG!

   The marginal revenue product curve applies to the factor market, while the marginal revenue curve applies to the product market. RIGHT!

The formula for marginal revenue product is

$$\frac{\text{Change in total revenue}}{\text{Change in quantity of input}}$$

while that for marginal revenue is

$$\frac{\text{Change in total revenue}}{\text{Change in quantity of output}}$$

Marginal revenue shows changes in total revenue as a result of increased output and therefore is appropriate in analyzing what happens in the product market.

Marginal revenue product shows how total revenue changes as a result of the increased use of a factor and therefore is appropriate in analyzing what happens in the factor market. Both curves are derived from the demand curve in the product market. However, in order to find marginal revenue product, it is necessary also to know the relationship between the quantity of input and quantity of output. That is why the marginal physical product becomes important.

6. The law of diminishing returns means that average total costs will rise as a firm expands. WRONG!

The law of diminishing returns applies only to changes in the use of one factor while all others remain constant. RIGHT!

If a firm could expand all factors of production proportionately, there might be no decline in productivity at all, and thus no increase in average total cost. If the firm could do so without affecting factor prices, there would then be no change in unit costs either. The law of diminishing returns applies to changes of only one factor or group of factors, *ceteris paribus* (all other factors being held constant).

7. No one is hurt when companies are taxed except the companies themselves. WRONG!

Part of the burden of taxes on a company may fall on the factors of production that a company employs. RIGHT!

Remember that the demand for factors is derived from the product market. If the sales tax, for example, affects the demand curve for a product, it will affect the demand curve for the factors used to produce the product.

# •ANSWERS•

## Using Key Terms
### Across
1. efficiency decision
7. equilibrium wage
13. elasticity of labor supply
14. labor supply
15. production process

## Down

2. derived demand
3. substitution effect of wages
4. law of diminishing returns
5. marginal physical product
6. income effect of wages
8. marginal revenue product
9. market supply of labor
10. cost efficiency
11. opportunity wage
12. demand for labor

## True or False

1. T
2. F   The intersection of supply and demand establishes the equilibrium wage. The minimum wage is typically set above the equilibrium wage by the government.
3. F   For wages to be higher without sacrificing jobs the MPP must increase (or the price of the product must increase).
4. T
5. T
6. F   The demand for labor is downward sloping because of diminishing returns caused by the fact that the amount of capital and space available to each worker decreases.
7. T
8. F   When fewer workers are hired total output is typically lower. It is also usually true, however, that when fewer workers are hired the MPP of the last worker increases.
9. F   The MPP multiplied by the price of the product equals the MRP which is the labor-demand curve.
10. T

## Multiple Choice

| | | | | | | | | | |
|---|---|---|---|---|---|---|---|---|---|
| 1. | b | 5. | a | 9. | d | 13. | b | 17. | b |
| 2. | b | 6. | c | 10. | c | 14. | b | 18. | d |
| 3. | c | 7. | a | 11. | d | 15. | c | 19. | c |
| 4. | d | 8. | b | 12. | c | 16. | a | 20. | a |

## Problems and Applications

## Exercise 1

1. See Table 15.1 Answer, column 2.

**Table 15.1 Answer**

| (1) Hourly wage (dollars per hour) | (2) Work effort (hours worked per day) | (3) Elasticity of supply |
|---|---|---|
| $ 0 | 0 | --- |
| 2 | 1 | 1.0 |
| 4 | 4 | 1.8 |
| 8 | 6 | 0.6 |
| 16 | 8 | 0.429 |
| 32 | 6 | -0.429 |

2. **Figure 15.1 Answer**

3.  b        4.  d        5.  b        6.  a

7.  See Table 15.1 Answer, column 3. The formula for the elasticity of labor supply is

$$\frac{\text{Percentage change in quantity of labor supplied}}{\text{Percentage change in wage rate}}$$

The elasticity of labor supply can be estimated (just as the elasticity of demand was estimated) by using the following midpoint formula:

$$\frac{(L_2 - L_1) \div [1/2 \times (L_2 + L_1)]}{(W_2 - W_1) \div [1/2 \times (W_2 + W_1)]} = \frac{(6 - 8) \div [(1/2 \times (6 - 8)]}{(32 - 16) \div [(1/2 \times (32 - 16)]} = \frac{3}{7}$$

In the formula, $L_1$ is the amount of labor offered at the wage $W_1$ in period 1 and $L_2$ is the amount of labor offered at the wage $W_2$ in period 2. (*Note:* Elasticity is negative only on the backward-bending part of the supply curve.)

225

# Exercise 2

1. T
2. c
3. **Table 15.2 Answer**

| (1) Labor | (4) Total revenue | (5) Marginal revenue product | (6) Marginal physical product |
|---|---|---|---|
| 0 | ---- | ---- | ---- |
| 1 | $15 | $15 | 15 |
| 2 | 27 | 12 | 12 |
| 3 | 36 | 9 | 9 |
| 4 | 42 | 6 | 6 |
| 5 | 45 | 3 | 3 |
| 6 | 46 | 1 | 1 |

4. b
5. T

# Exercise 3

1. **Table 15.3 Answer**

| (2) Labor | (5) Total revenue | (6) Marginal revenue product |
|---|---|---|
| 0 | $ 0 | $ ---- |
| 1 | 15 | 15 |
| 2 | 27 | 12 |
| 3 | 36 | 9 |
| 4 | 42 | 6 |
| 5 | 45 | 3 |
| 6 | 46 | 1 |

2. T

3. **Figure 15.2 Answer**

4. See Figure 15.2 Answer
5. 4
6. 42

# Exercise 4

1. $4.00, 1600
2. surplus
3. 900, 700
4. ". . . to help families coming off welfare."
5. demand, right

# CHAPTER 16
# Labor Unions

## Quick Review

The outcomes in the labor market, including the wage rate and level of employment, can be distorted by market power on either the supply or demand side. This chapter investigates power in labor markets by looking first at labor unions and then at powerful employers. We examine the following:

- How do large and powerful employers affect market wages?
- How do labor unions alter wages and employment?
- What outcomes are possible from collective bargaining between management and unions?

Power in labor markets means the ability to influence wage rates. Where the labor market is segmented by geographical, occupational, or industrial boundaries, a very few firms or unions may have market power. In extreme cases, a single labor union may contract all of one type of labor and thus be a monopoly, or a single firm may be the only buyer in a particular market, thereby becoming a monopsonist.

Unions typically negotiate over a large number of objectives. The most important is usually the wage rate. But a union's power is based on its membership. If wages rise, the number of workers hired may decline (law of demand). Unions therefore tend to reduce the number of people they permit to be employed and to bargain for higher wages than they would seek if the labor market were competitive.

In a competitive labor market the market equates the supply of labor with the demand for labor to determine the equilibrium wage. However, unions may behave like monopolists. They may restrict employment so that supply and the marginal wage rate are equated. The marginal wage rate is the change in total wages that results from employment of an extra unit of labor. The union tries to negotiate a wage as far above this marginal wage rate as possible. If a firm has market power, it will try to keep wages down to the marginal wage rate.

The dilemma faced by firms that have market power is the opposite of the one confronting labor unions: the more labor an employer seeks, the higher the wages will have to be. And when wages are raised for any worker, they must be raised for everyone. The marginal factor cost is therefore higher than the market wage rate. The marginal factor cost is the change in total wage costs that results from the hiring of an extra unit of labor. It is the marginal factor cost, not the market wage rate (i.e., on the labor-supply curve), that a firm equates with marginal revenue product (found on the labor-demand curve). Like unions, monopsonists fail to employ the amount of labor that would be employed in a competitive labor market. Unlike unions, employers will try to pay *less* than the competitive wage. They will force the wage somewhere between the marginal revenue product of labor and the market wage rate.

In bilateral monopolies, where power exists on both sides of the labor market, unions and employers engage in collective bargaining to negotiate a final settlement. The ultimate settlement for wages and employment depends on the skill of the negotiators.

The percentage of workers in the U.S. economy who belong to a union has been declining for forty years and union power has thus waned as well. Two noticeable trends have emerged as a result. Old industrial unions are being supplanted by unions of service workers, especially in the public sector, and private sector unions have been merging to enhance their power.

Whether unions have been effective in achieving their goals is a question that must be addressed empirically. There is general agreement that unions have raised relative wages significantly. Labor's *share* of national income has also increased, but this is thought to be due largely to changes in the structure of the economy, not union power. Union work rules are thought to restrain *productivity growth*. If this is true, it certainly provides an incentive for firms to raise product prices if wage settlements exceed productivity improvements. Finally, even though the unionization ratio is significantly lower than it used to be, organized labor is still a potent political force.

## Learning Objectives

After reading Chapter 16 and doing the following exercises, you should:

1. Understand the characteristics that are used to define the boundaries of labor markets.
2. Be able to demonstrate the meaning of the equilibrium wage rate.
3. Be able to describe the various types of labor buyers and suppliers.
4. Be familiar with the history of labor unions and their role in the economy.
5. Be able to define, compute, and graph the marginal wage curve and the demand curve for labor.
6. Be able to determine the optimal level of employment from a union point of view.
7. Know how to measure union power using the unionization ratio.
8. Be able to define, compute, and graph the marginal factor cost of labor and the supply curve of labor.
9. Be able to describe the monopsonist's desired equilibrium.
10. Understand how wages are determined in a market characterized by bilateral monopoly.
11. Be able to discuss the impact of unions in the U.S. economy.

## Using Key Terms

Fill in the puzzle on the opposite page with the appropriate term from the list of Key Terms at the end of the chapter in the text.

### Across

2. The change in total wages paid because of a one unit increase in the quantity of labor employed.
5. A market with only one buyer and one seller.
10. The change in total costs because of a one unit increase in the quantity of a factor employed.
11. A workplace in which all workers must join the union within 30 days after being employed.
12. The willingness and ability to work specific amounts of time at alternative wage rates.

### Down

1. The quantity of labor employers are willing and able to hire at alternative wages.
2. The change in total revenue because of an additional unit of input.
3. Direct negotiations between employers and unions to determine labor market outcomes.
4. Output per unit of input.
6. The wage rate at which the quantity of labor supplied equals the quantity of labor demanded.
7. The percentage of the labor force belonging to a union.
8. The ability to alter the market price of a good or service.
9. A market in which there is only one buyer.

# Puzzle 16.1

# True or False: *Circle your choice and explain why any false statements are incorrect.*

T   F   1.   The equilibrium wage rate is the rate at which the quantity of labor demanded equals the quantity supplied.

T   F   2.   When determining the optimum level of employment, monopsonists will equate the marginal wage and the marginal revenue product.

T   F   3.   When determining the optimum level of employment, monopolists in the labor market will equate the marginal wage and the labor supply curve.

T   F   4.   The marginal wage curve lies below the labor-demand curve because all worker's wages are lowered when one more worker is hired.

T   F   5.   Unions do not need to control the labor supply in order to have market power.

T   F   6.   Wars have aided union development, whereas depressions tend to hurt the union movement.

T   F   7.   The U.S. unionization ratio is about one-half of the labor force.

T   F   8.   A monopsony employer seeks to establish a wage rate that is lower than competitive standards.

T   F   9.   The collective bargaining process results in prices above the marginal revenue product curve.

T   F   10.  Unions are thought to be responsible for the rise in labor's share of national income and the rise in relative wages for unionized workers.

## Multiple Choice: *Select the correct answer.*

_____   1.   Typical goals of a labor union in the United States include:
    (a)   Job security.
    (b)   Wages.
    (c)   Fringe benefits.
    (d)   All of the above.

_____   2.   The reason that a union may worry about having too many members is that:
    (a)   The union faces a downward-sloping marginal revenue product curve.
    (b)   It may be unable to control all of its members.
    (c)   It may not be able to reach optimal employment, at which the marginal labor cost curve intersects the demand curve.
    (d)   None of the above.

_____   3.   Total wages paid to labor are maximized when workers are hired up to the point where:
    (a)   The marginal wage is equal to the market wage.
    (b)   The demand for labor is equal to the marginal factor cost.
    (c)   The market wage equals the marginal factor cost.
    (d)   The marginal wage equals zero.

_____ 4. Unions must distinguish between the marginal wage and the market wage, but nonunion workers generally do not:
   (a) Because the demand curve for labor from the union point of view slopes downward.
   (b) Because for a nonunion worker who has no market power, the demand curve appears flat.
   (c) Because for a nonunion worker who has no market power, the demand curve is the same as the marginal wage curve.
   (d) For all of the above reasons.

_____ 5. From a union's perspective, the optimal level of employment is determined by the intersection of:
   (a) The labor-demand curve and the labor-supply curve.
   (b) The marginal wage curve and the labor-supply curve.
   (c) The labor-demand curve and the marginal wage curve.
   (d) The labor-demand curve and the marginal factor cost curve.

_____ 6. The unionization ratio represents the:
   (a) Percentage of the total labor force belonging to unions.
   (b) Market power of unions relative to the market power of nonunion labor.
   (c) Proportion of industries that are dominated by unions.
   (d) Annual percentage growth in the total number of unions.

_____ 7. To be successful in changing wage rates and employment conditions, labor unions need to have control over only:
   (a) Their own members.
   (b) The supply of labor to the market.
   (c) The *MRP* of employers.
   (d) The production decision of employers.

_____ 8. A craft union:
   (a) Exerts market power by controlling the supply of labor to a particular industry.
   (b) Exerts market power by controlling the supply of labor to a particular firm.
   (c) Is an organization of workers with a particular skill.
   (d) Is an organization of workers in a particular industry.

_____ 9. At a union-imposed level of employment:
   (a) Employment is lower than at the competitive equilibrium.
   (b) The marginal wage is negative.
   (c) Employment and wages are both at the maximum possible levels.
   (d) Employment would not be increased by reducing the wage rate.

_____ 10. A monopsonist must pay a higher wage rate to hire additional workers because:
   (a) As a single seller in the market, it has market power.
   (b) As a single buyer in the market, it faces an upward-sloping supply curve for labor.
   (c) As a single seller in the market, it does not have to compete with other firms for customers.
   (d) As a single buyer in the market, it faces a flat supply curve for labor.

_____ 11. The difference between a competitive labor market and a monopsonistic labor market is:
   (a) That the monopsony will attempt to charge a higher wage than will be charged in a competitive market, *ceteris paribus*.
   (b) That the monopsony will hire less labor than will be hired in a competitive market, *ceteris paribus*.
   (c) That the shape of the marginal revenue product curve of a monopsony will differ from that of a competitive market.
   (d) All of the above.

_____ 12. The marginal factor cost for labor is:
   (a)   The net cost to a monopsonist of hiring an additional unit of labor.
   (b)   The net gain to a monopolist seller of labor if an additional unit of labor is hired.
   (c)   The demand for labor.
   (d)   The supply of labor.

_____ 13. If the employers in a competitive labor market decided to collude, *ceteris paribus,* then most likely:
   (a)   Wages would rise and employment would fall.
   (b)   Wages would rise and employment would rise.
   (c)   Wages would fall and employment would fall.
   (d)   Wages would fall and employment would rise.

_____ 14. A profit-maximizing monopsonist will hire workers to the point where the marginal factor cost curve intersects the:
   (a)   Marginal wage curve.
   (b)   Equilibrium wage.
   (c)   Marginal revenue product curve.
   (d)   Labor-supply curve.

_____ 15. The buyer's profit-maximizing level of input use occurs at:
   (a)   Marginal wage = marginal factor cost.
   (b)   $MRP$ = marginal wage.
   (c)   Marginal wage = zero.
   (d)   $MRP$ = marginal factor cost.

_____ 16. A workplace that requires workers to become a member within thirty days of being hired by a firm is:
   (a)   A craft union.
   (b)   An industrial union.
   (c)   A union shop.
   (d)   The AFL-CIO.

_____ 17. Which of the following correctly assesses the impact of unions in the U.S. economy?
   (a)   Unions have been successful in raising both the relative wages and the absolute wages of their members.
   (b)   Union work rules have contributed to inflation because productivity increases have generally exceeded wage increases.
   (c)   The political power of unions has grown because the unionization ratio has grown at the same rate as the labor force.
   (d)   Unions have been successful at raising relative wages but not absolute wages.

_____ 18. The trend in the U.S. toward the merger of unions is driven by the labor movement's desire to:
   (a)   Increase representation.
   (b)   Increase financial support.
   (c)   Enhance their political power.
   (d)   All of the above.

_____ 19. In a bilateral monopoly, wages and employment are determined by:
   (a)   Negotiation.
   (b)   The intersection of market supply and demand.
   (c)   The intersection of marginal cost and marginal revenue product.
   (d)   The intersection of marginal wage and market demand.

_____ 20. Unions have had an adverse impact on the efficiency of U.S. firms by supporting which of the following types of legislation?
   (a)    Civil rights legislation.
   (b)    Tariffs and quotas.
   (c)    Health and education programs.
   (d)    All of the above.

# Problems and Applications

## Exercise 1

This exercise provides practice in calculating the marginal factor cost of labor (marginal wage) and the marginal revenue product of labor for a monopsony situation.

1.   Suppose the data in Table 16.1 represent the wages, number of workers, and the price that you face when producing different amounts of Roaring Ripple, a new soft drink. Complete Table 16.1.

### Table 16.1
### Labor market with variable wage

| (1) Labor (workers per hour) | (2) Wage (dollars per hour) | (3) Ripple (quarts per hour) | (4) Price (dollars per quart) | (5) TC (dollars per hour) (1) x (2) | (6) MFC (dollars per worker) (ΔTC/ΔL) | (7) TR (dollars per hour) (3) x (4) | (8) MRP (dollars per worker) (ΔTR/ΔL) |
|---|---|---|---|---|---|---|---|
| 0 | $1 | 0  | $1 | $ _____ | $ ___ | $ _____ | $ ___ |
| 1 | 2  | 15 | 1  | _____ | _____ | _____ | _____ |
| 2 | 7  | 27 | 1  | _____ | _____ | _____ | _____ |
| 3 | 9  | 36 | 1  | _____ | _____ | _____ | _____ |

2.   The amount of Roaring Ripple you will produce to maximize your profits is _____ ; the wage you will pay your workers is _____ ; the marginal cost of labor will be _____ ; the number of employees you will hire will be _____ .

3.   T    F    For each new worker you hire, you must raise wages for all of the workers together, which means that the marginal cost of labor is different from the supply curve of labor.

4.   T    F    The wage at which the marginal cost of labor curve intersects the marginal revenue product curve is the equilibrium wage rate.

# Exercise 2

The differences in labor goals are the focus of this exercise.

Suppose that the supply and demand schedules in Table 16.2 apply to a particular labor market.

## Table 16.2
## Labor supply and demand

| Wage rate (dollars per hour) | $14 | 13 | 12 | 11 | 10 | 9 | 8 | 7 | 6 | 5 |
|---|---|---|---|---|---|---|---|---|---|---|
| Quantity of labor demanded (workers per hour) | 0 | 1 | 2 | 3 | 4 | 5 | 6 | 7 | 8 | 9 |
| Total wage bill (dollars per hour) | — | — | — | — | — | — | — | — | — | — |
| Marginal wage (dollars per worker) | — | — | — | — | — | — | — | — | — | — |

| Wage rate (dollars per hour) | $3 | 4 | 5 | 6 | 7 |
|---|---|---|---|---|---|
| Quantity of labor supplied (workers per hour) | 1 | 3 | 5 | 7 | 9 |
| Total wage (dollars per hour) | — | — | — | — | — |
| Marginal factor cost (dollars per worker) | — | — | — | — | — |

## Figure 16.1

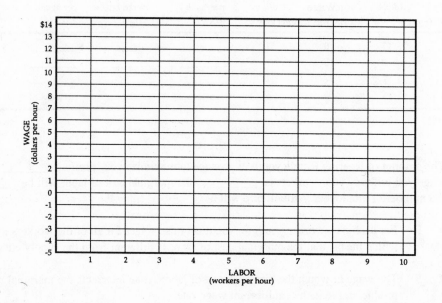

1. Compute the marginal wage and the marginal factor cost in the space provided in Table 16.2.

2. Graph labor demand, labor supply, marginal wage, and marginal factor cost curve in Figure 16.1.

3. The amount of labor hired in a competitive market would be _____ workers at a wage of _____ per hour.

4. The amount of labor that a union would want hired if it acted as a monopolist would be _____ workers at a wage of _____ per hour.

5. Suppose a union asks each member to contribute a certain percentage of income to the union. Therefore, when the wage bill is maximized the union maximizes the dues it receives. The amount of labor that would maximize union dues would be _____ workers at a wage of _____ per hour.

6. Suppose the union wishes to maximize the number of employees that it has so that it can become a political force at the ballot box. The maximum amount of labor that such a union would be able to recruit would be _____ workers at a wage of _____ per hour.

7. The amount of labor hired by a monopsonist would be _____ workers at a wage of _____ per hour.

Following are the names of the five types of labor market situations described in question 3-7:

        *A.*    Competition  (question 3)
        *B.*    Union monopolist  (question 4)
        *C.*    Union dues maximizer  (question 5)
        *D.*    Union vote maximizer  (question 6)
        *E.*    Monopsony  (question 7)

8. Label the wage-labor combination in Figure 31.1 corresponding to the letter of each of these types of labor markets.

9. Rank the above list of labor markets in order (highest to lowest) with respect to wage rates and then rank (lowest to highest) with respect to the total employment.  When there is a tie, place both types of market on the same line.

| | Wage | | Amount of labor |
|---|---|---|---|
| (rank) | (highest to lowest) | (rank) | (lowest to highest) |
| 1. _____ | | 1. _____ | |
| 2. _____ | | 2. _____ | |
| 3. _____ | | 3. _____ | |
| 4. _____ | | 4. _____ | |
| 5. _____ | | 5. _____ | |

10. T  F  Market power, regardless of whether it is possessed by the buyer or the supplier, results in output equal to or lower than in a competitive labor market.

11. T  F  Market power, regardless of whether it is possessed by the buyer or the supplier, results in wage rates higher than in a competitive labor market.

# Exercise 3

Reread the *In the News* article entitled "Free Agents In Sports: A Threat to Monopsony." Then answer the following questions.

1. Before 1976, team owners had _____ power in the labor market.

2. As players were allowed to become "free agents," player salaries (increased, decreased, did not change).

3. For a monopsonist, the marginal factor cost is (greater, less) than the wage rate because additional workers can be hired only if the wage rate for all workers (increases, decreases).

4. A monopsonist hires (more, fewer) workers at a (higher, lower) wage rate than would occur in a competitive market.

# Common Errors

The first statement in each "common error" below is incorrect. Each incorrect statement is followed by a corrected version and an explanation.

1. The marginal cost of labor curve is the same as the marginal cost curve, and therefore it is also the supply curve for a firm. WRONG!

   The marginal cost of labor curve is derived from the supply of labor and is applicable only to the labor market, not to the product market. RIGHT!

   The marginal cost of labor is given by the formula

   $$\frac{\text{Change in total wage cost}}{\text{Change in quantity of labor}}$$

   while the marginal cost curve is given by

   $$\frac{\text{Change in total wage cost}}{\text{Change in quantity of product}}$$

   While the marginal cost of labor applies only to labor costs in the labor market, the marginal cost curve applies to all costs in the product market.

2. In bilateral monopoly the optimal level of employment occurs where the marginal cost of labor curve intersects the marginal wage curve. WRONG!

   In bilateral monopoly, it is possible to determine the limits between which the labor employment and wage levels will fall but not the precise optimal levels. RIGHT!

   The buyer wishes to buy labor at the point where the marginal cost of labor curve intersects the labor-demand curve. Only through negotiation can a compromise be worked out. The final outcome reflects the relative market power of supplier and buyer.

3. Powerful unions can get whatever wage they want. WRONG!

   Powerful unions are limited by the demand for labor. RIGHT!

   If unions make and receive exorbitant wage demands, they may find the union membership dwindling as more employees are laid off. Frequently, unions moderate wage demands in order to prevent employers from going out of business, foreign competition from undercutting prices, and nonunionized workers from becoming attractive to employers. All of these considerations reflect the law of demand.

# •ANSWERS•

## Using Key Terms
### Across
2. marginal wage
5. bilateral monopoly
10. marginal factor cost
11. union shop
12. labor supply

### Down
1. demand for labor
2. marginal revenue product
3. collective bargaining
4. productivity
6. equilibrium wage
7. unionization ratio
8. market power
9. monopsony

## True or False

1. T
2. F  Monopsonists will equate marginal factor cost and marginal revenue product.
3. T
4. T
5. F  To maintain higher than equilibrium wages labor supply must be reduced.
6. F  Unions tend to gain power during downturns in the economy.
7. F  Only about one-seventh of the U.S. labor force is unionized.
8. T
9. F  The marginal revenue curve sets an upper limit for wages because it measures the value of each worker to the firm.
10. T

## Multiple Choice

| | | | | |
|---|---|---|---|---|
| 1. d | 5. b | 9. a | 13. c | 17. a |
| 2. a | 6. a | 10. b | 14. c | 18. d |
| 3. d | 7. b | 11. b | 15. d | 19. a |
| 4. d | 8. c | 12. a | 16. c | 20. b |

# Problems and Applications

## Exercise 1

1. **Table 16.1 Answer**

| (1) Labor | (2) Wage | (5) TC | (6) MFC | (7) TR | (8) MRP |
|-----------|----------|--------|---------|--------|---------|
| 0 | $1 | $ 0 | $ --- | $ 0 | $ --- |
| 1 | 2 | 2 | 2 | 15 | 15 |
| 2 | 7 | 14 | 12 | 27 | 12 |
| 3 | 9 | 27 | 13 | 36 | 9 |

2. 27 quarts per hour; $7 per hour; $12 per hour; 2 employees per hour
3. T
4. F

## Exercise 2

1. **Table 16.2 Answer**

| Wage rate (dollars per hour) | $14 | 13 | 12 | 11 | 10 | 9 | 8 | 7 | 6 | 5 |
|---|---|---|---|---|---|---|---|---|---|---|
| Quantity of labor demanded (workers per hour) | 0 | 1 | 2 | 3 | 4 | 5 | 6 | 7 | 8 | 9 |
| Total wage bill (dollars per hour) | 0 | 13 | 24 | 33 | 40 | 45 | 48 | 49 | 48 | 45 |
| Marginal wage (dollars per worker) | — | 13 | 11 | 9 | 7 | 5 | 3 | 1 | -1 | -3 |

| Wage rate (dollars per hour) | $3 | 4 | 5 | 6 | 7 |
|---|---|---|---|---|---|
| Quantity of labor supplied (workers per hour) | 1 | 3 | 5 | 7 | 9 |
| Total wage (dollars per hour) | $3 | 12 | 25 | 42 | 63 |
| Marginal factor cost (dollars per worker) | 3 | 4.5 | 6.5 | 8.5 | 10.5 |

2. **Figure 16.1 Answer**

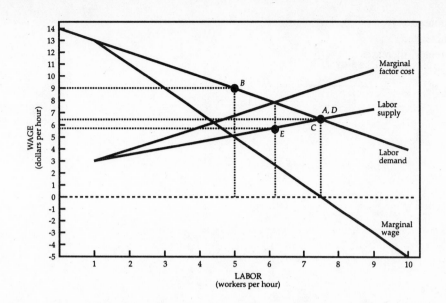

*Note*: When demand falls below the price at which workers are willing and able to work, there can be no greater employment. So the dues-maximizing and wage bill-maximizing unions will push employment to the competitive level. However, more inelastic demand can mean that wage bill-maximizing unions would produce less than the competitive level at a higher wage.

3. 7 (Labor supply and labor demand intersect at 7.5 workers.); $6.50
4. 5; $9.00
5. 7; $6.50. The wage bill is maximized where the marginal wage intersects the *x*-axis. But the equilibrium amount of labor, where labor supply equals labor demand, tells us the maximum number of workers which could be hired.
6. 7; $6.50
7. 6; $5.75. Remember that a monopsonist forces the wage down to the supply curve from which the wage is read.
8. See the letters marking the points in Figure 16.1 Answer.

9.

| Wage<br>(rank) | (highest to lowest) | Amount<br>of labor<br>(rank) | (lowest to highest) |
|---|---|---|---|
| 1. | Union monopolist | 1. | Union monopolist |
| 2. | Competition | 2. | Monopsony |
| | Union dues maximizer | 3. | Competition |
| | Union vote maximizer | | Union vote maximizer |
| 3. | Monopsony | | Union dues maximizer |

10. T
11. F  Monopsony results in a lower price than the competitive price.

241

# Exercise 3

1. monopsony
2. increased
3. greater, increases
4. fewer, lower

# CHAPTER 17

# Uncertainty, Risk, and Financial Markets

## Quick Review

Financial markets play a critical role in the economy, but the way in which they do so remains a mystery to many people. The objective of this chapter is to provide a basic analysis of how financial markets work. To do this we will focus on the following questions:

- What is traded in financial markets?
- How do the financial markets affect the economic outcomes of WHO, WHAT, and FOR WHOM?
- Why do financial markets fluctuate so much?

In answering these questions we'll look at how financial markets bring together those who wish to save more than they spend (the savers) and those who wish to spend more than they save (the dissavers). Financial markets provide access to the savings pool of funds. This is vital to the process of "spreading the risk" of failure over a large number of individuals. Three distinct financial markets, the stock market, the bond market, and the futures market aid in financial intermediation through which risk spreading occurs. By bringing together savers and spenders, financial intermediaries also reduce the costs of information and search. In doing so, they make the financial markets more efficient.

Financial intermediaries are concerned with the present value of future profits. Future dollars must be discounted by the opportunity cost of money or the market interest rate. Higher interest rates and a longer time until future payment will cause a decrease in the present discounted value of a future payment. Risk also has an impact on the expected value of future payments.

The stock market allows firms to raise capital by selling equities, that is, claims to ownership in a corporation which are then listed on one of several stock exchanges. Naturally, a stock market has both a supply side and a demand side. Changes in the nonprice determinants of the supply of, and the demand for, stocks lead to shifts of the respective curves and, in the process, cause the price to change. Changing expectations regarding the future profitability of particular corporations and the future course of the economy are especially important nonprice determinants on both the supply side and the demand side.

The bond market is a market in which debt instruments called bonds are bought and sold. Each bond is essentially an IOU which states the principal amount, interest, and terms on which the debt must be repaid. While the initial purchasers lend directly to the borrower, the bonds can then be traded in an organized market where, again, their price is determined by the supply and demand for bonds at the time the trade is made. Changes in investors' expectations concerning future interest rates and the borrowers' potential ability to pay interest and repay principal will affect the supply and demand for bonds. Bond yields are inversely related to bond prices.

Venture capitalists provide initial funding for entrepreneurial ventures. If the project is a success, they get profits; if not, losses. Financial markets help the economy in its search for the optimal mix of output by helping to mobilize savings, manage risk, and signal desired resource allocations.

## Learning Objectives

After reading Chapter 17 and doing the following exercises, you should:

1. Understand the primary function of financial markets.
2. Understand how financial markets increase efficiency.
3. Know what present discounted value means and how to calculate it.
4. Know that risk has an impact on the expected value of future payments.
5. Understand how companies raise funds through the stock market and the bond market.
6. Know some of the determinants of the demand for and supply of stocks and bonds, and know how changes in those determinants affect stock and bond prices.
7. Be able to explain why bond yields are inversely related to bond prices.
8. Understand the role of venture capitalists.

## Using Key Terms

Fill in the puzzle on the opposite page with the appropriate term from the list of Key Terms at the end of the chapter in the text.

### *Across*

1. Amount of corporate profit paid out for each share of stock.
8. The price of a stock share divided by earnings per share.
10. A limited liability form of business.
11. The rate of return on a bond is the current _____.
13. The face value of a bond.
14. The ability of an asset to be converted to cash.
15. The difference in rates of return on risky and safe investments.

### *Down*

2. The first sale to the general public of stock in a corporation.
3. An increase in the market value of an asset.
4. Shares of ownership in a corporation.
5. An institution that brings savers and dissavers together.
6. The value today of future payments, adjusted for interest accrual.
7. The probable value of a future payment, including the risk of nonpayment.
9. An IOU issued by corporations and government agencies.
12. Failure to make scheduled payments of interest or principal on a bond.

244

# Puzzle 17.1

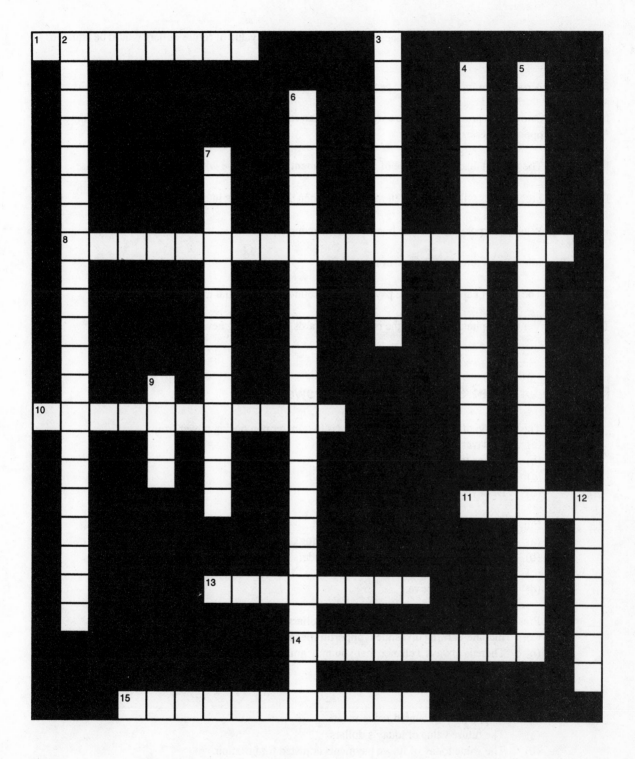

## True or False: *Circle your choice and explain why any false statements are incorrect.*

T  F  1.  Financial intermediaries change the mix of output by transferring purchasing power from dissavers to savers.

T  F  2.  If the opportunity cost of money was zero, the expected value of future dollars would be equal to their present value.

T  F  3.  A risk premium compensates people who invest in risky ventures that succeed.

T  F  4.  One reason present dollars are worth more than future dollars is that income-earning investment opportunities exist.

T  F  5.  The present discounted value of a future payment will decrease when interest rates decrease.

T  F  6.  Stock prices will increase, ceteris paribus, when the prevailing interest rate increases.

T  F  7.  When a corporation issues a bond, it is borrowing funds.

T  F  8.  Interest is a return on the use of money.

T  F  9.  The present value of a future payment is discounted by potential interest accumulation.

T  F  10.  Venture capitalists share in the risks and rewards by financing new ventures.


## Multiple Choice: *Select the correct answer.*

_____  1.  The function of financial intermediaries is to transfer purchasing power from:
    (a)  Dissavers to consumers.
    (b)  Savers to dissavers.
    (c)  Consumers to savers.
    (d)  Dissavers to savers.

_____  2.  Financial intermediaries:
    (a)  Reduce search and information costs for savers and investors.
    (b)  Transfer purchasing power from spenders to savers.
    (c)  Concentrate investment risk.
    (d)  Do all of the above.

_____  3.  Present dollars are worth more than future dollars because:
    (a)  Income-earning investment opportunities exist.
    (b)  There is always a chance that you may not receive the future dollars.
    (c)  Of the opportunity cost of money.
    (d)  All of the above.

_____  4.  The term present discounted value means:
    (a)  The future value of today's dollars.
    (b)  The value today of future payments adjusted for inflation.
    (c)  The value today of future payments adjusted for interest accrual.
    (d)  The value today of future payments adjusted for risk.

_____ 5. Higher interest rates:
(a) Reflect a higher opportunity cost of money.
(b) Raise the future value of current dollars.
(c) Lower the present value of future payments.
(d) All of the above.

_____ 6. The present discounted value of a future payment will decrease when the:
(a) Future payment is further into the future.
(b) Interest rate decreases.
(c) Risk of non-payment increases.
(d) Opportunity cost of money decreases.

_____ 7. The possibility of non-payment is taken into account in the calculation of the:
(a) Present discounted value.
(b) Future discounted value.
(c) Expected value.
(d) Profits.

_____ 8. The term expected value means:
(a) The future value of a current payment.
(b) The present value of a future payment.
(c) The probable value of a future payment.
(d) The difference in the rates of return on risky and safe investments.

_____ 9. Suppose that Beth has a 20 percent chance of not collecting $1000 in 3 years. If the interest rate is 10 percent, what is the expected value of the future payment?
(a) $150.
(b) $601.
(c) $751.
(d) $1065.

_____ 10. A motivation for holding stocks is:
(a) To receive interest payments on the firm's debt.
(b) To receive potential capital gains.
(c) To have a direct role in the operation of the corporation.
(d) All of the above.

_____ 11. The purpose of an initial public offering is to:
(a) Raise funds for investment and growth by selling shares of the company to the public.
(b) Change the membership of the Board of Directors.
(c) Borrow funds for investment and growth.
(d) See if there is a demand for a company's new product.

_____ 12. Which of the following determines the price of a stock?
(a) The amount of stock people are willing and able to purchase.
(b) The amount of stock people offer for sale.
(c) Expectations of future earnings.
(d) All of the above.

_____ 13. The price of a stock will increase, *ceteris paribus*, when:
   (a) When there is a shortage of the stock at the current price.
   (b) The demand for the stock increases.
   (c) The supply of the stock decreases.
   (d) All of the above.

_____ 14. A bond is:
   (a) A share in a corporation.
   (b) A coupon used to collect a dividend.
   (c) An insurance policy investors purchase to protect against the possibility of falling stock prices.
   (d) A promise to repay a loan.

_____ 15. If a corporation issues bonds which they cannot sell, this is an indication that:
   (a) Expectations of future sales are low.
   (b) The coupon rate is too low.
   (c) Dividends are too low.
   (d) All of the above.

_____ 16. When investors expect greater future profits from a company, the:
   (a) Demand for the company's bonds increases.
   (b) Price of the company's bonds increases.
   (c) Yield on the company's bonds decreases.
   (d) All of the above occur.

_____ 17. When the interest rate rises:
   (a) The demand for loanable funds falls and the supply of loanable funds falls.
   (b) The demand for loanable funds rises and the supply of loanable funds rises.
   (c) The demand for loanable funds falls and the supply of loanable funds rises.
   (d) The quantity of loanable funds demanded falls and the quantity of loanable funds supplied rises.

_____ 18. The present value of $100,000 to be received every year for 3 years when the discount rate is 10 percent is:
   (a) $300,000.
   (b) $248,742.
   (c) $133,100.
   (d) $330,000.

_____ 19. As the interest rate increases, the opportunity cost of money:
   (a) Increases for both lender and borrower.
   (b) Increases for the borrower but not the lender.
   (c) Decreases for both lender and borrower.
   (d) Decreases for the borrower but not the lender.

_____ 20. As the interest rate increases, *ceteris paribus*, the tradeoff between present and future consumption:
   (a) Is not affected.
   (b) Encourages present consumption.
   (c) Changes in favor of future consumption.
   (d) Makes it less appealing to sacrifice present consumption.

# Problems and Applications

## Exercise 1

This exercise shows how to compute the present discounted value of an investment. It also shows how important the interest rate and length of time until payment are in the present value calculation.

1.  Suppose you own 1,000 acres of forest land. Next year you could have the trees cut down for lumber and receive $1,320,000 (after taxes and all other expenses). The interest rate is 10 percent. Find the present discounted value of your 1,000 acres of forest land. _____

2.  Suppose interest rates rose to 20 percent. What would the present discounted value of cutting down the forest for lumber be at the 20 percent interest rate if the cost and profit were the same as at 10 percent? _____

3.  Suppose interest rates are at the original 10 percent. What would the present discounted value of cutting down the forest for lumber be if you had to wait two years to receive $1,320,000?
    _____

4.  T   F   When the interest rate rises, the present value of an investment rises.

5.  T   F   The longer one has to wait for a future payment, the less present value it has.

## Exercise 2

This exercise uses the loanable funds market to determine the market interest rate and investment.

1.  The supply and demand of loanable funds are shown in Figure 17.1. If the supply of loanable funds is $S_1$, then the equilibrium interest rate is _____ percent.

### Figure 17.1
### Investment demand, and the supply of loanable funds

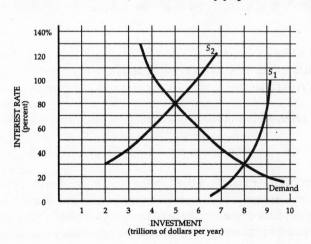

INVESTMENT
(trillions of dollars per year)

2.  At the equilibrium interest rate, the level of investment would equal $_____ trillion.

3.  If the supply of loanable funds shifts to $S_2$, this represents a(an) (increase, decrease) in loanable funds.

249

4. The equilibrium interest rate would (increase, decrease) to _____ percent and the level of investment would (increase, decrease) to $_____ trillion.

5. One reason for the shift in loanable funds in Figure 31.1 might be the (increase, decrease) in savings by consumers.

## Exercise 3

The media often carry information about the amount of money won in lotteries. The reality is often different than what is reported.

Reread pages 345 through 346 in the text about Frank and Shirley Carpaci and their lottery winnings. Then answer the following questions.

1. What was the advertised amount of the payoff from the winning lottery? _____

2. When discounted at 6.2%, what was the present value of the payout? _____

3. What would happen to the present value of the payout if it were discounted at an interest rate greater than 6.2%? _____

4. How many payments was the winner of the lottery to receive? _____

5. If the payoff was made in ten annual installments instead, what would have happened to the present value? _____

## Common Errors

The first statement in each "common error" below is incorrect. Each incorrect statement is followed by a corrected version and an explanation.

1. The primary function of financial intermediaries is to provide checking accounts for customers. WRONG!

   The primary function of financial intermediaries is to transfer income from savers to spenders. RIGHT!

   Financial intermediaries provide access to the savings pool for government and the business sector. They also reduce the search and information costs involved with lending and investment opportunities. As a result they change the mix of output and increase market efficiency.

2. As bond prices rise, the rate of return or current yield also rises. WRONG!

   As bond prices rise, the rate of return or current yield falls. RIGHT!

   The rate of interest earned on a bond, or the coupon rate, is stated on the bond certificate and does not change. The current yield represents the rate of return on a bond. It is calculated as the annual interest payment divided by the bond price. The price of a bond in the secondary bond market varies based on changes in expectations and opportunity cost. If the annual interest payment stays constant and the bond price increases, the rate of return or current yield falls.

# •ANSWERS•

## Using Key Terms
### Across
1. dividend
8. price earnings ratio
10. corporation
11. yield
13. par value
14. liquidity
15. risk premium

### Down
2. initial public offering
3. capital gain
4. corporate stock
5. financial intermediary
6. present discounted value
7. expected value
9. bond
12. default

## True or False

1. F  Financial intermediaries change the mix of output by transferring purchasing power from savers to dissavers.
2. F  The expected value calculation takes into account the possibility of not getting the future payment. Whenever this is a possibility, future dollars will be worth less than current dollars.
3. T
4. T
5. F  The present discounted value of a future payment will increase when interest rates decrease.
6. F  Stock prices will decrease when the prevailing interest rate increases because the opportunity cost of holding stocks will increase making stocks a less desirable investment option (i.e. the demand for stocks will decrease).
7. T
8. T
9. T
10. T

## Multiple Choice

| | | | | | | | | | |
|---|---|---|---|---|---|---|---|---|---|
| 1. | b | 5. | d | 9. | b | 13. | d | 17. | d |
| 2. | a | 6. | a | 10. | b | 14. | d | 18. | b |
| 3. | d | 7. | c | 11. | a | 15. | b | 19. | a |
| 4. | c | 8. | c | 12. | d | 16. | d | 20. | c |

251

## Problems and Applications

### Exercise 1

1. $\$1,320,000/(1.10)^1 = \$1,200,000$
2. $\$1,320,000/(1.20)^1 = \$1,100,000$
3. $\$1,320,000/(1.10)^2 = \$1,090,909$
4. F
5. T

### Exercise 2

1. 30 percent
2. $8 trillion
3. decrease
4. increase, 80 percent, decrease, $5 trillion
5. decrease

### Exercise 3

1. The advertised amount was $195 million.
2. $103.90 million.
3. If discounted at more than 6.2%, the present discounted value would be less than $103.90 million.
4. The text says that the payments were to be made over 24 years.
5. Ten annual installments would raise the present discounted value.

## CHAPTER 18

# Taxes: Equity vs. Efficiency

## Quick Review

Taxes are used to transfer command of resources from the private sector to the public sector and to redistribute income from the rich to the poor. The impact of taxes on the economy is not always easy to determine, and there appears to be a tradeoff between society's goals of equity and efficiency. Let's focus on the following questions:

- How are incomes distributed in the United States?
- How do taxes alter that distribution?
- How do taxes affect the rate and mix of output?

The distribution of income is a major concern of public policy; it concerns the FOR WHOM question. It should be remembered, however, that income is sometimes not required to get goods and services; welfare payments, for example, are sometimes made in kind. It is also necessary to distinguish between income and wealth, even though the two are obviously related, and both have implications for one's command over goods and services. Income is a flow and is measured over time; wealth is a stock and is measured at a point in time.

The size distribution of income concentrates on the way income is distributed among income-receiving units, such as households. For example, one may be interested in the fraction of total income received by those who constitute the lowest 20 percent of income recipients (households).

The Lorenz curve is a graph that compares the actual distribution of income with a distribution of income in which everyone receives the same income. The Lorenz curve is particularly useful in comparing income distribution before and after taxes. It is generally observed that in the United States, income is distributed somewhat more equally after taxes than before.

One must be extremely careful in talking about taxes and the tax system. Provisions in the tax law, called "loopholes," allow individuals to reduce the amount of income subject to tax. The loopholes also result in a violation of two important principles of taxation—horizontal equity and vertical equity. Because of this, economists use several tax rates—average tax rate, nominal tax rate, effective tax rate, and so on—to analyze the tax system. This is not an easy task. Taxes may also be shifted from one group to another. Even the employer's portion of the social security tax is thought to be borne by the employee. We should also not lose sight of the fact that other levels of government (state and local) tax income and property, too.

While the overall degree of inequality is difficult to determine, one cannot argue with the fact that income is distributed unequally in the United States. Whether the distribution is fair or not is an entirely different matter. Some feel more should be transferred from those with higher incomes to those with lower incomes. Others argue that such a redistribution of income would so damage the incentives of productive, high-income people that total production and income would decline.

Because of the many concerns about such issues as equity, efficiency, and the erosion of the tax base, Congress passed the Tax Reform Act of 1986. This act closed loopholes, reduced marginal tax rates, reduced the number of tax brackets, increased the tax burden of corporations relative to individuals, and provided tax relief for the poor. The new marginal tax rates didn't last long. Revisions in 1990 and 1993 added a fourth bracket, a new marginal tax rate and a surcharge.

Arguments over the equity of the federal income tax will not go away. Most recently Congressman Richard Armey has proposed a "flat tax" of 17% to replace the cumbersome, complex and sometimes contradictory IRS Code. His proposal would eliminate all deductions, credits and most exemptions and would not tax income from savings and investment (interest, dividends and capital gains). Armey's focus is on simplicity (all IRS forms would be eliminated in favor of a single postcard sized one) and on incentives to save and invest. Under this system, he argues, decisions to save and invest would be made on an economic basis rather than to simply avoid taxes.

Critics argue that many provisions Armey would throw out are there to encourage desired economic activity and that the flat tax would hit the middle class particularly hard and reduce the government's ability to alter the mix of output. Massive restructuring and redistribution of wealth and income are also a possibility.

## Learning Objectives

After reading Chapter 18 and doing the following exercises, you should:

1. Be able to distinguish between wealth and income.
2. Understand the size distribution of income and be able to interpret a Lorenz curve.
3. Be aware of the impact of taxes and transfers on the distribution of income.
4. Understand the principles of horizontal and vertical equity.
5. Be able to distinguish the marginal and average tax rates, and nominal and effective tax rates.
6. Understand the impact of tax "loopholes."
7. Be able to distinguish arguments for equality from arguments for equity.
8. Be aware of major reforms embodied in the Tax Reform Act of 1986 and the changes in 1990 and 1993.
9. Be able to distinguish among progressive, regressive, and proportional taxes.
10. Recognize that the most serious potential cost of greater equality would be damaged incentives.
11. Be aware of the arguments for and against the proposed "flat tax."

## Using Key Terms

Fill in the puzzle on the opposite page with the appropriate term from the list of Key Terms at the end of the chapter in the text.

### *Across*

4. The percentage change in the quantity supplied divided by the percentage change in tax rates.
7. A tax system in which tax rates rise as incomes rise.
14. Taxes paid divided by total income.
15. Taxes paid divided by taxable income.
16. The proportion of total income received by a particular group.
17. The change in total revenue associated with one additional unit of input.
20. The idea that people with higher incomes should pay more taxes.
21. A tax system in which tax rates fall as incomes rise.

### *Down*

1. The tax rate imposed on the last dollar of income.
2. The way total personal income is divided among households.
3. People with equal incomes should pay equal taxes.
5. Distribution of the real burden of a tax.
6. A graph that contrasts complete equality with the actual distribution of income.
7. Income received by households before taxes.
8. Goods and services received directly, without payment in a market transaction.

9. A mathematical summary of inequality based on the Lorenz curve.
10. A situation in which the market mechanism prevents optimal outcomes.
11. A situation in which government intervention fails to improve market outcomes.
12. A single-rate tax system.
13. Payments to individuals for which no current goods or services are exchanged.
18. The amount of income directly subject to nominal tax rates.
19. The market value of assets.

# Puzzle 18.1

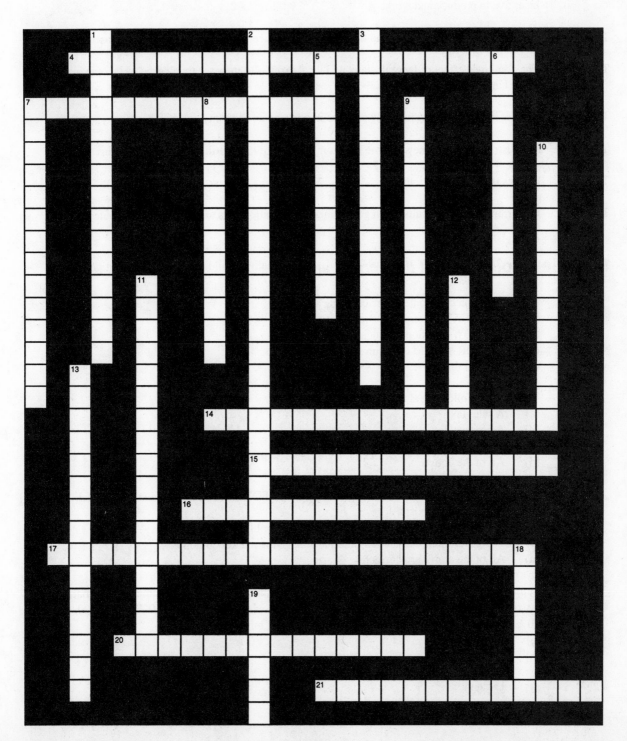

# True or False: *Circle your choice and explain why any false statements are incorrect.*

T  F  1.  Marginal tax rates must increase as income increases for a tax to be progressive, *ceteris paribus*.

T  F  2.  When people believe that the market's answer to the FOR WHOM question is suboptimal, taxes can be used as a policy lever to address the problem.

T  F  3.  A flat tax rate would take the same dollar amount from each taxpayer.

T  F  4.  The efficiency issue in taxation refers to the negative impact of higher marginal tax rates on the incentive to produce and work.

T  F  5.  Fewer workers are employed and the net wage is reduced when a payroll tax is imposed.

T  F  6.  The combined effect of federal, state, and local taxes is to increase the degree of income inequality in the United States.

T  F  7.  Greater income equality has only positive impacts on an economy.

T  F  8.  The distribution of money income is synonymous with the distribution of goods and services.

T  F  9.  A sales tax is a proportional tax.

T  F  10.  Government failure results when government intervention fails to improve market outcomes.

# Multiple Choice: *Select the correct answer.*

_____  1.  The distribution of income is basically the answer to:
  (a)  The WHAT question for society.
  (b)  The HOW question for society.
  (c)  The FOR WHOM question for society.
  (d)  None of the above.

_____  2.  Which of the following is typically a regressive tax?
  (a)  A sales tax.
  (b)  A property tax.
  (c)  The social security tax.
  (d)  All of the above.

_____  3.  When people believe that the market's answer to the FOR WHOM question is suboptimal:
  (a)  Market failure exists.
  (b)  Taxes can be used as a policy to address the problem.
  (c)  The government has an obligation to change the market outcome.
  (d)  All of the above are correct.

_____  4.  Suppose that in 1999 Ms. Gonzales had a taxable income of $80,000. Assume that the marginal tax rates are 10% of the first $20,000, 20% of the income in excess of $20,000 to $60,000, and 30% of any income over $60,000. Ms. Gonzales' tax bill was:
  (a)  $8,000.
  (b)  $16,000.
  (c)  $24,000.
  (d)  $36,000.

_____ 5. If income is distributed unequally:
   (a) The Lorenz curve would be a straight line.
   (b) The line of equality sags below the Lorenz curve.
   (c) The Lorenz curve sags below the line of equality.
   (d) The Gini coefficient would be greater than zero.

_____ 6. The U.S. tax system results in a slight reduction in inequality of after-tax income because:
   (a) Of the progressive nature of state and local taxes.
   (b) Of the progressive nature of the federal income tax.
   (c) The rich have fewer available loopholes than the poor.
   (d) The poor receive such generous welfare benefits.

_____ 7. Government attempts to create a more equitable income distribution by increasing marginal tax rates may:
   (a) Reduce output.
   (b) Increase unemployment.
   (c) Reduce government tax receipts.
   (d) All of the above.

_____ 8. The argument _in favor_ of greater equality of income distribution in the United States hinges on:
   (a) The idea that greater equality does not affect incentives.
   (b) The idea that low-income earners would be more willing and able participants in the economy if income were distributed more equally.
   (c) The idea that those with high incomes wield greater political power and strengthen the democratic process.
   (d) All of the above.

_____ 9. In making comparisons of income among countries, care must be exercised because:
   (a) In poor countries much of what is produced does not pass through markets and thus does not get counted in the nation's income.
   (b) In countries such as Sweden and Great Britain, the government provides more goods and services directly than in the United States.
   (c) In-kind benefits should be included in real income in all countries.
   (d) All of the above are true.

_____ 10. The tax elasticity of labor supply measures the:
   (a) Response of workers to a change in the tax rate.
   (b) Response of workers to a change in prices.
   (c) Change in the amount of taxes workers must pay when tax rates change.
   (d) Response of employers to a change in the tax rate.

Use the following information to answer questions 11-12. The tax schedule is hypothetical to keep the calculations simple.

Suppose an individual has a total income of $100,000, has a taxable income of $50,000, and pays taxes of $5,000.

_____ 11. This individual's _____ tax rate is 5 percent.
   (a) Effective.
   (b) Nominal.
   (c) Marginal.
   (d) Incidence.

_____ 12. This individual's _____ tax rate is 10 percent.
    (a)    Marginal.
    (b)    Effective.
    (c)    Nominal.
    (d)    Incidence.

_____ 13. The principle of taxation that says people with equal incomes should pay equal taxes is called:
    (a)    Vertical equity.
    (b)    Horizontal equity.
    (c)    Progressive.
    (d)    Regressive.

_____ 14. Transfer payments are an appropriate mechanism for correcting:
    (a)    Market power.
    (b)    Government failure.
    (c)    Natural monopoly.
    (d)    Inequity.

_____ 15. Food stamps, public housing, and subsidized public education are examples of:
    (a)    Free goods.
    (b)    "In-kind" benefits or income.
    (c)    Tax expenditures.
    (d)    Money incomes.

_____ 16. If the tax elasticity of supply is negative 0.6 and tax rates increase by 20 percent, the quantity of labor supplied would:
    (a)    Increase by 12 percent.
    (b)    Decrease by 12 percent.
    (c)    Increase by 33.3 percent.
    (d)    Decrease by 33.3 percent.

_____ 17. The flat tax:
    (a)    Reduces the government's ability to alter the mix of output.
    (b)    Encourages economic activity through deductions and credits.
    (c)    Includes many tax brackets.
    (d)    All of the above.

_____ 18. By instituting a sales tax, a tax plan would:
    (a)    Be more progressive since it takes a larger fraction of income as income falls.
    (b)    Increase horizontal equity.
    (c)    Increase vertical equity.
    (d)    Shift the Lorenz curve for after-tax income away from the line of equality.

_____ 19. A tax is progressive if it takes a:
    (a)    Larger number of dollars as income rises.
    (b)    Larger number of dollars as income falls.
    (c)    Smaller fraction of income as income falls.
    (d)    Smaller fraction of income as income rises.

_____ 20. New loopholes in the personal income tax law tend to:
    (a)    Make the system more regressive.
    (b)    Increase horizontal equity.
    (c)    Increase the tax base.
    (d)    All of the above.

# Problems and Applications

## Exercise 1

This exercise will help you understand the Lorenz curve.

1.  Complete column 3 in Table 18.1 using the data from column 2. Then draw a Lorenz curve based on column 3 in Figure 18.1.

### Table 18.1
### Size distribution of personal income, by household income group, 1988

| (1) Quintile of income recipients (households) | (2) Percent of total household income received | (3) Percent of income received (cumulative) |
| --- | --- | --- |
| Lowest fifth | 3.8% | _____% |
| Second fifth | 9.6 | _____ |
| Third fifth | 16.0 | _____ |
| Fourth fifth | 24.2 | _____ |
| Highest fifth | 46.3 | _____ |

### Figure 18.1
### Lorenz curve

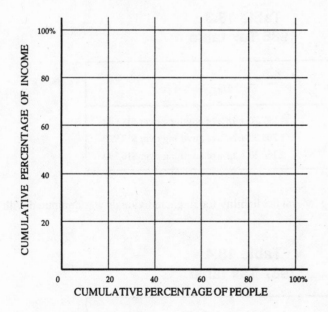

2.  The information given in Table 18.1 is for 1988 income. Income in 1988 was distributed (equally, unequally).

3.  Draw the line of absolute equality in Figure 18.1 and label it. Shade in the area between the Lorenz curve and the line of equality. The shaded area is a measure of the degree of _____ .

4. In Figure 18.1 draw a second Lorenz curve that indicates the distribution of wealth in the United States for the same year. Use the hypothetical data from Table 18.2. Calculate column 3 first.

### Table 18.2
### Hypothetical size distribution of wealth, by wealth-holding group

| (1) Quintile of wealth owners | (2) Wealth owned | (3) Wealth owned (cumulative) |
|---|---|---|
| Lowest fifth | 0.5% | _____% |
| Second fifth | 5.0 | _____ |
| Third fifth | 12.0 | _____ |
| Fourth fifth | 20.0 | _____ |
| Highest fifth | 62.5 | _____ |

5. Although the data in Table 18.2 are hypothetical, they do actually indicate the direction of inequality of wealth ownership relative to the distribution of income. Wealth is (more, less) equally distributed than income.

## Exercise 2

This exercise will use the tax reform legislation for the 1987 tax year to show how to determine the impact of a tax change on vertical and horizontal equity. It will help you complete problem 1 for Chapter 18 in the text.

For the 1986 tax year the federal tax liability for single individuals was computed on the basis of the schedule shown in Table 18.3.

### Table 18.3
### 1986 Tax table

| If your taxable income Is above: | But below: | Then your tax is: |
|---|---|---|
| $11,650 | $13,920 | $1,297.70 + 18% of anything over $11,650 |
| 13,920 | 16,190 | 1,706.30 + 20% of anything over $13,920 |
| 16,190 | 19,640 | 2,160.30 + 23% of anything over $16,190 |

For the 1987 tax year the corresponding federal tax liability for single individuals was computed with the schedule found in Table 18.4.

### Table 18.4
### 1987 Tax table

| If your taxable income Is above: | But below: | Then your tax is: |
|---|---|---|
| $ 1,800 | $16,800 | $  198.00 + 15% of anything over $  1,800 |
| 16,800 | 27,000 | 2,448.00 + 28% of anything over $16,800 |

1. What would the marginal tax rates be for a single taxpayer with a taxable income of $17,000 in 1986? _____ In 1987? _____ On the basis of this information, does it appear that the tax reform of the Reagan administration increased work incentives for single taxpayers with a taxable income of $17,000? _____

2. For the three taxpayers listed in Table 18.5, compute the taxable income, taxes in the years 1986 and 1987, and difference in taxes for the two years.

### Table 18.5
### Taxable income and tax computations

| Taxpayer | Gross income | Exemptions and deductions | Taxable income | 1986 Tax | 1987 Tax | Difference |
|----------|--------------|---------------------------|----------------|----------|----------|------------|
| 1 | $30,000 | $18,000 | $_____ | $_____ | $_____ | $_____ |
| 2 | 30,000 | 13,000 | _____ | _____ | _____ | _____ |
| 3 | 50,000 | 38,000 | _____ | _____ | _____ | _____ |

3. On the basis of Table 18.5 did the tax reform package lower taxes for single taxpayers in the taxable income range of $12,000 to $17,000? _____

4. In Table 18.6 rank each taxpayer on the basis of the effective tax rate. Then complete the table by filling in the nominal, effective, and marginal tax rates for each taxpayer.

### Table 18.6
### Rankings for 1987

| Rank | Tax payer | Nominal tax rate | Effective tax rate | Marginal tax rate |
|------|-----------|------------------|--------------------|--------------------|
| 1 | _____ (highest) | _____% | _____% | _____% |
| 2 | _____ (middle) | _____ | _____ | _____ |
| 3 | _____ (lowest) | _____ | _____ | _____ |

5. How should horizontal equity be determined?
   (a) The two taxpayers with the same nominal incomes should be compared for their marginal tax rates.
   (b) The two taxpayers with the same nominal incomes should be compared for their effective tax rates.
   (c) The effective tax rate of the taxpayer with the highest nominal income should be compared with the effective tax rates of taxpayers with lower nominal incomes.
   (d) The marginal tax rate of the taxpayer with the highest nominal income should be compared with the marginal tax rates of taxpayers with lower nominal incomes.

6. How should vertical equity be determined?
   (a) The two taxpayers with the same nominal incomes should be compared for their marginal tax rates.
   (b) The two taxpayers with the same nominal incomes should be compared for their effective tax rates.
   (c) The effective tax rates of the taxpayer with the highest nominal income should be compared with the effective tax rates of taxpayers with lower nominal incomes.
   (d) The marginal tax rate of the taxpayer with the highest nominal income should be compared with the marginal tax rates of taxpayers with lower nominal incomes.

7.  T   F   For single taxpayers with taxable incomes between $12,000 and $17,000, the tax-reform package reduced vertical equity from 1986 to 1987. (*Hint:* See last column in Table 18.5)

## *Exercise 3*

Around April 15 of every year many articles appear which discuss changes in the tax laws from the previous year. This exercise will use one of the cartoons in the text to show the kind of information to look for to identify and classify changes in the tax system.

Look at the cartoon on page 374 in the text. Then answer the following questions.

1.  What word indicates a change in policy has occurred or has been proposed?_____

2.  What three words indicate a change in horizontal or vertical equity resulting from the change?
    _____

3.  The change in equity indicated in the article concerns:
    (a)   Vertical equity.
    (b)   Horizontal equity.

## Common Errors

The first statement in each "common error" below is incorrect. Each incorrect statement is followed by a corrected version and an explanation.

1.  Income and wealth are the same thing. WRONG!

    Income and wealth mean distinctly different things. RIGHT!

    The distinction between income and wealth is critical to sound economic analysis. Income is a flow and has a time dimension. For example, one states one's income in dollars *per year*. Wealth is a stock and is measured at a point in time; for example, you may say you have $5,000 in your savings account *today*. Some people with apparently great wealth may have very little income, as in the case of someone who owns land known to contain oil. On the other hand, someone who has much income may have little wealth; some famous entertainers earn large incomes, save little (accumulate no wealth), and wind up in bankruptcy. Of course, wealth and income may go hand in hand: the incomes of some oil magnates flow *from* their wealth. But clearly the two terms imply different things about one's economic well-being and command over goods and services.

2.  Equity and equality of income distribution mean the same thing. WRONG!

    Equity and equality of income distribution mean different things. RIGHT!

    Many arguments over the division of the income pie, whether at the national level, the corporate level, or the university level, are laced with the terms "equity" and "equality" used interchangeably. They are *not* interchangeable. Equality of income distribution means that each person has an equal share. Equity of income distribution implies something about fairness. In a free society some will surely be more productive than others at doing what society wants done. The brain surgeon's services have greater value than the hairdresser's. The surgeon's income will exceed that of the hairdresser—that is, they'll be unequal. But is that inequitable? This is a matter of judgment. It's safe to say, however, that if one were not allowed to keep some of the rewards for being more productive than average, our economy would suffer. An equitable distribution of income in our society will require some inequality. How much? There is no sure answer to that question, only a series of compromises.

# •ANSWERS•

## Using Key Terms
### Across
4.  tax elasticity of supply
7.  progressive tax
14. effective tax rate
15. nominal tax rate
16. income share
17. marginal revenue product
20. vertical equity
21. regressive tax

### Down
1.  marginal tax rate
2.  size distribution of income
3.  horizontal equity
5.  tax incidence
6.  Lorenz curve
7.  personal income
8.  in-kind income
9.  Gini coefficient
10. market failure
11. government failure
12. flat tax
13. income transfers
18. tax base
19. wealth

## True or False

1.  T
2.  T
3.  F  A flat tax takes the same percentage of income from each taxpayer.
4.  T
5.  T
6.  F  The combined effect is to slightly decrease the level of income inequality in the U.S.
7.  F  Greater income equality can have negative impacts on work incentives and efficiency.
8.  F  Wealth is also a determinant of who receives goods and services.
9.  F  A sales tax is a regressive tax because lower income groups tend to spend a higher proportion of their income than upper income groups.
10. T

## Multiple Choice

| | | | | |
|---|---|---|---|---|
| 1. c | 5. c | 9. d | 13. b | 17. a |
| 2. d | 6. b | 10. a | 14. d | 18. d |
| 3. d | 7. d | 11. a | 15. b | 19. c |
| 4. b | 8. b | 12. c | 16. b | 20. a |

# Problems and Applications

## Exercise 1

1. **Table 18.1 Answer**

| (1) Quintile of income recipients (households) | (3) Percent of income received (cumulative) |
|---|---|
| Lowest fifth | 3.8% |
| Second fifth | 13.4 |
| Third fifth | 29.4 |
| Fourth fifth | 53.6 |
| Highest fifth | 99.9 |

See Figure 18.1 Answer.

**Figure 18.1 Answer**

2. unequally
3. See line of absolute equality and shaded area in Figure 18.1 Answer; inequality.

4. **Table 18.2 Answer**

| (1) Quintile of wealth owners | (3) Wealth owned (cumulative) |
|---|---|
| Lowest fifth | 0.5% |
| Second fifth | 5.5 |
| Third fifth | 17.5 |
| Fourth fifth | 37.5 |
| Highest fifth | 100.0 |

See Figure 18.1 Answer.

5. less

# Exercise 2

1. 23 percent for 1986 (the percentage used in the formula is the marginal tax rate); 28 percent for 1987; no

2. **Table 18.5 Answer**

| Taxpayer | Taxable income | 1986 Tax | 1987 Tax | Difference |
|---|---|---|---|---|
| 1 | $12,000 | $1,360.70 | $1,728 | $367.30 |
| 2 | 17,000 | 2,346.60 | 2,504 | 157.40 |
| 3 | 12,000 | 1,360.70 | 1,728 | 367.30 |

3. no

4. **Table 18.6 Answer**

| Rank | Tax payer | Nominal tax rate | Effective tax rate | Marginal tax rate |
|---|---|---|---|---|
| 1 | 2 | 14.7% (=2,504/17,000) | 8.4% (=2,504/30,000) | 28% |
| 2 | 1 | 14.4% (=1,728/12,000) | 5.8% (=1,728/30,000) | 15 |
| 3 | 3 | 14.4% (=1,728/12,000) | 3.5% (=1,728/50,000) | 15 |

5. b
6. c
7. T    The difference in total taxes paid was greater at a $12,000 taxable income than it was at a $17,000 taxable income, as shown in the last column of Table 18.5 Answer.

# Exercise 3

1. "it," when referring to some generic policy that has changed
2. "favors the rich"
3. a

# CHAPTER 19

# Transfer Payments: Welfare and Social Security

## Quick Review

The distribution of income is an age-old problem. Even in the most affluent societies some individuals and families have incomes and living standards that society feels are too low. This is certainly true in the United States where programs to provide relief have multiplied since the 1960s. Existing programs have been broadened to include more recipients and new programs have been funded. The programs are very costly to provide and administer and have become a political hot potato requiring every presidential candidate to declare the need for reform. We conduct our study of this topic by examining the following questions:

- What are the goals of major income transfer programs?
- How are transfer benefits computed?
- How do transfer payments alter market behavior?

Approximately half of every U.S. tax dollar is spent on income transfers, and almost every U.S. household receives some of these transfer dollars. Most of the transfer payments received by poor families are in the form of "in-kind" transfers such as food stamps, medical aid, and housing assistance. Other transfer payments, such as Social Security, are cash transfers. All income transfers result in a redistribution of income, but not all income transfers go to the poor. Welfare programs are means-tested and require some type of income eligibility test, while social insurance programs offer event-conditioned benefits. They insure people against events such as old age or unemployment. The majority of income transfer payments in the U.S. are the result of social insurance programs, not welfare.

In 1996, Congress created a new welfare program called Temporary Aid to Needy Families (TANF). This program allows states to play a much greater role in deciding who receives welfare, under what conditions, and for how long. But, the unintended impact of welfare is to encourage undesirable behavior. Welfare benefits perpetuate dependence, since they do not increase human capital or job opportunities, and welfare benefits may *worsen* the poverty problem by discouraging recipients from working.

The latter is known as the work-welfare dilemma as it is argued that income transfers reduce the incentive to seek earned income which allows individuals to fend for themselves. The designers of welfare programs recognize that many of the programs put in place result in a person being as well off without working as he or she is working! In fact, if work-related expenses are taken into account, a person might be worse off if he or she participates in the labor market. Modifications of existing programs have taken this into account by adjusting the marginal tax rate on earned income. The basic problem is that low marginal tax rates encourage more work effort, but make more people eligible for welfare. High marginal tax rates discourage work effort, but make fewer people eligible for welfare.

The Social Security program faces the same work disincentives as the welfare program. The program provides income for older people who do not work, but it imposes high marginal tax rates on those who do work. Because of the way the program is designed, people retire earlier than they would otherwise. The result is a reduction in total output. By eliminating the work test, the economic cost of the Social Security program could be reduced. The marginal tax rate on the wages of older workers would change from 50 percent to zero. The American Association of Retired Persons favors this change. This would eliminate the work disincentive and total output would increase. However, the total cost of the Social Security program would increase because all older people would receive their full retirement benefit. Payroll taxes would have to increase to cover the additional costs.

## Learning Objectives

After reading Chapter 19 and doing the following exercises, you should:

1. Know the impact of transfer payments in the U.S.
2. Be able to distinguish between cash transfers and "in-kind" transfers.
3. Understand the role of human capital and derived demand in the poverty dilemma.
4. Know what the basic government welfare programs are, which level of government administers them, and who is eligible for the various programs.
5. Be able to describe the work disincentive that results from the welfare program and Social Security.
6. Understand how welfare eligibility changes as income increases.
7. Be able to describe how a welfare recipient's real income changes as money income increases.
8. Know some of the recent initiatives to reform the welfare system and Social Security.

## Using Key Terms

Fill in the puzzle on the opposite page with the appropriate term from the list of Key Terms at the end of the chapter in the text.

### *Across*
1. The willingness and ability to work specific amounts of time at alternative wage rates.
4. An incentive to engage in undesirable behavior.
5. The percentage of income transfers that goes to the intended recipients and purposes.
6. The shortfall between actual income and the poverty threshold.
7. Means-tested income transfer programs.
11. Programs that provide event-conditioned income transfers.
12. The percentage of base wages paid out in benefits is the _____ _____ rate.
13. Direct transfers of goods and services rather than cash.

### *Down*
2. The income level at which welfare eligibility ceases.
3. Payment to individuals for which no good or service is exchanged.
4. The tax rate imposed on the last dollar of income.
8. The percentage change in quantity of labor supplied divided by the percentage change in tax rates is the _____ _____ of labor supply.
9. Income transfers of direct cash payments.
10. The _____ participation rate is the percentage of the working-age population working or seeking employment.

# Puzzle 19.1

# True or False: *Circle your choice and explain why any false statements are incorrect.*

T   F   1.   The Social Security payments received by retired persons are an in-kind transfer payment.

T   F   2.   Whether a given family is below the official poverty line depends only on its money income and the number of family members.

T   F   3.   The availability of welfare benefits shifts the labor supply curve to the right.

T   F   4.   The higher the marginal tax rate of any given welfare program, the greater the damage to the work incentives of recipients, *ceteris paribus*.

T   F   5.   The break-even level of income is the amount of income a person can earn before losing all welfare benefits.

T   F   6.   Increasing "disregards" will lower the break-even level of income.

T   F   7.   Almost every U.S. household receives some form of income transfer payments.

T   F   8.   Social Security is a welfare program.

T   F   9.   If welfare benefits for each household in poverty equaled the poverty gap, people who are not poor would have a strong incentive to become poor.

T   F   10.   The primary economic cost of the Social Security program is the financial costs of administering the program.

# Multiple Choice: *Select the correct answer.*

_____   1.   Transfer payments include:
   (a)   Unemployment benefits for the unemployed.
   (b)   In-kind transfers.
   (c)   Social Security benefits.
   (d)   All of the above.

_____   2.   Increased income transfers are undesirable because:
   (a)   They create dependency.
   (b)   Work disincentives result.
   (c)   Total output decreased.
   (d)   All of the above.

_____   3.   Which of the following is a goal of an in-kind transfer program but not a cash transfer program?
   (a)   To change the market's answer to the WHO question.
   (b)   Equity.
   (c)   To insure that recipients get the type of aid intended.
   (d)   All of the above are correct.

_____   4.   Medicaid and food stamps are received by:
   (a)   Anyone that applies.
   (b)   Only the elderly.
   (c)   Only the poor.
   (d)   Mostly upper income households in the U.S. due to inequities in the system.

_____ 5. Social insurance programs:
  (a) Are event conditional.
  (b) Insure people against specific problems, e.g. unemployment.
  (c) Are not welfare programs.
  (d) All of the above are correct.

_____ 6. Income-transfer programs can:
  (a) Change the answer to the WHAT to produce question.
  (b) Change the answer to the FOR WHOM to produce question.
  (c) Result in reduced output.
  (d) All of the above are correct.

_____ 7. If welfare benefits for each household in poverty equaled the poverty gap:
  (a) The effective marginal tax rate for welfare recipients would be 100 percent.
  (b) People who are not poor would have a strong incentive to become poor.
  (c) Poverty would be eliminated.
  (d) All of the above would occur.

_____ 8. Suppose a poverty program provides a basic benefit of $3,000, and a marginal tax rate of 0.25. The break-even level of income is:
  (a) $8,000.
  (b) $12,000.
  (c) $18,000.
  (d) $4,000.

_____ 9. The official poverty index is based on:
  (a) Family size.
  (b) Cash income.
  (c) Age of the household head.
  (d) All of the above.

_____ 10. A good reason for excluding in-kind transfers from income calculations is:
  (a) That the more poor there are, the more jobs there will be for bureaucrats.
  (b) That people would be forced above the poverty line by consuming things like medical services.
  (c) That it is impossible to place a value on most of the services provided.
  (d) All of the above.

Use the following welfare benefit formula to answer the following questions.
Welfare Benefit = Maximum benefit - 3/4 [Wages - (work expenses + child care costs)]

_____ 11. Based on the information given above, the marginal tax rate is:
  (a) Zero percent.
  (b) 25 percent.
  (c) 75 percent.
  (d) 100 percent.

_____ 12. Suppose that Mr. Henry works 1200 hours per year at a wage of $8 per hour, has child care expenses of $1600 per year and work expenses of $1400. If Mr. Henry's state has a maximum welfare benefit of $8000 per year, based on the welfare formula given above, Mr. Henry's welfare benefit will be:
  (a) Zero. His income has exceeded the limit.
  (b) $3050.
  (c) $4950.
  (d) $6600.

271

_____ 13. Social security benefits paid by the federal government:
   (a) Are income transfers financed by taxes on workers and employers.
   (b) Are classified as in-kind benefits.
   (c) Have no effect on the decision regarding for whom output is to be produced.
   (d) All of the above.

_____ 14. Which of the following programs does *not* provide in-kind benefits?
   (a) The food stamp program.
   (b) The housing assistance program.
   (c) Temporary Aid to Needy Families (TANF).
   (d) Medicaid.

_____ 15. When authorities choose to "disregard" income earned by welfare recipients, they are:
   (a) Intentionally helping the welfare recipient cheat.
   (b) Attempting to improve work incentives.
   (c) Looking out for their own jobs because the more income they disregard, the more poor there will be.
   (d) Being arbitrary in their administration of the program.

_____ 16. Higher marginal tax rates in welfare programs will:
   (a) Decrease the incentive to work.
   (b) Decrease total welfare costs.
   (c) Reduce the number of people on welfare.
   (d) Do all of the above.

_____ 17. The Social Security program tends to:
   (a) Increase work incentives for both older and younger workers.
   (b) Increase work incentives for older workers but not younger workers.
   (c) Decrease work incentives for both older and younger workers.
   (d) Decrease work incentives for older workers but not younger workers.

_____ 18. If the Social Security program is privatized:
   (a) Work disincentives for younger workers will be reduced.
   (b) Income inequalities would increase.
   (c) Another kind of public transfer program may have to be implemented for those elderly who made bad investments.
   (d) All of the above could occur.

_____ 19. The primary economic cost of the Social Security program is the:
   (a) Financial costs of administering the program.
   (b) Reduction in total output the program causes because of work disincentives.
   (c) Redistribution of income from younger to older workers.
   (d) Benefits paid.

_____ 20. The primary benefit of the Social Security program is the:
   (a) Increased work incentives for older workers.
   (b) More equitable distribution of income that results.
   (c) Jobs created by the additional spending.
   (d) All of the above are benefits.

# Problems and Applications

## Exercise 1

This exercise examines welfare benefits and the marginal tax rate on benefits.

Assume the welfare benefit is calculated as:

Benefit = maximum benefit - wages

1. Every additional dollar of wages (increases, reduces) welfare benefits by the same amount.

2. T    F         In this case there is a disincentive to work because the marginal tax rate is 100 percent.

3. Now assume the welfare benefit formula changes to:

    Benefit = maximum benefit - 0.5(wages)

    What is the marginal tax rate? _____

4. A decrease in the marginal tax rate will encourage (more, less) work effort and make (more, fewer) people eligible for welfare.

5. Use the formula in question 3. Assume the maximum benefit is $10,000. If a welfare recipient earns $4000 in a part-time job, his or her total income will be _____.

6. The breakeven level of income is the amount of income a person can earn before losing (some, all) welfare benefits.

7. The breakeven level of income in question 5 is _____.

## Exercise 2

This exercise focuses on the Social Security program.

1. The Social Security program is a _____ transfer program because it sends checks to recipients.

2. T    F         The primary economic cost of the Social Security program is benefits it pays to retired workers.

3. Assume a person is entitled to a maximum award of $12,000 in Social Security benefits. But this person continues to work upon reaching retirement age and earns $10,000 per year. Given the following benefit formula:

    Benefit amount = maximum award - 0.60(wage - $6000)

    What is the Social Security benefit for this individual? _____

4. What is the total income for this individual? _____

# Common Errors

The first statement in each "common error" below is incorrect. Each incorrect statement is followed by a corrected version and an explanation.

1. The federal government runs the welfare system. WRONG!

   The welfare system consists of programs administered by federal, state, and local governments. RIGHT!

   It's true that the federal government is heavily involved in the welfare system, but state and local governments are involved as well. As a matter of fact, the benefits that a poor person may receive vary from state to state. The differentials in benefits have been the reason for the migration of some poor people from low-benefit states to high-benefit states. The federal government is trying to reduce its role in this area, however.

2. Welfare recipients are typically minority families headed by able-bodied males. WRONG!

   There is no average welfare recipient. RIGHT!

   The stereotype of the welfare recipient seems firmly entrenched in the minds of American taxpayers. The poor are a very heterogeneous group, however, with many more whites than minority-group members. Most work when they can find employment. Some work all year long and are still poor.

# •ANSWERS•

## Using Key Terms

### Across
1. labor supply
4. moral hazard
5. target efficiency
6. poverty gap
7. welfare programs
11. social insurance
12. wage replacement
13. in-kind transfers

### Down
2. break even level of income
3. transfer payment
4. marginal tax rate
8. tax elasticity
9. cash transfers
10. labor force

## True or False

1. F  They are a cash transfer payment.
2. T
3. F  The availability of welfare benefits reduces the incentive to work thus shifting the labor supply curve to the left.
4. T
5. T
6. F  Increasing disregards will raise the break-even level of income.
7. T
8. F  Social Security is event-based and is therefore not a welfare program.
9. T
10. F  The primary economic cost of the Social Security program is the reduction in total output the program causes because of work disincentives.

## Multiple Choice

| | | | | | | | | |
|---|---|---|---|---|---|---|---|---|
| 1. | d | 5. | d | 9. | d | 13. | a | 17. c |
| 2. | d | 6. | d | 10. | b | 14. | c | 18. d |
| 3. | c | 7. | d | 11. | c | 15. | b | 19. b |
| 4. | c | 8. | b | 12. | b | 16. | d | 20. b |

## Problems and Applications

### Exercise 1

1. reduces
2. T
3. 50 percent
4. more, more
5. $10,000 - 0.5($4000) = $10,000 - $2000 = $8000    $8000 + $4000 = $12,000
6. all
7. $10,000/0.5 = $20,000

### Exercise 2

1. cash
2. F  The primary economic cost is the decrease in total output because workers retire early.
3. $12,000 - 0.6($10,000 - $6000) = $12,000 - 0.6($4000) = $12,000 - $2400 = $9600
4. $10,000 + $9600 = $19,600

# CHAPTER 20
# International Trade

## Quick Review

Even the most casual observer of economic activity understands that trade between the United States and other nations is very important. Hardly a day goes by without hearing or reading some reference to exports, imports, the "trade deficit," the value of the dollar in foreign-exchange markets, and the like. In this chapter we ask some basic questions about trade, such as:

- What benefit, if any, do we get from international trade?
- How much harm do imports cause, and to whom?
- Should we protect ourselves from "unfair" trade by limiting imports?

In recent decades the United States has become much more dependent on foreign trade than ever before. We export a wide variety of goods, especially agricultural products and capital goods, to many countries, and import from advanced industrial nations such as Japan, Germany, and Canada and such poor countries as Mexico and Uruguay. Oil is our most important import. Each nation trades with many others and although overall trade must balance (total exports must equal total imports), exports and imports between pairs of countries seldom do. Bilateral trade imbalances (surpluses and deficits) are the rule rather than the exception.

Countries are motivated to trade because by doing so they can produce together more total output than they could in the absence of trade. Specialization and trade allow both members of a trading partnership to consume beyond their respective production-possibilities curves. That is, consumption possibilities will exceed production possibilities. The economic reason for this result is rooted in the "law of comparative advantage." This dictum says that as long as the opportunity costs of producing goods in two countries differ, it will always be possible for those countries to specialize and trade to their mutual advantage. Neither the absolute size of the countries nor their absolute costs of production are important. What does count is the relative (comparative) opportunity cost of producing alternative goods.

It is obvious that specialization and trade benefit trading nations. While trade increases total world output, it is the terms under which trade takes place that determine how the gains are distributed between trading partners. In spite of trade's overall benefits, special interest groups often exert strong pressure *against* foreign trade. Those who would lose their markets and jobs to imported goods and foreign workers often strongly and successfully oppose free trade.

Industries that need raw materials that are being exported may exert pressure on government to place restrictions on the export of those raw materials. The government may place a tariff or quota on imported goods or provide aid to the affected domestic industry. The government may subsidize industries that are hurt by foreign trade. We have occasionally asked our trading partners to voluntarily limit their exports to us so as to ease the pressure on threatened firms and industries. Government has sometimes made assistance (cash, training, or relocation) available to those whose jobs were lost to foreign competition.

Most of the world's industrialized countries belong to the General Agreement on Tariffs and Trade (GATT). This organization, which was created in 1947, commits the world's trading partners to pursue free-trade policies. This includes the dismantling of both tariff and nontariff barriers to trade in goods and services. The organization had significant success in early "rounds," but it has had more difficulty in making important gains recently. Overall, tariffs have been reduced from an average of 40 percent in 1948 to less than four percent today, and trade has expanded greatly as a result. The Uruguay round of GATT expanded the application of free trade rules to agricultural goods and to services and created the World Trade Organization to adjudicate disputes

The Economic Union (EU) and the North American Free Trade Agreement (NAFTA) are examples of trading blocks designed to reduce trade barriers. Any successful trading arrangement will bring about a reallocation of resources, but the overall effect will be a net gain in jobs and output for all the participants. NAFTA brought gains to U.S. producers of agricultural products, metal products, autos and others, and estimated losses in construction, medicine, lumber, etc.

## Learning Objectives

After reading Chapter 20 and doing the following exercises, you should:

1. Know some basic facts about U.S. trade patterns.
2. Understand the macroeconomic impact of international trade.
3. Understand why specialization and trade increase both production possibilities and consumption possibilities.
4. Be able to explain comparative advantage using opportunity costs.
5. Know how to determine the limits to the terms of trade.
6. Be able to calculate the gains from specialization and trade at given terms of trade.
7. Be able to show how trade allows a country to consume beyond its production-possibilities curve.
8. Recognize the sources of pressure that result in restricted trade.
9. Know some of the arguments used by those wishing to restrict trade.
10. Be able to discuss tariff and nontariff barriers to trade.
11. Be able to discuss the reasons for the rise of regional trading arrangements.

## Using Key Terms

Fill in the puzzle on the opposite page with the appropriate term from the list of Key Terms at the end of the chapter in the text.

### *Across*

2. Alternative combinations of goods and services that can be produced with available resources and technology.
3. Alternative combinations of goods and services that a country can consume.
5. The ability to produce a good at a lower opportunity cost than another country.
9. A negative trade balance.
11. The sale of goods in export markets at prices below domestic prices.
13. A limit on the quantity of a good that may be imported.
14. The most desired goods and services that are foregone in order to obtain something else.
15. A tax imposed on imported goods.
16. The amount of good A given up for good B in trade.

### *Down*

1. An agreement to reduce the volume of trade in a specific good.
4. Determined by the intersection of market demand and market supply.
6. The ability of a country to produce a good with fewer resources than other countries.

7. A prohibition on exports or imports.
8. The amount by which exports exceed imports.
10. Goods and services sold to foreign buyers.
12. Goods and services purchased from foreign sources.

## Puzzle 20.1

# True or False: *Circle your choice and explain why any false statements are incorrect.*

T  F  1.   The United States buys large quantities of goods and services from other countries but foreign countries buy very few of our goods and services.

T  F  2.   A reduction of trade barriers should result in reduced prices and increased consumption, *ceteris paribus*.

T  F  3.   The United States has a higher reliance on foreign trade, as measured by the ratio of exports to GDP, than most other nations.

T  F  4.   Comparative advantage refers to the ability to produce output with fewer resources than any other country.

T  F  5.   If one country has a comparative advantage in producing one of two goods, the other country must have a comparative advantage in the other good.

T  F  6.   It is impossible for a country to consume a mix of goods and services beyond its production-possibilities curve.

T  F  7.   The terms at which countries will trade one good for another will occur between their respective domestic opportunity costs.

T  F  8.   Everybody wins when countries specialize and trade.

T  F  9.   From the consumer's point of view, quotas have the potential to inflict more damage than do tariffs because additional imports are not available at any price.

T  F 10.   Tariffs and quotas raise the price of imported goods to consumers.

# Multiple Choice: *Select the correct answer.*

_____   1.   Suppose the production of 1 ton of steel in the United States requires the same amount of resources as the production of 100 gallons of oil. In Canada, 2 tons of steel requires the same amount of resources as 200 gallons of oil. This means that:
     (a)   Neither country has a comparative advantage.
     (b)   Canada has the comparative advantage in steel.
     (c)   The United States has an absolute advantage in steel.
     (d)   The United States has the comparative advantage in steel.

_____   2.   In Germany, suppose 6 cameras or 4 bicycles can be produced with 1 unit of labor. In Japan, suppose 9 cameras or 5 bicycles can be produced with 1 unit of labor. Therefore:
     (a)   Japan has an absolute advantage in the production of both goods.
     (b)   Japan has a comparative advantage in the production of both goods.
     (c)   Germany has a comparative advantage in the production of cameras.
     (d)   Japan has a comparative advantage in the production of bicycles.

_____   3.   If a country is completely self-reliant in producing goods for its own consumption needs, then:
     (a)   It is consuming more than it could with trade.
     (b)   Its consumption possibilities will equal its production possibilities.
     (c)   It is promoting specialization.
     (d)   It will achieve a higher standard of living by exporting.

_____ 4. The expansion of world output as a result of trade is mainly due to the effects of:
   (a)   Higher trade barriers.
   (b)   Improved terms of trade.
   (c)   Specialization according to comparative advantage.
   (d)   Specialization according to absolute advantage.

_____ 5. When one country can produce a given amount of a good using fewer inputs than any other country:
   (a)   It has an absolute advantage in producing the good.
   (b)   It has a comparative advantage in producing the good.
   (c)   Specialization will definitely increase worldwide consumption possibilities.
   (d)   All of the above.

_____ 6. "Terms of trade" refers to:
   (a)   The opportunity costs incurred in trade.
   (b)   The rate at which goods are exchanged.
   (c)   The degree to which one country has an absolute advantage.
   (d)   Which country pays the transportation costs when trade occurs.

_____ 7. To say that a country has a comparative advantage in the production of wine is to say that:
   (a)   It can produce wine with fewer resources than any other country can.
   (b)   Its opportunity cost of producing wine is greater than any other country's.
   (c)   Its opportunity cost of producing wine is lower than any other country's.
   (d)   The relative price of wine is higher in that country than in any other.

_____ 8. America's tariffs on foreign goods result in:
   (a)   Lower domestic prices than those that would prevail in their absence.
   (b)   A stimulus to efficient American firms that are not protected.
   (c)   Higher employment and output in protected industries than would otherwise be the case.
   (d)   A more efficient allocation of resources than would occur in their absence.

_____ 9. A principal objective of GATT is to:
   (a)   Reduce barriers to trade.
   (b)   Settle domestic tax disputes internationally.
   (c)   Equalize income tax structures in various countries.
   (d)   Protect domestic producers from foreign competition.

_____ 10. World output of goods and services increases with specialization because:
   (a)   The world's resources are being used more efficiently.
   (b)   Each country's production possibilities curve is shifted outward.
   (c)   Each country's workers are able to produce more than they could before specialization.
   (d)   All of the above are correct.

_____ 11. A "beggar-thy-neighbor policy" is:
   (a)   An attempt by a poor country to get more foreign aid and assistance.
   (b)   The imposition of trade barriers for the purpose of expanding exports.
   (c)   The imposition of import barriers for the purpose of curbing inflation.
   (d)   The imposition of trade barriers to increase domestic employment.

Suppose the production possibilities of Japan and the U.S. are given in Table 20.1. Use Table 20.1 to answer questions 12 and 13.

## Table 20.1
## Output per worker day in the United States and Japan

| Country | TV sets (per day) | Bicycles (per day) |
|---|---|---|
| Japan | 2 | 10 |
| United States | 1 | 8 |

_____ 12. Which of the following statements is true?
  (a)    The United States has an absolute advantage in the production of bicycles.
  (b)    Japan has an absolute advantage in the production of bicycles only.
  (c)    Japan has an absolute advantage in the production of TV sets only.
  (d)    Japan has an absolute advantage in the production of both bicycles and TV sets.

_____ 13. Suppose the terms of trade are established in such a way that 1 TV set equals 5 bicycles. Which of the following statements would be true?
  (a)    These terms of trade provide gains for the United States, but Japan is worse off.
  (b)    These terms of trade provide gains for Japan, but the United States is worse off.
  (c)    These terms of trade provide gains for the United States, and Japan is no worse off.
  (d)    These terms of trade provide gains for Japan, and the United States is no worse off.

_____ 14. Suppose the country of Montgomery has specialized in the production of a good but has not yet entered into a trade. At this point in time, Montgomery:
  (a)    Has moved to a level of production outside its production possibilities curve.
  (b)    Has shifted its production possibilities curve outward.
  (c)    Has moved along its existing production possibilities curve.
  (d)    Has moved to a level of consumption outside its production possibilities curve.

_____ 15. "Dumping" is said to occur when:
  (a)    Foreign producers sell more of a particular good in the United States than domestic producers sell.
  (b)    Foreign producers sell their goods in the United States at prices lower than the U.S. average cost of production.
  (c)    Foreign producers sell their goods in the United States at prices lower than those prevailing in their own countries.
  (d)    The foreign countries have trade surpluses and the United States has a trade deficit.

_____ 16. What should happen to the equilibrium price and quantity in a market as a result of a tariff on imports?
  (a)    Equilibrium price and quantity should both go up.
  (b)    Equilibrium price should go up, and equilibrium quantity should go down.
  (c)    Equilibrium price should go down, and equilibrium quantity should go up.
  (d)    Equilibrium price and quantity should both go down.

_____ 17. With regard to international trade, the market mechanism:
  (a)    Provides a profit incentive to producers who specialize in the goods and services for which a comparative advantage exists.
  (b)    Provides a profit incentive to producers who trade in the goods and services for which a comparative advantage exists.
  (c)    Determines the terms of trade.
  (d)    Does all of the above.

_____ 18. International trade:
   (a) Lowers prices to consumers.
   (b) Alters the mix of domestic production.
   (c) Redistributes income toward export industries.
   (d) All of the above.

_____ 19. Suppose that Brazil has a comparative advantage in coffee and Mexico has a comparative advantage in tomatoes. Which of the following groups would be worse off if these two countries specialize and trade?
   (a) Brazilian tomato producers.
   (b) Brazilian coffee producers.
   (c) Mexican tomato producers.
   (d) Everyone is better off when specialization and trade take place.

_____ 20. If we add together all the gains from specialization and trade and then subtract all the losses, the net result would be:
   (a) Zero; the gains and losses would cancel out.
   (b) Positive; a net gain for the world and each country.
   (c) Negative; a net loss for the world and each country.
   (d) Impossible to tell; the net result could be zero, positive, or negative.

# Problems and Applications

## *Exercise 1*

This exercise shows how trade leads to gains by all trading partners through specialization and comparative advantage.

Suppose that Japan has 20 laborers in total and that the United States has 40 laborers. Suppose their production possibilities are given in Table 20.2. (*Be careful:* The table tells you that a worker in Japan can produce 2 TV sets per day *or* 10 bicycles per day, *not* two TV sets *and* 10 bicycles!)

### Table 20.2
### Output per worker day in the United States and Japan

| Country | TV sets (per day) | Bicycles (per day) |
|---|---|---|
| Japan | 2 | 10 |
| United States | 1 | 8 |

1. Draw the production-possibilities curves for each country in Figure 20.1. Assume constant costs of production.

## Figure 20.1

2. Suppose that before trade Japan uses 12 laborers to produce bicycles and 8 laborers to produce television sets; suppose also that in the United States 20 workers produce bicycles and 20 produce television sets. Complete Table 20.3.

## Table 20.3
## Output produced and consumed without trade

| Country | TV sets (per day) | Bicycles (per day) |
|---|---|---|
| Japan | _____ | _____ |
| United States | _____ | _____ |
| Total | _____ | _____ |

3. Before trade, the total output of television sets is _____ ; of bicycles, _____ .

4. What is the opportunity cost of 1 television set in Japan? _____ In the United States? _____

5. What is the opportunity cost of 1 bicycle in Japan? _____ In the United States? _____

6. If Japan and the United States specialize according to their respective comparative advantages, Japan will produce _____ and the United States will produce _____ . They will do so because the opportunity cost of bicycles in terms of television sets is (lower, higher) in the United States than in Japan, and the opportunity cost of television sets in terms of bicycles is (lower, higher) in Japan than in the United States.

7. After specialization, the total output of television sets is _____ and the total output of bicycles is _____ . (*Hint:* Assume 20 Japanese produce only TV sets, and 40 Americans produce only bicycles.)

8. This output represents an increase of _____ bicycles and _____ television sets over the pre-specialization output. (*Hint:* Compare answers to problems 3 and 7.)

# Exercise 2

This exercise will help you understand how the terms of trade are determined. Refer to Exercise 1 for the data.

If Japan and the United States are to benefit from the increased production, trade must take place. The Japanese will be willing to trade television sets for bicycles as long as they get back more bicycles than they could get in their own country.

1. The terms of trade will be between 1 television set equals _____ bicycles and 1 television set equals _____ bicycles.

2. If the terms of trade were 4 bicycles equals one television set:
   (a) Neither country would buy bicycles, but both would buy TV sets.
   (b) Neither country would buy TV sets, but both would buy bicycles.
   (c) Both countries would buy bicycles and TV sets.

3. Suppose that the two countries agree that the terms of trade will be 6 bicycles equals 1 television set. Let Japan export 20 television sets per day to the United States. Complete Table 20.4. Assume that Japan produces 40 television sets per day and the United States produces 320 bicycles.

## Table 20.4
## Consumption combination after trade

| Country | TV sets (per day) | Bicycles (per day) |
|---|---|---|
| Japan | _____ | _____ |
| United States | _____ | _____ |
| Total | 40 | 320 |

4. As a result of specialization and trade, the United States has the same quantity of television sets and _____ more bicycles per day. (Compare Tables 20.3 and 20.4.)

5. As a result of specialization and trade, Japan has the same number of bicycles and _____ more television sets per day.

Now suppose that at the exchange rate of 6 bicycles to 1 TV set, Japan would like to export 10 TV sets and import 60 bicycles per day. Suppose also that the United States desires to export 90 bicycles and import 15 television sets per day.

6. At these terms of trade there is a (shortage, surplus) of television sets.

7. At these terms of trade there is a (shortage, surplus) of bicycles.

8. Which of the following terms of trade would be more likely to result from this situation?
   (a) 5 bicycles equal 1 television set.
   (b) 6 bicycles equal 1 television set.
   (c) 7 bicycles equal 1 television set.

## Exercise 3

When protection is provided to producers of a particular product, consumers of that product are harmed because they must pay higher prices than in the absence of protection. In addition, the effects of the protection in one market spill over into related factor and product markets, thus distorting both production and consumption patterns. This exercise will help you to discover how this occurs.

Reread the World View article entitled "Sugar Quota a Sour Deal," and then answer the following questions.

1. What was the estimated overall cost to U.S. consumers in 1995 due to the quota on sugar?

2. If the U.S. sugar quota was abolished, which of the following would be the most likely equilibrium world price for sugar, *ceteris paribus*?
   (a)     7 cents per pound.
   (b)     15 cents per pound.
   (c)     22 cents per pound.
   (d)     24 cents per pound.

3. If the sugar quotas were abolished, what would you predict to happen to the number of sugar producers in the United States?_____

4. Suppose the next best use of land used to produce sugar beets in the U.S. was to produce wheat. What would you predict to happen to the price of wheat in the U.S. market, *ceteris paribus*, if the sugar quota was abolished?_____

5. What would you predict to happen to the marginal revenue product of labor and the level of employment of labor in the Caribbean sugar industry, *ceteris paribus*?_____
_____

## Common Errors

The first statement in each "common error" below is incorrect. Each incorrect statement is followed by a corrected version and an explanation.

1. A country must have an *absolute advantage* in order to gain from trade with another country. WRONG!

   A country must have a *comparative advantage* in order to gain from trade with another country. RIGHT!

   Mutually advantageous trade requires only that the opportunity costs of producing goods differ between the two countries, *ceteris paribus*. Another way of stating this is that the production-possibilities curves of the two countries must have different slopes. The two circumstances noted above are indicated in Figure 20.2 below.

**Figure 20.2**

In diagram (a), in which country B has an absolute advantage over country A, the production-possibilities curves have the same slope; thus mutually advantageous trade *is not* possible. In diagram (b), each country has a comparative advantage because the production-possibilities curves of the two countries have different slopes; thus mutually advantageous trade *is* possible.

2.  Foreign trade costs a country jobs. WRONG!

    Although jobs may be lost, new ones will be created by the opportunities opened up with trade. RIGHT!

    When countries specialize and trade according to the law of comparative advantage, some particular workers and firms may be hurt by imports, but the economy as a whole gains by trade. More output per resource input will be attainable. Because the economy is able to reach full employment with trade as well as without trade, there is no reason to assume there will be fewer jobs.

3.  A country is well off only as long as it exports more than it imports. WRONG!

    Countries may, at times, be well off when they experience a trade surplus; they may also be well off when they have a trade deficit. RIGHT!

    Both trade deficits and trade surpluses can be problems if either situation persists for a long period of time. Trade surpluses mean that a country is giving more of its limited, precious resources in trade than it is acquiring from other countries. The currencies of deficit countries tend to depreciate, which means they will be unable to buy as many foreign goods with a unit of currency.

4.  Countries tend to enter into trade to get things they cannot produce themselves. WRONG!

    Countries very often trade for things they could produce themselves. RIGHT!

    *Be careful!* Countries often trade for things they could produce themselves because the relative costs of domestic production would be prohibitive. Take baskets as an example. Producers in the U.S. could certainly produce baskets if they really wanted to. The technique is not difficult to learn and the materials are abundant. But baskets do not lend themselves to machine production, and hand labor is expensive here. The cost in terms of goods forgone would be tremendous. (So would the price of the baskets.) We're better off specializing in something like computers, where we have a comparative advantage, and trading for baskets, where we clearly do not have a comparative advantage.

5. The effects of protection affect only workers in the protected industry and the domestic consumers of the protected commodity. WRONG!

The effects of protection spread to many other markets both here and abroad as producers and consumers adjust their production and consumption patterns. RIGHT!

Protection and output changes in any market are bound to set off additional changes in related markets. Higher prices for a protected product lead consumers to seek out substitutes with lower prices. This should increase the demand for the substitute and set off a host of other changes in related input and product markets. Similarly, if the protected commodity is used as an input, an increase in its price will lead to a search for substitutes with lower prices and have consequent impacts on related markets. In the case of sugar, corn based high-fructose corn syrup has replaced sugar to such an extent that corn growers, fearing a reduction in the demand for their output, now lobby their congressional delegations to maintain the sugar quota! Similar impacts can be expected in the markets of foreign producers.

# •ANSWERS•

## Using Key Terms
### Across
2. production possibilities
3. consumption possibilities
5. comparative advantage
9. trade deficit
11. dumping
13. quota
14. opportunity cost
15. tariff
16. terms of trade

### Down
1. voluntary restraint agreement
4. equilibrium price
6. absolute advantage
7. embargo
8. trade surplus
10. exports
12. imports

## True or False

1. F  Approximately 11 percent of U.S. GDP is exported. In dollar terms, the U.S. is the world's largest exporter of goods and services.
2. T
3. F  Despite the fact that the U.S. is the world's largest importer, the U.S. only exports and imports a relatively small percentage of its GDP.
4. F  Comparative advantage refers to the ability to produce output at a smaller opportunity cost than another country, i.e. giving up fewer alternative goods and services.
5. T
6. F  With specialization and free trade it is possible for a country to consume a mix of goods and services beyond its production-possibilities curve although it is never possible for a country to produce beyond its production-possibilities curve.

7. T
8. F Although countries as a whole benefit from specialization and free trade, there are always individuals and groups that may lose, e.g. import-competing firms.
9. T
10. T

## Multiple Choice

| | | | | | | | | | |
|---|---|---|---|---|---|---|---|---|---|
| 1. | a | 5. | a | 9. | a | 13. | c | 17. | d |
| 2. | a | 6. | b | 10. | a | 14. | c | 18. | d |
| 3. | b | 7. | c | 11. | d | 15. | c | 19. | a |
| 4. | c | 8. | c | 12. | d | 16. | b | 20. | b |

## Problems and Applications

### Exercise 1

1. **Figure 20.1 Answer**

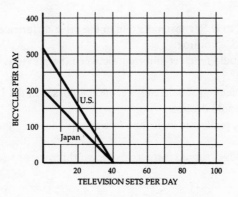

2. **Table 20.3 Answer**

| Country | TV sets | Bicycles |
|---|---|---|
| Japan | 16 | 120 |
| United States | 20 | 160 |
| Total | 36 | 280 |

3. 36; 280
4. 5 bicycles; 8 bicycles
5. 1/5 television set; 1/8 television set
6. television sets; bicycles; lower; lower
7. 40; 320
8. 40; 4

# Exercise 2

1. 5; 8
2. a
3. **Table 20.4 Answer**

| Country | TV sets | Bicycles |
|---|---|---|
| Japan | 20 | 120 |
| United States | 20 | 200 |
| Total | 40 | 320 |

4. 40
5. 4
6. shortage, The Japanese wish to export fewer (10) TV sets than Americans want to import (15).
7. surplus, The Americans wish to export more (90) bicycles than the Japanese want to import (60).
8. c    The shortage of TV sets will cause their price to increase.

# Exercise 3

1. The estimated cost to U.S. consumers due to the price difference between the U.S. market and the world market was $1.5 billion.
2. c    The market should reach equilibrium between the previous world price and the protected U.S. price.
3. The absence of protection should cause economic losses in the U.S. sugar industry and the number of firms should decline.
4. As sugar producers reallocate their land to wheat production, the market price of wheat should fall.
5. Their marginal product should increase as the world price of sugar rises; the level of employment should increase.

# CHAPTER 21

# International Finance

## Quick Review

All of the trade between nations discussed in the previous chapter must somehow be financed. And since each country has its own money, we have to ask several critical questions:

- What determines the value of one country's money as compared to the value of another's?
- What causes the international value of currencies to change?
- Should government intervene to limit currency fluctuations?

To facilitate trade and to eliminate the need for barter, markets for foreign exchange have developed. Their function is to determine the exchange rate at which two currencies will trade. The foreign-exchange market is like any other market—it consists of a supply schedule and a demand schedule. Supply and demand mean the same thing here as they do in any other market. The commodity being traded in this case is the money of one country for the money of another. Demand and supply determine the equilibrium price (exchange rate) and quantity of foreign exchange that is traded.

When the international value of a currency increases, the currency is said to appreciate. When a currency's international value decreases, the currency is said to depreciate. The exchange rate responds to changes in underlying forces, as reflected in shifts of the supply and demand curves. Changes in relative income levels, changes in relative prices, changes in product availability, relative interest-rate changes, and speculative activities are examples of the determinants that cause supply and demand curves to shift and alter exchange rates.

To keep track of the foreign-exchange flows that accompany the flow of goods and services, each country summarizes its transactions in a statement called the "balance of payments." The balance of payments is based on double-entry bookkeeping and must therefore balance, even though individual accounts may not.

There are good reasons why countries resist exchange rate movements. On a micro level, those doing business involving foreign currency will know the current exchange rate, but must forecast its future value when making contracts. This is very difficult and causes a great deal of uncertainty. Furthermore, any change in a country's exchange rate automatically alters the price of all its exports and imports. The interests of exporters and importers are thus diametrically opposed when a currency appreciates or depreciates due to market forces. On a macro level, changes in exchange rates can complicate the conduct of domestic monetary and fiscal policy. As a result, governments sometimes feel forced to intervene in foreign exchange markets.

Under a fixed-rate system, governments enter on the supply side to prevent an unwanted appreciation and on the demand side to prevent a depreciation. The overall conduct of intervention requires a country to accumulate reserves (foreign currencies, gold, etc.) at some times and disburse them at others. Both trade policy (tariffs, quotas, etc.) and domestic monetary and fiscal policy are sometimes used to prevent undesirable trends in exchange rates. When monetary and fiscal policy are used to address balance of payments and currency problems the general rule is that deficit countries are required to forsake full employment and surplus countries must give up price stability.

The United States and its major trading partners abandoned the fixed-rate Bretton Woods system in 1973 and replaced it with a flexible exchange rate system. In an ideal setting, a flexible rate system would not require government intervention because the exchange rate would automatically adjust to the equilibrium rate. In practice this has not been the case, however, and a system of "managed rates" has evolved in which governments still intervene, but now with the idea of narrowing, rather than eliminating, fluctuations.

A change in the value of one country's currency can affect other countries if the countries are linked through trade, geography, or by agreement. Recently Asia, Mexico, Brazil, and Russia have all experienced currency crises. In each case, the countries asked for outside help in the form of a currency bailout. Typically a bailout is facilitated by the International Monetary Fund (IMF) and the world's strongest economies. There are arguments both for and against currency bailouts.

## Learning Objectives

After reading Chapter 21 and doing the following exercises, you should:

1.  Understand that an exchange rate is simply a price.
2.  Know the forces that operate on the demand side of the foreign exchange market.
3.  Know the forces that operate on the supply side of the foreign exchange market.
4.  Understand how supply and demand interact to determine the equilibrium exchange rate.
5.  Understand the essentials of balance-of-payments accounting.
6.  Be able to demonstrate graphically the forces that cause a currency to appreciate or depreciate.
7.  Understand why there is resistance to exchange-rate changes.
8.  Be able to describe several exchange-rate systems and their consequences.
9.  Understand the macroeconomic and microeconomic consequences of exchange-rate movements.
10. Be able to describe a balance-of-payments problem.
11. Be aware of the recent history of the international value of the dollar.

## Using Key Terms

Fill in the puzzle on the opposite page with the appropriate term from the list of Key Terms at the end of the chapter in the text.

### *Across*

2.  Places where foreign currencies are bought and sold.
4.  The amount by which the quantity demanded exceeds the quantity supplied.
6.  A system in which governments intervene in foreign-exchange markets to limit exchange-rate fluctuations.
8.  Stocks of gold held by a government to purchase foreign exchange.
9.  A rise in the price of a currency relative to another.
10. The price of one currency in terms of another currency.
11. A fall in the price of one currency relative to another.
13. A mechanism for fixing the exchange rate.
14. The price at which the quantity demanded equals the quantity supplied.
15. An excess demand for domestic currency at current exchange rates.

## Down

1. An excess demand for foreign currency at current exchange rates.
2. Holdings of foreign exchange by official government agencies.
3. Floating exchange rates.
5. A summary record of a country's international economic transactions.
7. An abrupt depreciation of a currency whose value was fixed or managed by the government.
12. A situation in which the value of imports exceeds the value of exports.

# Puzzle 21.1

293

## True or False: *Circle your choice and explain why any false statements are incorrect.*

T  F  1.  The U.S. demand for French francs represents a supply of dollars to the foreign-exchange market.

T  F  2.  Increased foreign travel by Americans tends to cause the dollar to appreciate, *ceteris paribus*.

T  F  3.  Trade protection can be used to prop up fixed exchange rates.

T  F  4.  When the dollar price of German marks increases, German machinery becomes more expensive to U.S. residents.

T  F  5.  If the dollar appreciates against the franc, this change will be harmful to California vineyard owners.

T  F  6.  Under a flexible-exchange-rate system, there is no need for foreign-exchange reserves.

T  F  7.  If the U.S. price level rises more rapidly than the Japanese price level, *ceteris paribus*, U.S. exports to Japan will rise.

T  F  8.  When exchange rates are fixed, the balance of payments is zero.

T  F  9.  If there is a deficit in the capital account, it must be offset by a surplus in the current account.

T  F  10.  A country experiencing trade surpluses faces higher foreign debt and interest costs.

## Multiple Choice: *Select the correct answer.*

_____  1.  An increase in the dollar price of other currencies will tend to cause:
    (a)  American goods to be cheaper for foreigners.
    (b)  American goods to be more expensive for foreigners.
    (c)  Foreign goods to be cheaper to residents of the United States.
    (d)  Foreign goods to be more expensive to residents of foreign countries.

_____  2.  Suppose that a flexible exchange rate exists between the U.S. dollar and the Japanese yen. An increase in the supply of yen (a rightward shift in the supply curve of yen) will tend to:
    (a)  Increase U.S. imports of Japanese goods.
    (b)  Push the U.S. balance of trade in the direction of a surplus.
    (c)  Lower the yen price of the dollar.
    (d)  Raise the dollar price of the yen.

_____  3.  Changes in the value of the euro affect the economies of:
    (a)  Only those countries using the euro as currency.
    (b)  All European countries but there would no significant impact on countries outside Europe.
    (c)  Potentially the entire world.
    (d)  There would be no significant impact on any economies as long as exchange rates are flexible.

_____  4.  If the exchange rate between U.S. dollars and Japanese yen changes from $1 = 100 yen to $1 = 110 yen:
    (a)  All Japanese producers and consumers will lose.
    (b)  U.S. auto producers and autoworkers will gain.
    (c)  U.S. consumers of Japanese TV sets will gain.
    (d)  Japanese tourists to the U.S. will gain.

5. A country will experience a reduction in its balance-of-payments deficit, *ceteris paribus*, if:
   (a) Its level of GDP rises relative to foreign levels of GDP.
   (b) Its prices fall relative to foreign price levels, *ceteris paribus*.
   (c) The domestic price of the foreign currency falls.
   (d) It lowers its tariffs.

6. A result of the Asian Crisis of 1997-98 was:
   (a) A general increase in the value of the U.S. dollar in relation to Southeast Asian currencies.
   (b) A major decrease in the level of U.S. exports to Southeast Asia.
   (c) Political unrest in many Southeast Asian countries.
   (d) All of the above.

7. Greater volatility of floating exchange rates results in:
   (a) Greater costs because of uncertainty.
   (b) Balance-of-payments instability.
   (c) Smaller market shortages and surpluses of currencies.
   (d) Depletion of foreign reserves.

8. Which of the following changes will tend to cause a shift in the domestic demand curve for foreign currencies?
   (a) Changes in domestic incomes, *ceteris paribus*.
   (b) Changes in domestic prices of goods, *ceteris paribus*.
   (c) Changes in consumer taste for foreign goods, *ceteris paribus*.
   (d) All of the above.

9. An increase in the U.S. trade deficit could be caused by:
   (a) A depreciation of the dollar in terms of other currencies.
   (b) An appreciation of the dollar in terms of other currencies.
   (c) The imposition of a tariff on imported goods.
   (d) An increase in the capital-account deficit.

10. In a floating-exchange-rate system, the capital-account balance equals:
    (a) The negative of the current-account balance.
    (b) Foreign purchases of U.S. assets minus U.S. purchases of foreign assets.
    (c) The balance of payments minus the sum of the trade balance, the services balance, and unilateral transfers.
    (d) All of the above.

11. American citizens planning a vacation abroad would welcome:
    (a) Appreciation of the dollar.
    (b) Depreciation of the dollar.
    (c) Devaluation of the dollar.
    (d) Evaluation of the dollar.

12. A change in the exchange rate for a country's currency alters the prices of:
    (a) Exports only.
    (b) Imports only.
    (c) Both exports and imports.
    (d) Only domestic goods and services.

13. In a floating exchange-rate regime, the overall "balance" of the balance of payments must be:
    (a) Equal to zero.
    (b) Positive if exports of goods and services exceed imports of goods and services.
    (c) Positive if the capital account is in surplus.
    (d) Negative if the current account is in deficit.

14. When exchange rates are flexible, they are:
    (a) Determined by proclamation of the monetary authorities of a country.
    (b) Determined by the relative levels of gold reserves.
    (c) Permitted to vary with changes in supply and demand in the foreign exchange market.
    (d) Determined by the provisions of the Bretton Woods agreement.

15. If the U.S. dollar depreciates, the United States should experience in the long run:
    (a) A lower inflation rate.
    (b) A smaller deficit on the U.S. trade balance.
    (c) A larger deficit on the U.S. current account.
    (d) A larger deficit on the U.S. capital account.

16. The major drawback to a system of managed exchange rates is that:
    (a) A country's efforts to manage exchange-rate movements may arouse suspicion and retaliation.
    (b) A country's efforts to affect changes in exchange rates are almost totally ineffective.
    (c) Government efforts to alter exchange rates usually result in violent disruptions of the domestic economy.
    (d) It requires enormous gold reserves.

17. If French speculators believed the yen was going to appreciate against the dollar, they would:
    (a) Purchase francs.
    (b) Purchase dollars.
    (c) Purchase yen.
    (d) Sell yen.

18. Suppose that at the prevailing yen-dollar exchange rate, there is an excess demand for yen. To prevent the dollar from depreciating, the United States might:
    (a) Raise taxes.
    (b) Reduce government spending.
    (c) Raise interest rates.
    (d) Do all of the above.

19. A currency bailout:
    (a) Occurs when an economy is lent money in order to increase or maintain the value of its currency.
    (b) Can help avoid a "domino effect" of depreciating currencies in other economies.
    (c) Can be ultimately self-defeating because it saves the country receiving the bailout from implementing politically unpopular domestic policies which could have prevented the problem in the first place.
    (d) All of the above are correct.

20. The capital account includes:
    (a) Trade in goods.
    (b) Trade in services.
    (c) Unilateral transfers.
    (d) Foreign purchases of U.S. assets.

# Problems and Applications

## *Exercise 1*

This exercise provides practice in determining exchange rates.

1. Table 21.1 depicts the hypothetical demand for and supply of British pounds in terms of U.S. dollars. Use the information in Table 21.1 to plot the demand and supply of British pounds at the exchange rates indicated in Figure 21.1. Then answer questions 2-4.

### Table 21.1
### Monthly demand for and supply of British pounds in the United States

| Dollars per British pound | Quantity demanded | Quantity supplied |
|---|---|---|
| 4.50 | 100 | 700 |
| 4.00 | 200 | 600 |
| 3.50 | 300 | 500 |
| 3.00 | 400 | 400 |
| 2.50 | 500 | 300 |
| 2.00 | 600 | 200 |
| 1.50 | 700 | 100 |

### Figure 21.1
### Demand and supply curves for pounds

2. What is the equilibrium rate of exchange? _____

3. At a price of $2 per pound there would be excess:
   (a) Demand, and the exchange rate for pounds would rise.
   (b) Demand, and the exchange rate for pounds would fall.
   (c) Supply, and the exchange rate would rise.
   (d) Supply, and the exchange rate would fall.

4.   Suppose that Americans suddenly increased their demand for British exports.  The dollar price of pounds would (rise, fall).

5.   T   F   Whenever one currency depreciates, another currency must appreciate.

6.   As a result of the increased demand for British exports, the pound price of the dollar would (rise, fall).

## Exercise 2

This exercise shows why one currency appreciates when another currency depreciates.  It also shows why the demand for dollars represents the supply of other currencies, while the supply of dollars represents the demand for other currencies in the foreign-exchange markets.  In learning these things, you will get practice in making calculations with exchange rates.

1.   Table 21.2 includes the sources of demand and supply of dollars.  In the first column, check off the items that are the source of the demand for dollars.  In the second column, check off the items that are the source of the supply of dollars. (*Hint*: There are two kinds of speculators—those who think the dollar will rise and those who think it will fall.  You must sort the two types of speculators to determine which type will supply dollars and which will demand dollars.)

### Table 21.2
### Sources of supply and demand for dollars and pounds

|  | (1) Demand for $ | (2) Supply of $ | (3) Demand for £ | (4) Supply of £ |
|---|---|---|---|---|
| Foreign demand for American exports | ____ | ____ | ____ | ____ |
| Foreign demand for American investments | ____ | ____ | ____ | ____ |
| Speculation that the dollar will appreciate | ____ | ____ | ____ | ____ |
| American demand for imports | ____ | ____ | ____ | ____ |
| American demand for investments in foreign countries | ____ | ____ | ____ | ____ |
| Speculation that the dollar will depreciate | ____ | ____ | ____ | ____ |

2.   If we assume there are just two currencies in the world, the dollar ($) and the pound (£), then the items in Table 21.2 also account for the supply and demand for the pound.  Once again place checks in the appropriate blanks of Table 21.2 to indicate which items will constitute the demand for pounds and which items will constitute the supply of pounds.

3.   T   F   In a two country world the sources of demand for dollars are the same as the sources of the supply of the pound, and the sources of the supply of dollars are the same as the sources of the demand for pounds.

4.   T   F   The sources of demand for dollars are the same as the sources of supply for all other currencies in terms of dollars.  The sources of supply of dollars are the same as the sources of demand for all other currencies in terms of dollars.

5.   Let's return to our assumption that there are only two countries.  Use your observations in the previous two questions and your knowledge of converting one currency into another to find the quantities of dollars supplied (column 3) and quantities of dollars demanded (column 6) in Table 21.3.  Use the information in Table 21.3, which is the same as the data we used in Exercise 1 above, to compute the supply and demand for pounds.

## Table 21.3
## Supply and demand for dollars ($) and pounds (£)

| (1)<br>Price of a £<br>($ / £) | (2)<br>Quantity of £<br>demanded | (3)<br>Quantity of $<br>supplied | (4)<br>Price of a $<br>(£ / $) | (5)<br>Quantity of £<br>supplied | (6)<br>Quantity of $<br>demanded |
|---|---|---|---|---|---|
| 4.50 | 100 | _____ | _____ | 700 | _____ |
| 4.00 | 200 | _____ | _____ | 600 | _____ |
| 3.50 | 300 | _____ | _____ | 500 | _____ |
| 3.00 | 400 | _____ | _____ | 400 | _____ |
| 2.50 | 500 | _____ | _____ | 300 | _____ |
| 2.00 | 600 | _____ | _____ | 200 | _____ |
| 1.50 | 700 | _____ | _____ | 100 | _____ |

6.  Complete column 4 of Table 21.3 by converting the price of pounds (£) in terms of dollars ($) in column 1 to the price of dollars in terms of pounds. (*Hint*: they are reciprocals of each other. Remember that to find the price of any good or currency, that good or currency appears in the denominator!)

7.  From the data on the demand for the dollar (columns 4 and 6 of Table 21.3), draw the demand curve for the dollar in Figure 21.2. From the data on the supply of the dollar (columns 3 and 4 of Table 21.3), draw the supply curve for the dollar in Figure 21.2.

## Figure 21.2
## Demand and supply of dollars

8.  The equilibrium value of the dollar is _____ , and the equilibrium quantity of dollars is _____.

9.  When you multiply the equilibrium quantity of dollars by the equilibrium exchange rate for the dollar in terms of pounds (£), you find the quantity of pounds is _____. When you find the reciprocal of the equilibrium exchange rate for the dollar, you find the exchange rate for pounds is _____.

10. T   F   When you multiply the equilibrium quantity of dollars by the equilibrium exchange rate for the dollar in terms of pounds (£), you have calculated the equilibrium quantity of pounds. (Compare your answer to question 9 in this exercise with your answer to question 2, Exercise 1 above.)

11. T  F    The equilibrium exchange rate for the dollar equals the equilibrium exchange rate for the pound.

## Exercise 3

The media often feature articles about international financial issues.

Read the article entitled "Nobel Prize Was Nobler in October." Then answer the following questions.

1. According to the article, what was the dollar value of the Nobel Prize at the time it was announced?_____

2. How much was it worth two months later?_____

3. Why did the value change so much? _____

## Common Errors

The first statement in each "common error" below is incorrect. Each incorrect statement is followed by a corrected version and an explanation.

1. The price of a dollar in terms of yen is the number of dollars per yen. WRONG!

   The price of a dollar in terms of yen is the number of yen per dollar. RIGHT!

   This mistake can cost a bundle if you are in a foreign country and don't know how to distinguish the price of a dollar from the price of the other currency. In Japan you don't want to give $100 for a single yen note when you should be receiving 100 yen for $1! Remember that the item for which you want a price must appear in the denominator of the price. For example, the price of tomatoes is the number of dollars divided by the number of tomatoes that are purchased. Similarly, the price of a yen is the number of dollars divided by the number of yen that are purchased. The price of a dollar is the number of yen divided by the number of dollars that are purchased.

2. The supply and demand for dollars in the foreign-exchange market is the same thing as the supply and demand for money (dollars) targeted by the Fed. WRONG!

   The supply and demand for dollars in the foreign-exchange market is a totally different concept from the supply and demand for money. RIGHT!

   Remember that the price of money was the interest rate when we were focusing on the supply and demand for money. In the foreign-exchange market the price is the exchange rate, not the interest rate. Furthermore, the supply and demand for money (dollars), which is the focus of the Fed, occurs geographically within the United States. The foreign-exchange market occurs between countries—literally on the phone lines between banks of different countries. We can visualize the foreign-exchange market as an area totally outside of borders in which money temporarily enters for the purpose of being exchanged. While domestic monetary policies may influence the amount of money going into the foreign-exchange market, the link is often indirect. In fact, when the Fed tightens monetary policy to reduce the supply of dollars, the foreign-exchange market may see an *increase* in the supply of dollars as foreigners seek the higher interest rates from a tighter U.S. monetary policy.

3. A country is well off if its currency appreciates steadily over a long period of time. WRONG!

   Both appreciating currencies and depreciating currencies create problems. RIGHT!

   *Be careful!* There are problems associated with steadily appreciating currencies *and* with steadily depreciating currencies. People sometimes view a depreciating currency as a source of national shame and dislike the higher cost (and inflation) associated with higher prices of foreign goods. However, depreciation may make a country's exports more competitive, may lead to more jobs, and may help correct a trade deficit. By contrast, a country with an appreciating currency develops employment problems and a loss of competitiveness against other countries, even if it has more buying power as a result of its stronger currency.

4. When countries have trade deficits, money really flows out. When they have surpluses, money really flows in. WRONG!

   Money is not physically sent in most transactions, but the claim to ownership is. RIGHT!

   Most foreign trade is transacted by check and is just a "flow" of bookkeeping entries. Even when gold is sold, it seldom *physically* flows anywhere. In the case of the United States, under a fixed-exchange-rate system, it stays in Fort Knox even though someone else owns it. Thus, it is the claim to ownership that flows, not the money. When countries run trade deficits, their trading partners add to their claims against them. For countries with a trade surplus, the reverse is true.

5. There are balance-of-payments surpluses and deficits under floating exchange rates. WRONG!

   The balance of payments is always zero under floating exchange rates. RIGHT!

   Under fixed exchange rates, the government must balance surpluses and deficits on the balance of payments with changes in reserves. With floating exchange rates, there is no reserve currency and any transfers abroad by the government are simply classified as unilateral transfers and are included in the current account. By definition, the current account and the capital account balance each other under a floating exchange-rate system.

# •ANSWERS•

## Using Key Terms
### Across
2. foreign-exchange markets
4. market shortage
6. managed exchange rates
8. gold reserves
9. appreciation
10. exchange rates
11. depreciation
13. gold standard
14. equilibrium price
15. balance-of-payments surplus

### Down
1. balance-of-payments deficit
2. foreign exchange reserves

3. flexible exchange rate
5. balance of payments
7. devaluation
12. trade deficit

## True or False

1. T
2. F   Increased foreign travel by Americans tends to increase the demand for foreign currency, thus increasing the supply of U.S. dollars and reducing the value of the dollar.
3. T
4. T
5. T
6. T
7. F   U.S. goods will be relatively more expensive to Japan thus reducing exports.
8. F   Fixed exchange rates tend to cause balance-of-payments deficits and surpluses because they cause shortages and surpluses of currencies.
9. T
10. F   A country experiencing trade deficits will have higher foreign debt and interest rates because that country will have to borrow to finance the additional goods and services it is consuming over what it is producing.

## Multiple Choice

| 1. | a | 5. | b | 9. | b | 13. | a | 17. | c |
|----|---|----|---|----|---|-----|---|-----|---|
| 2. | a | 6. | d | 10. | d | 14. | c | 18. | d |
| 3. | c | 7. | a | 11. | a | 15. | b | 19. | d |
| 4. | c | 8. | d | 12. | c | 16. | a | 20. | d |

## Problems and Applications

## *Exercise 1*

1. **Figure 21.1 Answer**

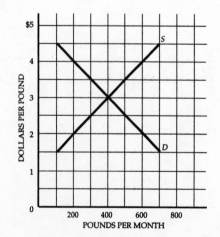

302

2.  $3 per British pound          3.  a          4.  rise          5.  T          6.  fall

# Exercise 2

### Table 21.2 Answer

|  | (1)<br>Demand<br>for $ | (2)<br>Supply<br>of $ | (3)<br>Demand<br>for £ | (4)<br>Supply<br>of £ |
|---|---|---|---|---|
| Foreign demand for American exports | X | — | — | X |
| Foreign demand for American investments | X | — | — | X |
| Speculation that the dollar will appreciate | X | — | — | X |
| American demand for imports | — | X | X | — |
| American demand for investments in foreign countries | — | X | X | — |
| Speculation that the dollar will depreciate | — | X | X | — |

3.  T
4.  T
5. and 6.    **Table 21.3 Answer**

| Price of a £<br>($ / £)<br>(1) | | Quantity of £<br>demanded<br>(2) | | Quantity of $<br>supplied<br>(3) | Price of a $<br>(£ / $)<br>(4) | Quantity of £<br>supplied<br>(5) | Quantity of $<br>demanded<br>(6) |
|---|---|---|---|---|---|---|---|
| 4.50 | x | 100 | = | 450   | 0.222 = 1/4.50 | 700 | 3,150 |
| 4.00 | x | 200 | = | 800   | 0.25  = 1/4    | 600 | 2,400 |
| 3.50 | x | 300 | = | 1,050 | 0.29  = 1/3.50 | 500 | 1,750 |
| 3.00 | x | 400 | = | 1,200 | 0.33  = 1/3    | 400 | 1,200 |
| 2.50 | x | 500 | = | 1,250 | 0.40  = 1/2.50 | 300 | 750   |
| 2.00 | x | 600 | = | 1,200 | 0.50  = 1/2    | 200 | 400   |
| 1.50 | x | 700 | = | 1,050 | 0.67  = 1/1.50 | 100 | 150   |

7.  **Figure 21.2 Answer**

303

8. 1/3 £ per dollar; $1,200
9. 400 (= 1,200 x 1/3); $3 per pound [= 1/(1/3)]
10. T
11. F    The equilibrium exchange rate for the dollar equals the *reciprocal* of the equilibrium exchange rate for the pound.

## Exercise 3

1. $1.2 million
2. $958,000
3. The Swedish krona depreciated which caused the value of the prize to decrease.

# CHAPTER 22

# The New Capitalist Revolutions: Russia, China, Cuba

## Quick Review

The collapse of communism has accelerated since the late 1980s. In 1991 the Soviet Union became fifteen separate republics. Each of the republics had to establish their own methods for allocating their resources and developing answers to the WHAT, HOW, and FOR WHOM questions. It was inevitable that, with the collapse of the Soviet Union, Fidel Castro would have to decide how to run the Cuban economy without the massive Soviet subsidies which propped up his system for over three decades. China remains a centrally-planned economy, but it has recently allowed some capitalist innovation to occur. All around the world former communist countries are being forced to abandon central planning, however reluctantly, in favor of the market mechanism.

In this chapter we look back at the communist ideology and the central planning which was used to implement it. Then we investigate the inherent problems of attempting to plan a large, diverse, and complex economy. Finally, we look at "transitional problems" as the formerly planned economies move toward market-based systems of resource allocation. Specifically, we attempt to answer the following questions:

- What is the appeal of central planning?
- What are the basic problems of central planning?
- What impedes the transition to market economies?

Every economy has to answer the WHAT, HOW, and FOR WHOM questions. In the United States these questions are answered when consumers attempt to maximize satisfaction with limited incomes, business people attempt to maximize profits, and voters express their preferences about the way they are governed. In planned economies, the big decisions, such as the division of output between capital goods and consumer goods, are made by a central authority.

The central authority (i.e., the planners) attempts to allocate resources to achieve specific objectives. Very often these objectives include a particular income distribution and a strong military establishment. Planners use such techniques as input-output analysis to allocate their scarce resources; in contrast, in a market economy prices automatically signal where resources are to move. Prices are used in planned economies to perform a rationing function, but not the allocation function that they perform in a market economy.

Trade between nations is difficult in centrally planned economies because prices, which are set by planners rather than by markets, are not accepted internationally. Currencies are not convertible, barter results, and countries do not follow the dictates of comparative advantage. These are additional problems to be overcome during the transition from planning to markets.

The movement from central planning to market-based systems of resource allocation is not an easy task and every economy attempting this transition must experience changes in the form of price reform, currency reform, private ownership of property, and institutional reform. Price reform means abandoning prices set by planners in favor of prices established in free markets. The implicit surpluses and shortages which were suppressed under the old system must be allowed to bring about necessary changes in resource and product markets. Some prices shoot up and others collapse while the markets seek equilibrium. The inevitable inflation which follows must be followed by currency reform. Consumers and producers in both internal and external markets must be able to rely on the real value of the medium of exchange, or it will cease to play that role and inefficient barter will result. While currency and price reform are the foundation for a market-directed economy, the necessary cornerstone is the emergence of private property. Private property provides the incentives necessary for good economic decisions. This has been very difficult for the former communists to accept since virtually all property had been owned by the state. Privatization of former state assets (land and capital) has been accomplished in many countries, but it has never been easy.

Finally, institutional reform must take place. This means workers are no longer guaranteed employment with state owned firms where inefficiency and low productivity were rampant. Inevitably, unemployment skyrockets while currency, price and property reforms are in progress. It cannot be avoided. The cost in human terms, especially for the very old and very young, is great.

## Learning Objectives

After reading Chapter 22 and doing the following exercises, you should:

1. Know the historical background of communism and the appeal of central planning.
2. Recognize that every economy is restricted by its production-possibilities curve and the choices that result.
3. Recognize the very serious difficulties encountered in "planning" for large economies.
4. Recognize that every economy, no matter how it's organized, must answer the WHAT, HOW, and FOR WHOM questions.
5. Understand the roles that prices play in market and planned economies.
6. Know what input-output analysis is and how it is used by planners.
7. Know the relative strengths and weaknesses of market and planned economies.
8. Understand that suppressed inflation is the symptom of even more serious underlying problems of planned economies.
9. Know that inconvertible currencies lead to inefficiency in the allocation of resources both domestically and internationally.
10. Know that price, currency, and institutional reforms must be accompanied by privatization in the transition to a market-directed economy and the difficulties which accompany the reforms.
11. Be aware of the Cuban approach to reform.

## Using Key Terms

Fill in the puzzle on the opposite page with the appropriate term from the list of Key Terms at the end of the chapter in the text.

### *Across*

3. Any currency widely accepted as payment in international markets.
5. An economy in which all nonlabor means of production are owned by the state.
10. Direct exchange of one good for another.
11. An economy that relies on the market mechanism to allocate goods and services.
12. An economy in which basic allocation decisions are made by market forces.
13. Alternative combinations of goods and services that can be produced with available resources and technology.
14. An increase in production possibilities.
15. The amount by which the quantity demanded exceeds the quantity supplied.

## Down

1. Inflationary imbalances reflected in market shortages and the rationing of goods.
2. The ability to produce a specific good at a lower opportunity cost than another country.
4. A situation in which people are employed but contribute little or nothing to total output.
6. The use of prices and sales to signal desired output.
7. A stateless, classless economy with no private property in which everyone shares in production and consumption according to their abilities and needs.
8. Expenditures on new plant and equipment plus changes in inventories.
9. Consumer saving because of shortages of goods.
13. The difference between total cost and total revenue.

## Puzzle 22.1

## True or False: *Circle your choice and explain why any false statements are incorrect.*

T   F   1.   The historical order of Marx's stages is (from first to last) . . . capitalism, socialism, communism.

T   F   2.   When the official price for goods and services is below the equilibrium price in a market, prices no longer perform their rationing function efficiently.

T   F   3.   Marx envisioned communism as a state-controlled economy in which there would be no private property.

T   F   4.   In the planned economies of Eastern Europe unemployment was nonexistent.

T   F   5.   The basic function of prices in a centrally planned economy is to signal to producers that some products are relatively scarce and others are relatively plentiful.

T   F   6.   A system which requires complete income equality eliminates material incentives to motivate workers.

T   F   7.   Income equality is greater in the United States than in the planned economies.

T   F   8.   Central planning agencies use input-output tables to determine which goods and services can be produced with available resources and technology.

T   F   9.   When currencies are not convertible, they cease to perform their medium-of-exchange function in the domestic economy.

T   F  10.   When limited availability of goods leads to involuntary saving, workers are encouraged to work harder.

## Multiple Choice: *Select the correct answer.*

_____  1.   The motivating principle of the communism Marx envisioned would be:
     (a)   Protection for the capitalist class because they are the ones who do the saving.
     (b)   Private ownership of factors of production because this would provide an incentive to accumulate.
     (c)   "From each according to his ability, to each according to his need."
     (d)   Freedom in the pursuit of private economic gain.

_____  2.   Capitalism is an economic system in which:
     (a)   Basic allocation decisions are made by market forces.
     (b)   Labor is rewarded according to need.
     (c)   All factors of production are controlled by the government.
     (d)   The principles of democracy govern the marketplace.

_____  3.   In a market economy, the coordination of producer and consumer decisions is accomplished by markets; in a planned economy, such decisions are typically coordinated by:
     (a)   The workers.
     (b)   The plant managers.
     (c)   A central planning authority.
     (d)   The proletariat.

4. In a socialist economy input-output tables can be used to:
   (a) Choose the best production processes.
   (b) Allocate the right amount of resources to each sector.
   (c) Choose the optimal amount of investment.
   (d) Choose the optimal amount of consumption.

5. Planned economies typically suffer from:
   (a) Underemployment but not unemployment.
   (b) Both unemployment and underemployment.
   (c) Neither unemployment nor underemployment.
   (d) Unemployment but not underemployment.

6. In both planned and market economies, increased capital formation requires:
   (a) Lower interest rates.
   (b) Increased saving.
   (c) Increased consumption.
   (d) Reduced business taxes.

7. In the move from a communist system to a market system which of the following changes have to be made?
   (a) State-owned property to privately-owned property.
   (b) Profits must be permitted.
   (c) Prices determined by supply and demand rather than central planners.
   (d) All of the above would have to change.

8. Resource allocation can be accomplished without major shortages and surpluses using:
   (a) Input-output analysis in a planned socialist economy.
   (b) Input-output analysis in the market mechanism.
   (c) Prices in an economy which relies on the market mechanism.
   (d) Prices in a planned socialist economy.

9. Suppressed inflation takes the form of:
   (a) Market surpluses.
   (b) Market shortages.
   (c) Prices above equilibrium levels.
   (d) Output above equilibrium levels.

10. The major communist criticism of market economies relates to the market's answer to the:
    (a) FOR WHOM question.
    (b) WHAT question.
    (c) HOW question.
    (d) EFFICIENCY question.

11. Which of the following statements justifies the rejection of the market mechanism by planned economies?
    (a) If prices were used to allocate resources, planning goals would be jeopardized.
    (b) If prices were used to allocate resources, capital-goods production would be reduced.
    (c) If prices were used to allocate resources, income-distribution goals would be impaired.
    (d) All of the above justify such a rejection.

12. In an effort to establish economic equity, central planners are likely to cause:
    (a) Uncontrolled inflation.
    (b) Economic inefficiency.
    (c) Massive unemployment.
    (d) All of the above.

13. Involuntary saving occurred in the Soviet Union because:
    (a)   Workers were provided pensions which were not available until the worker retired.
    (b)   Workers purchased government securities in compulsory programs.
    (c)   Consumer goods were not available because government used the resources for investment.
    (d)   Workers were shoved into higher marginal tax brackets as their real incomes increased.

14. Using heavy price controls and severe quotas on the production of consumer goods, the Soviet Union:
    (a)   Reduced suppressed inflation.
    (b)   Created market shortages.
    (c)   Lowered enforced saving.
    (d)   All of the above.

15. Which of the following has been used as an incentive to increase worker productivity under the former Soviet Union?
    (a)   Terror.
    (b)   Income bonuses.
    (c)   "Ownership" of small plots of land.
    (d)   All of the above.

16. Planned socialist economies tend to hold prices of necessities:
    (a)   Above market equilibrium prices, which results in surpluses.
    (b)   Below market equilibrium prices, which results in shortages.
    (c)   Below market equilibrium prices, which results in surpluses.
    (d)   Above market equilibrium prices, which results in shortages.

17. A communist country's efforts to eliminate cyclical unemployment typically causes:
    (a)   Disguised unemployment.
    (b)   Inflation.
    (c)   Structural unemployment.
    (d)   Frictional unemployment.

18. When currencies are nonconvertible:
    (a)   The official rate is determined in the black market.
    (b)   The currency is not useful for trade in the domestic market.
    (c)   Foreign suppliers often require hard currencies in payment for goods.
    (d)   The official rate is determined by negotiations between governments.

19. Countries that use barter instead of currencies in international trade will:
    (a)   Not be able to specialize in production to the extent they would if currencies were used.
    (b)   Not be able to consume on their true consumption-possibilities curve.
    (c)   Be forced to devote more resources to the arrangement of trade than if currencies were used.
    (d)   All of the above.

20. The transition from communism to capitalism would most likely result in:
    (a)   Massive unemployment.
    (b)   Negative GDP growth rates.
    (c)   Social and political tension.
    (d)   All of the above.

# Problems and Applications

## *Exercise 1*

The production-possibilities curve for a planned economy is shown in Figure 22.1. Assume that the economy is operating at point $A$. Suppose the planners decide that the society must increase its production of defense goods from the amount indicated by $D_1$ to the amount indicated by $D_2$.

**Figure 22.1**
**Production possibilities**

*Production possibilities and opportunities*

1. The opportunity cost of increasing the output of defense goods from $D_1$ to $D_2$ is:
   (a)   Zero, since there are unemployed resources in the economy.
   (b)   $0C_2$ of consumer goods.
   (c)   $0C_1$ of consumer goods.
   (d)   $C_1, C_2$ of consumer goods.

2. To get the workers to switch from the production of consumer goods to the production of defense goods, the planners will be most successful if they:
   (a)   Raise the wages of workers who produce defense goods.
   (b)   Lower the wages of workers who produce consumer goods.
   (c)   Raise the wages of workers who produce defense goods relative to those of workers who produce consumer goods.
   (d)   Raise the wages of workers who produce consumer goods relative to those of workers who produce defense goods.

3. If more defense goods are to be produced, resources will have to be taken away from consumer goods, and consumers will have fewer consumer goods to purchase. Suppose the demand and supply of consumer goods are as indicated in Figure 22.2. The equilibrium price-quantity combination is:
   (a)   $P_2, C_1$.
   (b)   $P_1, C_1$.
   (c)   $P_2, C_2$.
   (d)   $P_3, C_2$.

## Figure 22.2
## Supply and demand for consumer goods

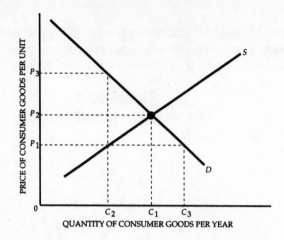

*Taxes and price limitations (ceilings)*

4. To prevent producers from having an incentive to produce too many consumer goods, the planners might hold down prices to $P_1$. Which of the following results would you expect?
   (a) Excess inventories.
   (b) Excess profits.
   (c) Long queues of people waiting to buy.
   (d) All of the above.

5. When the planners cut production from $C_1$ to $C_2$, the result is a:
   (a) Surplus at prices below $P_1$.
   (b) Shortage at prices below $P_2$.
   (c) New equilibrium at $P_3$, $C_2$.
   (d) None of the above.

6. To get consumers to restrain their consumption to output $C_2$, the planners could levy a tax equal to the distance:
   (a) $0P_3$.
   (b) $0P_1$.
   (c) $P_2$, $P_3$.
   (d) $P_1$, $P_3$.

*Subsidies, price supports, and floors*

7. Suppose the government wishes to control diseases by making more medical services available. Figure 22.3 shows the demand and supply curves for medical services. The equilibrium price-quantity is:
   (a) $P_1$, $M_1$.
   (b) $P_2$, $M_2$.
   (c) $P_3$, $M_3$.
   (d) $P_1$, $M_3$.

## Figure 22.3
## Supply and demand of medical services

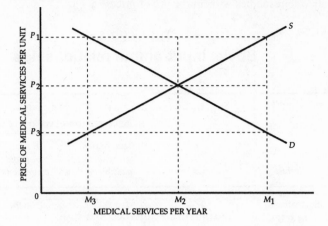

8. Suppose the government wants $M_1$ of medical services produced. If the government sets a price like $P_1$ so that the desired quantity of medical services would be supplied, you would expect:
   (a) Underemployment of medical personnel.
   (b) Shortages of medical services.
   (c) Improvements in health to the degree that the government targets.
   (d) All of the above.

9. In order to encourage fuller use of the services available at $M_1$, the government could introduce a subsidy per unit of medical service of:
   (a) $P_1, P_3$.
   (b) $M_3, M_1$.
   (c) $P_2, P_3$.
   (d) $P_1, P_2$.

10. If the government wanted $M_1$ of medical services to be offered, wanted to subsidize no one, and wanted to keep the price at $P_3$, it would have to build medical facilities to provide:
   (a) $M_3, M_1$ of medical services.
   (b) $0M_1$ of medical services.
   (c) $0M_2$ of medical services.
   (d) $0M_3$ of medical services.

11. At a price of $P_3$, private medical practices would provide:
   (a) $M_3, M_1$ of medical services.
   (b) $0M_1$ of medical services.
   (c) $0M_2$ of medical services.
   (d) $0M_3$ of medical services.

   (*Hint:* The supply curve reflects what would be provided in the private market.)

313

# Exercise 2

This exercise should give you an idea of how to use input-output analysis. It should also give you an idea of how difficult it is to allocate resources without the use of prices.

## Table 22.1
## Soviet input-output relationships

| (1) | (2) | (3) | (4) | (5) | (6) |
|---|---|---|---|---|---|
| | | | Input requirement per unit of: | | |
| Sector number | Inputs | Automobiles | Tractors and agricultural machinery | Bread, flour, and confections | Electric and thermal power |
| 1 | Specialized M & E | 0 | 0.00004 | 0.00054 | 0 |
| 2 | Fish products | 0 | 0 | 0.00040 | 0 |
| 3 | Sugar | 0.00000 | 0.00006 | 0.05334 | 0.00000 |

1. You are a planner faced with the Soviet input-output relationships shown in Table 22.1 in the text and Table 22.1 above. You are responsible for ensuring that the bread, flour, and confections industry (column 5 in Table 22.1) has all of the required inputs needed to produce 100,000 rubles of bread, flour, and confections. You succeed in obtaining all of the necessary requirements except those produced by three industries. Table 22.2 shows the amounts (column 2) of the various requirements in these three industries that you are able to obtain. In column 3 of Table 22.2 write the input-output coefficients for each of these sectors (use Table 22.1 above).

2. You should be able to calculate the amounts of the three requirements in Table 22.2 that you would need to produce 100,000 rubles of bread, flour, and confectionery goods. Place these amounts in column 4 of Table 22.2. (*Hint:* The coefficients in column 3 tell the fraction of the total cost of bread, flour, and confectionery goods that goes into each input.)

## Table 22.2
## Shortfall for requirements in three industries to produce bread, flour, and confections

| (1) | (2) | (3) | (4) | (5) | (6) |
|---|---|---|---|---|---|
| Industry | Amount obtained (rubles) | Input-output coefficient | Amount (rubles) needed to produce 100,000 rubles of output 100,000 x (3) | Fraction of target that can be met (2) ÷ (4) | Maximum production possible given input available 100,000 x (5) |
| Specialized M & E (sector 1) | 45.0 | _____ | _____ | _____ | _____ |
| Fish products (sector 2) | 30.0 | _____ | _____ | _____ | _____ |
| Sugar (sector 3) | 533.4 | _____ | _____ | _____ | _____ |

3. You are now ready to find the percentage of bread, flour, and confectionery goods you can make with the available inputs that you have. In column 5 of Table 22.2 you can compute the ratio of

314

what you have available of each input to the amount needed to reach your target of 100,000 rubles of bread, flour, and confection output. This same ratio tells the fraction of your 100,000-ruble production target that you will be able to produce. Compute this maximum production in column 6, Table 22.2.

4.  Which input causes the production of bread, flour, and confectionery goods to be the lowest?
    (a)   Specialized M & E.
    (b)   Fish products.
    (c)   Sugar.

5.  Assuming that production can be increased only if you have enough of each input and that production can be expanded only in proportion to the available inputs, the maximum output of bread, flour, and confectionery goods that can be produced with available inputs is:
    (a)   1,000 rubles.
    (b)   10,000 rubles.
    (c)   100,000 rubles.
    (d)   90,000 rubles.
    (e)   83,333 rubles.
    (f)   75,000 rubles.

6.  Since you are able to meet only one-tenth of your target for bread, flour, and confectionery products, you will have (surpluses, shortages) of all of the inputs to these products except sugar.

7.  For each of the commodities in Table 22.3, compute the amount of surplus you have of each of the listed inputs as a result of your inability to use them. The input-output coefficients are from Table 22.1 in the text. Since you had enough of each of these inputs to produce 100,000 rubles of bread, flour, and confectionery goods, you can assume that column 3 in Table 22.3 represents the amount of each input you were allocated. (*Hint:* Find the input coefficient and then compute the amount of factor needed as you did in Table 22.2.) Since you can use only 10 percent of the factors you were allocated, because of the sugar shortages, your surplus will be 90 percent (column 4) of what you were allocated (column 3).

## Table 22.3
## Excess inputs as a result of sugar shortage

| *(1)*<br><br>Input | *(2)*<br>Input-output coefficient for bread, flour, and confections. (See Table 22.1 in the text.) | *(3)*<br><br>Amount (rubles) needed to produce 100,000 rubles of output | *(4)*<br><br>Amount unused 0.9 x (3) |
|---|---|---|---|
| Coal (sector 5)<br>Electric and<br>    thermal power<br>    (sector 9) | ———  ——— | ———  ——— | ———  ——— |

8.  You are also the planner for automobile production. You have to produce 1 million rubles of output of automobiles. If you fail you will go to Siberia. You receive the allocation that you need from all sectors except for the two shown in Table 22.4. Complete Table 22.4 as you did Table 22.2 of this study guide, this time using the automobile column (column 1) in Table 22.1 in the text to find the input-output coefficients.

## Table 22.4
## Shortfall of requirements to produce one million rubles of automobiles

| (1)<br><br>Input | (2)<br><br>Amount<br>obtained<br>(rubles) | (3)<br><br>Input-output<br>coefficient | (4)<br>Amount (rubles)<br>needed to produce<br>1 million rubles<br>of output<br>1,000,000 x (3) | (5)<br>Fraction of<br>target that<br>can be met<br>(2) ÷ (4) | (6)<br>Maximum production<br>possible given<br>available inputs<br>1,000,000 x (5) |
|---|---|---|---|---|---|
| Coal (sector 5) | 1,945.8 | _____ | _____ | _____ | _____ |
| Electric and<br>thermal power<br>(sector 9) | 11,592.9 | _____ | _____ | _____ | _____ |

9. How would you be able to reach your automobile target?
   (a) Transfer bread, flour, and confectionery products to the automobile industry.
   (b) Transfer cars to the bread, flour, and confectionery industry.
   (c) Transfer sugar, fish products, and specialized M & E to the automobile industry.
   (d) Transfer coal and electric and thermal power from the automobile industry to the bread, flour, and confectionery industry.
   (e) Transfer coal and electric and thermal power from the bread, flour, and confectionery industry to the automobile industry.

10. How much more coal (in rubles) does the automobile industry need from the bread, flour, and confectionery industry in order to reach its target without any waste?
    (a) 1,171 rubles.
    (b) 214.2 rubles.
    (c) 117.1 rubles.
    (d) 2,160 rubles.

11. Are there still surpluses of inputs for some industry after the automobile target is reached? _____

## Exercise 3

This exercise will use one of the articles in the text to show the kind of information to look for to identify the type of economic system used in another country.

Reread the article "China Debates Whether to Slow Reforms" in the text.

1. How would you classify the way the economy of this country has been organized in the past? (circle one)
   Communism          Socialism          Mixed economy          Free market

2. What passage is consistent with the way you have classified the past economy? _____ _____

3. What passage indicates an example of the way the economy is changing to a new economic structure (for example, from communism to capitalism)? _____ _____

4. What passage indicates the impact the Asian crisis has had on reforms? _____ _____

# Common Errors

The first statement in each "common error" below is incorrect. Each incorrect statement is followed by a corrected version and an explanation.

1. Prices serve no function in a planned economy. WRONG!

   Prices are used to allocate resources and goods in accordance with central plans. RIGHT!

   In planned economies prices are not allowed to perform the same functions as in a market economy. Prices do not generally provide the signal for resources to move (their allocation function), but they do perform the rationing function. Luxury goods have high prices, and necessities carry lower price tags.

2. The average city dweller in China subsists on an income of approximately $340 per year. WRONG!

   The average Chinese city dweller is at about the U.S. poverty line. RIGHT!

   This "common error" points up the difficulty of making comparisons of living standards across international boundaries. Simple dollar comparisons gloss over the radical differences in economic organization. Some of the things that carry high price tags in the United States, such as medical services, carry low price tags in China. Housing is another example. Many services that are provided without charge by the state in China must be paid for by the consumer in the United States. Such differences create significant distortions, so simple comparisons are very misleading. After adjustments, it appears that the average Chinese city dweller has an income roughly equivalent to that at the U.S. poverty line.

3. Capitalism is a system characterized by democracy. WRONG!

   Capitalism is an economic system in which individuals own the factors of production and use the market mechanism. RIGHT!

   Do not confuse the classification of political systems with the classification of economic systems. It is conceivable—even if not historically common—for tyrannies to practice capitalism and democracies to practice communism. An economic system focuses on the ownership of the means of production and the mechanism by which goods are exchanged. A political system focuses on the issue of collective decision making.

## •ANSWERS•

## Using Key Terms
### Across
3. hard currency
5. socialism
10. barter
11. market economy
12. capitalism
13. production possibilities
14. economic growth
15. market shortage

## Down

1. suppressed inflation
2. comparative advantage
4. disguised unemployment
6. market mechanism
7. communism
8. investment
9. involuntary saving
13. profit

## True or False

1. T
2. T
3. F   Marx did envision a society in which there was no private property; however, he did not see the need for a central authority, i.e. a state, because in his view the only function of the state was to pursue the interests of the dominant class.
4. F   Although, officially, unemployment did not exist, disguised unemployment (underemployment) was widespread.
5. F   Prices in a centrally planned economy are typically government controlled and do not fluctuate in response to shortages and surpluses.
6. T
7. F   One of the major objectives of planned economies is to create a more equal distribution of income.
8. T
9. F   When currencies are not convertible, they do not perform their medium of exchange function in the international economy.
10. F   Limited availability of goods is a disincentive to work harder because access to more goods and services is the primary reward for hard work.

## Multiple Choice

| | | | | |
|---|---|---|---|---|
| 1. c | 5. a | 9. b | 13. c | 17. a |
| 2. a | 6. b | 10. a | 14. b | 18. c |
| 3. c | 7. d | 11. d | 15. d | 19. d |
| 4. b | 8. c | 12. b | 16. b | 20. d |

## Problems and Applications

### Exercise 1

| | | | | | |
|---|---|---|---|---|---|
| 1. d | 3. a | 5. b | 7. b | 9. a | 11. d |
| 2. c | 4. c | 6. c | 8. a | 10. a | |

# Exercise 2

1-3. **Table 22.2 Answer**

| (1) Industry | (2) Amount obtained | (3) Input-output coefficient | (4) Amount needed | (5) Fraction of target | (6) Maximum production |
|---|---|---|---|---|---|
| Specialized M & E | 45.0 | 0.00054 | 54 | 5/6 | 83,333 |
| Fish products | 30.0 | 0.00040 | 40 | 3/4 | 75,000 |
| Sugar | 533.4 | 0.05334 | 5,334 | 1/10 | 10,000 |

4. c
5. b
6. surpluses
7. **Table 22.3 Answer**

| (1) Input | (2) Input-output coefficient | (3) Amount needed | (4) Amount unused |
|---|---|---|---|
| Coal | 0.00238 | 238 | 214.2 |
| Electric and thermal power | 0.00284 | 284 | 255.6 |

8. **Table 22.4 Answer**

| (1) Input | (2) Amount obtained | (3) Input-output coefficient | (4) Amount needed | (5) Fraction of target | (6) Maximum production |
|---|---|---|---|---|---|
| Coal | 1,945.8 | 0.00216 | 2,160 | 0.9008 | 900,800 |
| Electric and thermal power | 11,592.9 | 0.01171 | 11,710 | 0.9900 | 990,000 |

9. e        10. b        11. yes

# Exercise 3

1. communism
2. Communist leaders
3. "Just over a year ago, the country was engaged in restructuring its obsolete state enterprises, inadequate housing system and insolvent banks."
4. "The crisis has . . . put on hold reforms . . . "